PRACTICAL
FURNITURE DESIGN

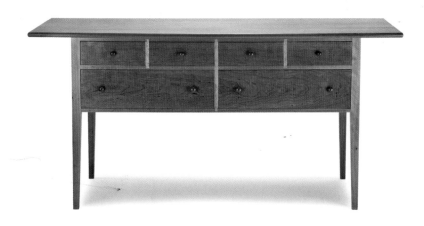

The Editors of Fine Homebuilding & Fine Woodworking

The Taunton Press

 The Taunton Press

The Taunton Press, Inc., 63 South Main Street, PO Box 5506, Newtown, CT 06470-5506
e-mail: tp@taunton.com

Editor: Jessica DiDonato
Copy editor: Seth Reichgott
Jacket/Cover design: Jean-Marc Troadec, Design & Typography
Layout: Laura Lind Design
Indexer: Jay Kreider

Library of Congress Cataloging-in-Publication Data
Practical furniture design : from drawing board to smart construction / editors of Fine
woodworking.
      p. cm.
   ISBN 978-1-60085-078-3
   1. Furniture design. I. Fine woodworking.
   TT196.P76 2009
   684.1'04--dc22

                              2008032426

Printed in the United States of America
10 9 8 7 6 5 4 3 2 1

The following manufacturers/names appearing in *Practical Furniture Design* are trademarks:
Amana®, Livos®, Masonite®, Multi-Router®, Quadraset™

Acknowledgments

Special thanks to the authors, editors,
art directors, copy editors, and other
staff members of *Fine Woodworking*
who contributed to the development
of the articles in this book.

Contents

Introduction

For me design is the most exciting aspect of woodworking, whether I'm working in a traditional mode and trying to get the details right, or attempting to make a piece no one has ever seen before. I've learned not to skimp on the process. Fine woodworkers face a cruel irony: Those who make things to last a lifetime have a lifetime to live with their mistakes.

This book brings together *Fine Woodworking* magazine's most trusted voices on furniture design, experts who will show you in a few pages what it took them years to work out. They'll guide you through the whole process, from finding inspiration, to using sketches and models, to getting the construction details right, so your furniture will remain strong, stylish, and useful for generations to come. This is a book you will return to again and again.

To kick things off, I'll offer three of my favorite tips. When editors sit down with submissions to the Readers Gallery in the magazine, or judge furniture shows around the country, you'd be surprised at how similar the conversations are, and how often they touch on the following issues.

Tip one is to make your furniture look handmade, as opposed to factory-made. Factories have to rush; you don't. Take the time to choose your boards carefully, and be thoughtful about grain and figure; the wood itself can make or break the look of a project. Factories also oversand, or sand crudely, dubbing over crisp edges and details. And they love router bits, which offer a quick way to make things look "fancy." So be careful how you use your router. Big roundovers are usually a bad idea. Think twice about all those flutes and ogees. Do they clash with the period or style of the piece?

Tip two is to keep things in proportion. Are the legs too thick for the piece? Consider everything: tabletop overhang, width of an apron, sizes of rails and stiles, shapes made by doors and drawers. And ask yourself if the details—inlay, moldings, pulls—are in proportion too. Many a piece has gone astray with a thick racing stripe of stringing or banding. Sketches, models, and small mockups are your friends here.

Tip three is not to overdo contrast. The exotic, intoxicating variety of woods has seduced many a craftsman. If the contrasting area is large, such as a door panel, make the difference subtle—think curly cherry with regular cherry. If the contrasting material is extreme, use it in small doses—beads, wedges, pulls?

Now on to the experts. They'll take it from here.

—Asa Christiana, Editor of
Fine Woodworking

Designing Furniture: A Survival Guide

BY GARRETT HACK

Designing a piece of furniture should be fun, not intimidating. Yet I know woodworkers who think nothing of building complicated jigs or mastering difficult finishes but feel lost when it comes to designing a piece of furniture truly their own.

The most important thing you can do is to train your eye. Look at furniture you like. Look in books, or go to museums, galleries, and new or antique furniture stores. Discover what appeals to you and why.

Absorb ideas from the past and synthesize them into your own vision. Jot down your discoveries as you make them. Measure the back of a particularly comfortable chair or the height of the seat. Keep a sketchbook of inspiring ideas; you never know how you might use some detail or rough sketch later.

Gaining confidence as a designer is more subtle than, say, learning to cut dovetails, but it's just another skill. I'll give you the loose process I follow when designing furniture and some tools and techniques that will help you along the way.

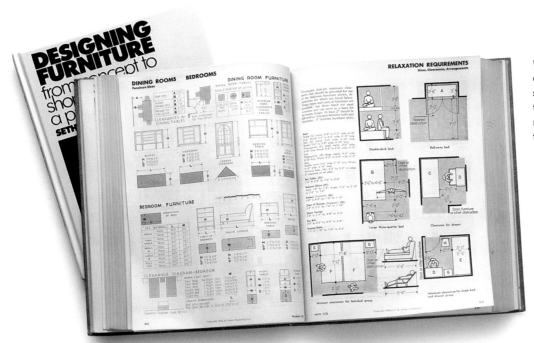

WHERE TO START. Furniture design books and architectural standard guides are good places to look for practical measurements based on average body types and ergonomic factors.

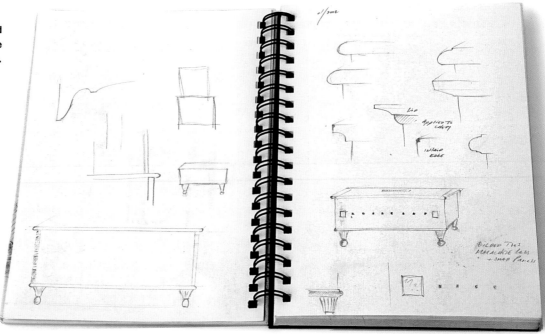

Start with What You Know

A good place to start a design is with the givens—there are always some. Say you're designing a piece with drawers. What are you going to store and how much space does it take up? This might mean measuring a stack of sweaters or sizing up particularly useful drawers you already use. If you're designing a table, consider whether it will be used next to a sofa or a bed or worked at while standing or sitting. How large does the top need to be?

Architectural Graphic Standards (John Wiley & Sons, 2000) is one place to get the starting points for a design. This book gives practical dimensions for a wide range of furniture.

Work Out the Lines and Proportions

Now, armed with (or saddled with, depending on how you look at it) the practical dimensions, work on the overall proportions and lines of the piece. Proportion is the size relationship of the parts. It's the width of a table compared with its length or the height of each drawer face compared with the ones above and below it. But don't think only about the proportions of parts you can see; the negative spaces formed between the parts are also important. Tables and chairs create lots of negative spaces, interesting ones that can mirror and reinforce the positive, as is the case with the shapely curved back splats of 18th-century chairs.

Avoid the tiresome stock lumberyard dimensions of ¾ in., 1½ in., and 3½ in. for door rails and stiles, dividers between drawers, table aprons, and other highly visible parts. A variety of sizes and proportions is the most visually stimulating.

Drawings and Mock-Ups

Typically I make lots of small sketches to get a sense of my design before making accurate full-scale drawings. Drafting full scale is always best for working out the shape of curves, details, or tricky joinery, and for recognizing potential problems before you get there. It's a useful way to see exactly what you're designing and whether the shapes and proportions are pleasing.

A full-size drawing offers other benefits. You can transfer angles and dimensions (such as shoulder lines) directly from the drawing to the parts, making fewer errors than reading measurements off a tape. Once you get curves and contours the way you like them, you can make patterns directly from the drawing.

Drawings, however, often aren't enough to help you visualize a three-dimensional piece of furniture. At some stage a mock-up of all or part of the piece might be the best way to visualize the design. Tape together cardboard cutouts or nail together some scraps. Stand back and look at your mock-up (and drawing) from different angles. Work on something else and come back to your design with a fresh eye. Use your eyes—not your tape—to work out the dimensions of parts, such as the thickness of a tabletop, the height of the table, or the width of its apron.

Once you know what works, you can break some of the rules. Exaggerate dimensions: Design a long, narrow table or a strongly vertical chest of drawers. Instead of a progression of deepening drawers down the front of a case, add a couple of smaller ones toward the middle. Keep in mind, however, the balance of the piece. It might be solid on its feet but feel unsettling to the viewer.

Keep Construction in Mind

Aside from the practical dimensions that the design must accommodate, construction is another real-world consideration. The most ingenious design is no good if it's incredibly difficult to build. It's better (and more profitable) to build something simple that looks complicated, rather than something complicated that looks simple. So think about construction early in the design process.

Insight into how to design the joinery and build a piece often comes from experience—if you have it. If I had never made a gate-leg table, I'd look at as many examples as possible to see other makers' designs and solutions. There is no one way to build anything, but there are easier and harder ways to do it. Some ways are stronger, too.

VARIATIONS ON A THEME. Square pegs and rectangular wedges made of ebony work together visually in the base of a trestle table (left). A black-and-white checkered pattern is repeated in the stringing and banding on the legs of this demilune table (far left), and the motif is echoed in the border of the oval inlay.

Choose Appropriate Woods

Wood choice is both an aesthetic and technical consideration. Wood color, figure, and hardness, how primary and secondary woods enhance or contrast each other, and how your wood will age are all concerns. A piece made of ash or oak, both of which have very strong grain, will be very different from the same piece made of quieter cherry or flashier bird's-eye maple. Harder woods will take fine details and hold up to wear and tear, but you may want the patina that softwoods develop with everyday use. Think through the various parts and the availability of stock wide or thick enough to make them. Of course, wood selection sometimes comes down to what you have on hand or what you can get.

NOTHING LIKE THE REAL THING. These models of edge treatments are for the chest in the sketchbook on the facing page.

Get Down to Details

Although choosing woods, refining proportions, and devising construction strategies are important aspects of a design, the details are the most important—and the most elusive. These are the small touches that draw your eye and delight your senses. Some details are purely practical: a chamfer to blunt and thus protect an edge from wear. Others are purely decorative: an inlay line around a drawer. Great details can do both; for instance, beads disguise the gap around a door, round an edge prone to wear, and add a nicely molded outline. Some designs are rich with details. Others rely on beautiful woods and surfaces alone.

The challenge is not finding details you like—they are everywhere you look—but using them in a way that enhances rather than clutters your design. Don't give your viewers so much variety that they feel confused and overwhelmed. Treat details as variations on a theme. Use similar woods, colors, patterns, and repeating shapes and sizes to create unity in the piece. In a cherry cabinet you might use dark rosewood to pin the joints on the doors, for the knobs, and perhaps for cock beading on the drawers. A part of the crown molding could echo the bead shape.

Details are hard to see on paper but easy to mock up. Wondering about a molding shape or how big to make a chamfer? Go cut some. Test samples also give you practice making a difficult detail, can be sent to a client, and can be saved for future reference.

Part of the thrill of making something unique is leaving some things to be discovered as you build. Give yourself the flexibility to let the design evolve. Curve an edge that was to be straight, refine a leg to a more pleasing taper, deepen a rail where you can now see you need it. Even mistakes can add something to the fun; they'll force you to come up with creative solutions you just might use again.

GARRETT HACK is a contributing editor to *Fine Woodworking* magazine.

A Guide to Good Design

BY GRAHAM BLACKBURN

Even if you should be blessed with a good eye, it's not easy to design a piece of furniture without using some underlying paradigm for determining its dimensions and the inner proportions of its parts. Whether it's a design method passed on from craftsman to apprentice or the inherent sense of balance that humans possess, without such a paradigm to follow it is perfectly possible to build something that is structurally sound and functionally adequate but not pleasing to the senses. A piece of furniture that disregards proven design may look clumsy, unbalanced, or awkward.

The Geometry of Furniture Design

Chief among the many paradigms that designers have used—and continue to use—to ensure balance and good proportions in furniture design is the golden ratio (also referred to as the golden mean). Represented by the Greek letter phi (ϕ), the golden ratio can be expressed as the equation $(1 + \sqrt{5})/2 = \phi$. For practical purposes, we can think of phi as equal to 1.618, and visualize it by dividing any given line so that the longer part is 1.618 times greater than the shorter part. One of many intriguing principles of the golden ratio is that the shorter portion of the

The Golden Ratio

The golden ratio, represented with the Greek letter phi (ϕ), is based on an equation ($[1 + \sqrt{5}]/2 = \phi$) that produces a decimal that proceeds infinitely without repetition. For practical purposes, it is rounded off to 1.618.

A x 1.618 (ϕ)   **A**

THE GOLDEN RATIO IN ITS SIMPLEST FORM

If you bisect any given line using phi, the longer portion is 1.618 times greater than the shorter portion. Interestingly, the whole line is also 1.618 times greater than its longest bisection.

A
A x ϕ

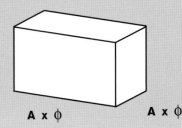

A x ϕ A x ϕ

THE GOLDEN RECTANGLE

The long dimension of a golden rectangle is 1.618 times greater than the shorter dimension.

THE GOLDEN SOLID

A golden solid incorporates multiple golden rectangles that are proportionate to one another.

The Golden Ratio in Nature and in Art

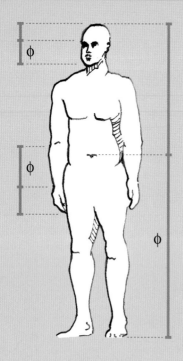

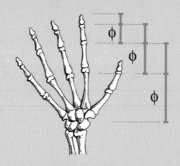

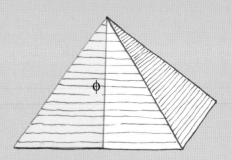

PHI IN THE HUMAN BODY

The eyes divide the head at the golden ratio. The navel divides the body's height at the golden ratio. The wrist divides the arm, from elbow to fingertip, at the golden ratio. The bones on an average human hand are related to each other in phi proportions from wrist to fingertip.

PHI IN THE PYRAMIDS

The Great Pyramid of Giza is constructed with the golden ratio at its core. The height of its side is equal to 1.618 times the length of half its base.

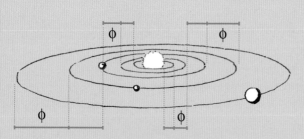

PHI IN THE HIGHBOY

The high chest of drawers, known as the Pompadour, made in Philadelphia between 1762 and 1790, uses the golden ratio to determine many of its measurements. The carcase is a golden rectangle. The position of the waist is determined by dividing the overall height by phi. And the two lower drawers also are golden rectangles.

PHI IN THE SOLAR SYSTEM

The distances between the sun and the first five planets in the solar system are close to the golden ratio in their relationship to one another, taking into account that they measure different distances throughout their orbits and are not on the same linear plane. Astronomers have used the golden ratio to locate planets in their orbits.

PHI IN THE PARTHENON

The Parthenon uses the golden ratio for its overall dimensions. When squared, it leaves a second, smaller golden rectangle, which when squared determines the height of the columns. Many other elements and details were determined with this method.

line is in the same proportion to the longer part as the longer part is to the whole line.

A naturally occurring proportion The golden ratio underlies much of nature and the way our universe is constructed. Examples abound on every level, from astrophysics to quantum mechanics. Planetary orbits and even the very structure of the human figure abide by it. Being so fundamental and pervasive in nature, the ratio appeals to us at a subconscious level as being essentially right. As such, it has been used for centuries by designers of everything from the pyramids to furniture masterpieces.

The golden rectangle The golden ratio relates to furniture design most commonly by way of a rectangle that is constructed using phi for its two dimensions. Known as the golden rectangle, it is sized so that the length is 1.618 times larger than the width (or vice versa). These proportions can be used to determine the overall dimensions of furniture as well as interior parts, such as doors and drawers.

The golden solid Furniture is three dimensional, and the golden ratio can be applied to all three dimensions by turning a golden rectangle into a golden solid. Take, for instance, a simple case. When viewing its profile, the height may be the long dimension of a golden rectangle. However, when viewed from the front, the height may be the short dimension of a proportionate golden rectangle.

Applying the Golden Ratio to Furniture Proportions

A word of caution before applying the golden ratio as a design paradigm: Remember that form must follow function. Even the most sublimely proportioned piece of furniture can be a failure if it does not function because it is too small or too large or otherwise unable to be used comfortably. Practical considerations, therefore, must come first.

In fact, most furniture designs require that you start with some given dimensions:

A table must be a certain height, a cabinet may have to fit a particular space, or a bookcase may require a fixed number of shelves. But almost certainly you will be left with many other decisions regarding dimensions to which you can apply this proportion. It will be worth the effort to see whether the golden ratio might work for these other elements. Deciding on dimensions by eye alone—or worse, on the basis of the lumber that is conveniently at hand—is a less certain way of achieving a well-balanced, nicely proportioned piece.

Individual elements Whether the overall dimensions of a piece are proportioned using the golden ratio, individual parts—such as table legs or even the relative sizes of framing members such as stiles, rails, and muntins—can be determined with the golden ratio. The golden ratio also offers one way to solve the problem of designing graduated drawers. Each consecutive drawer can increase in size by multiplying the depth of one drawer by phi to get the depth of the next-largest drawer. The method can be applied just as effectively to other elements, such as shelving or partitions.

Any measurement on a piece of furniture originally may have been determined by functional and structural requirements, but many adjustments can be made that add inner harmony. Using the golden ratio when designing furniture will enable you not only to produce a pleasing whole but also to ensure that all of the constituent parts, such as door panels and drawers, are fundamentally related.

Practical Adjustments

Designing something with perfect proportions is rarely possible in the real world. Almost every piece of furniture or woodwork will need to accommodate constraints imposed by details of function, joinery, or economics. But even the attempt to approach perfection (which may be defined as measurements that correspond precisely

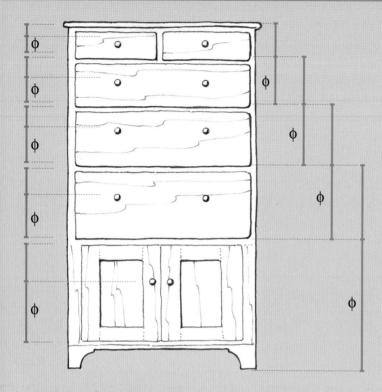

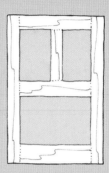 

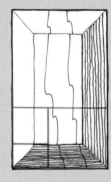

GRADUATED DRAWERS

This Shaker-style chest of drawers uses phi increments, which can be determined with a Fibonacci series (see "Four Ways to Construct a Golden Rectangle" on p. 12), to establish the height of the graduated drawers as well as the positions of the drawer pulls.

DOOR ELEMENTS

In a door, the golden ratio can be used to size the panels (above left) as well as the widths of the muntin, stiles, and rails (above right), which increase in size by multiples of phi.

PANEL PROPORTIONS

The overall dimensions of this panel form a golden rectangle. Squaring the rectangle to produce smaller, proportionate golden rectangles helps determine how much of the panel should be raised.

to a system like the golden ratio) is virtually guaranteed to produce a better result than designing with no regard for any such paradigm. Even if you are close to perfect proportions, the eye is inclined to accommodate slight imperfections and fill in the gaps. Don't think that everything has to fit the formula exactly.

Last, remember that we often adjust things by eye to make a piece look lighter or better balanced, and we do so by using techniques that are part of the everyday woodworking vocabulary. They include the calculated use of grain direction to imply

movement; highly figured grain to help the eye see curves where none exist; finished edges and corners that give the impression of thickness or thinness; the use of molding to adjust an apparent golden rectangle or solid; the use of tapered legs to give the appearance of more closely approximating an ideal proportion; and the mixing and matching of many other design paradigms.

GRAHAM BLACKBURN is a furniture maker, author, illustrator, and the publisher of Blackburn Books (www. blackburnbooks.com) in Bearsville, New York.

Scaling a Credenza

The dimensions on several elements of this credenza were determined by scaling a golden rectangle. The horizontal golden rectangle of the credenza's legs is formed by squaring the larger vertical golden rectangle of the credenza's overall profile.

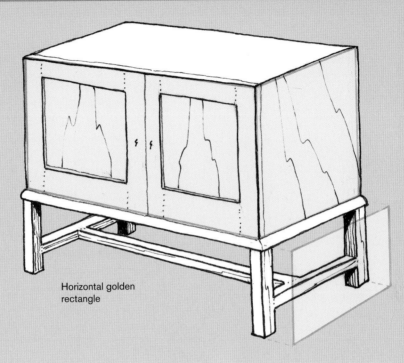

Case side and base form a vertical golden rectangle.

Horizontal golden rectangle

Horizontal golden rectangle

Tabletop Proportions

One simple application for a golden rectangle is a tabletop. To further make use of the proportions, the outer perimeter of the table legs also forms a golden rectangle.

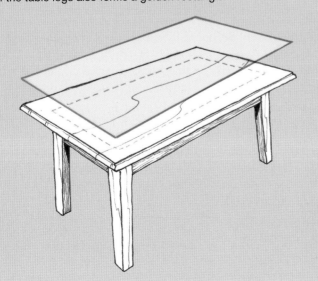

Table Dimensions

The tabletop, legs, and apron can be determined using the golden ratio. In this example, the fillet to round-over, the tabletop to leg, and the leg to apron are related by phi.

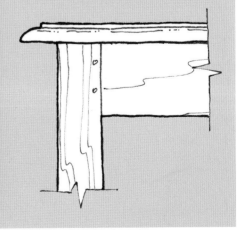

Four Ways to Construct a Golden Rectangle

Before you can conveniently use the golden ratio to design a piece of furniture, you must know how to produce it. You could simply multiply or divide any given measurement by 1.618, but this typically results in very clumsy numbers. It is much easier to construct an arbitrarily sized golden rectangle and then adjust the size to match your requirements. There are several simple methods to do this.

USE THE TRIANGLE METHOD

Construct a right-angle triangle with a base that is twice the length of the height. Then use a compass to draw an arc with a radius equal to the height of the triangle. The center point of this arc is located on the triangle where the vertical line and the hypotenuse meet. Next, using the location on the triangle where the base and the hypotenuse meet as a center point, draw an arc with a radius equal to the first bisection of the hypotenuse. The point at which this second arc bisects the base of the triangle divides the line into two portions that are related by the golden ratio. The two sections can be used to form the width and height of a golden rectangle.

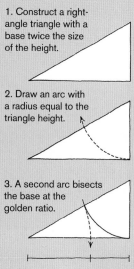

1. Construct a right-angle triangle with a base twice the size of the height.

2. Draw an arc with a radius equal to the triangle height.

3. A second arc bisects the base at the golden ratio.

4. Rotate the shorter section 90 degrees to complete the golden rectangle.

DIVIDE AND EXTEND A SQUARE

Divide a square in half with a vertical line, then draw a line continuing the baseline beyond the square. Draw an arc with a compass using the diagonal of one half of the square as a radius, with the center point on the baseline at the point of bisection. The point where the arc meets the continued baseline determines the extended line. The original baseline is now 1.618 times the length of the extension. These two lengths can be used to form the width and height of a golden rectangle.

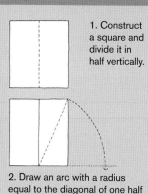

1. Construct a square and divide it in half vertically.

2. Draw an arc with a radius equal to the diagonal of one half of the square.

Original base is 1.618 times the size of the new extended section.

3. Rotate the shorter section 90 degrees to complete the golden rectangle.

SCALE A GOLDEN RECTANGLE

Using a golden rectangle of any size, you can create another golden rectangle with different dimensions. Simply draw a golden rectangle and bisect it with a diagonal line that stretches from one corner to another. Then extend the diagonal line. Any rectangle that shares this diagonal, whether it is smaller or larger, will be golden.

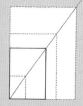

Any rectangle that shares this diagonal is golden.

APPLY THE FIBONACCI SERIES

Yet another way to derive measurements that reflect the golden ratio is to use a method known as the Fibonacci series, which is a sequence of numbers, with each number equal to the sum of the two preceding numbers. A simple series starting with 1 produces the following: 1, 2, 3, 5, 8, 13, 21, 34, 55, 89, 144, 233, and so on.

A Fibonacci series is useful because any number divided by the previous number—with the exception of the first few values—is roughly equal to phi. This explains why dimensions such as 3 by 5 and 5 by 8 are so common. They are based on phi.

Perhaps more useful to the furniture designer is that a Fibonacci series can be generated using any two numbers. Starting with two given dimensions for a furniture piece, add them together to produce the third value, and continue this pattern to create a series of other potential dimensions related by phi. For example, a case piece with a 15-in.-deep by 22-in.-wide top would produce the following Fibonacci series: 15, 22, 37, 59, 96, 155, 251, 406, and so on. Once again, discarding the first few values, you now have a series of pairs of numbers with a phi ratio, which might be used as a basis for other dimensions.

One thing to note is that although the first two values are expressed in inches, the successive numbers in a Fibonacci series could be expressed in any unit of measure, such as fractions of an inch. Therefore, a door panel on the case piece used as an example here could measure 25 1/64 in. by 40 96/64 in. and still be proportionate to the 15-in. by 22-in. case top.

Sam Maloof on Design

BY ASA CHRISTIANA

Though he is most widely known for his chairs and rockers, Sam Maloof has designed some 500 different pieces of furniture, including many tables and case pieces, as well as two homes. His original house, in a lemon grove in Alta Loma, was displaced by a freeway. The state declared it a historic landmark and moved it in 2001 to a new, larger site a few miles uphill, where it is now open to visitors. At the time, Maloof was dealing with the death of Freda, his wife and lifelong business partner, so he embraced the relocation as a chance for a new start. For one thing, it allowed him to design and build a second house to live in.

Maloof's new property offered lots of opportunities to create. There was the chance to design cavernous new lumber sheds, which he placed so they frame his view of the San Gabriel Mountains. He also has a spot picked out for a gallery to showcase the work of emerging artists.

On Trusting His Eye

"I draw with my bandsaw—with no lines or anything. A very well-known blacksmith said, 'I use my hammer as my pencil; I use my anvil as my table.' I use my bandsaw as my pencil. When I'm working, I'm looking at both (edges of the cut) and I'm looking at the saw, too. I don't recommend it to people—I'm afraid they'd cut their fingers off.

"I don't have any of the parts manufactured by parts makers. I could very easily; it would save me a lot of time. When I make a chair, I make it and evolve it to the very finish. I've made it for that individual."

On the Evolution of the Rocker

"**I** was making my spindles kind of fat (at the bottom), so they did give me this lower lumbar part. They just came (straight) down. They sat good, but then I started doing them so they actually curve, and I thought, well, this is the way to do it. They're very sensuous, and I still make them this way now.

"I like the combination of hard lines and soft lines very much. It (arose from) an error. My son was working with me and he was daydreaming or something, and he cut too deep. I said, 'Well, let's see what we can do about it.' So I saved it by making a hard line.

"I make the rocker (with a reversing curve at the tips) so if a child gets in it, they can't push it back too far.

"Then the horns (at the top of the back posts), they don't mean anything, but when you go to move the rocker, you hold on there. And then the seat is very deep in the back, so when you sit, it automatically just slides you right back to where you get good lumbar support."

HARD LINES ACCENTUATE THE SOFT CURVES. Maloof's earlier rockers (above) are characterized by upholstered seats, round spindles that swell outward to support the back, and a stretcher system for strength. Later (left), he developed a sculpted wood seat; curved, flattened spindles; and an interlocked, screwed joint at the seat rail that allowed him to omit the stretchers for a cleaner look. He also added hard edges to the soft sculpted curves.

On the "Maloof Round"

ROUND EDGES AND INSET DRAWERS. One of Maloof's favorite design elements is rounded case edges with flat doors and drawer fronts set back.

"I didn't want to have an edge on the drawers where it (would have to be) flush. But I could have the round on the outside that made a beautiful detail, and if (the drawers) weren't quite accurate, they still looked accurate—I'll be very blunt about it.

"I did it that way before other people did it, and all of a sudden I saw a lot of people up north doing it. And instead of calling it the Maloof round, they called it the California round. I could name people . . . "

Talent Is Innate, but Must Be Nurtured

As a boy, Maloof already was designing and drawing things, a sketch pad always at hand. His first serious job was as a graphic artist in Los Angeles. When he joined the Army during World War II, his superiors discovered his drawing skills and put him to work as a mapmaker. Today, after delivering pieces to the White House and the Smithsonian Institution, after being hailed as a national treasure, he still is sketching and designing, changing his furniture and surroundings, looking forward always.

It's hard to pin down Maloof on the question of design. Basically, he knows beauty when he sees it. He believes that design can't be taught—the talent is either there or it is not—but he allows that one's innate talent can be nurtured.

For woodworkers who wish to improve their design skills, he recommends frequent drawing and sketching. "I still do that. I think of something, and I'll pick up a piece of paper, and I'll do a sketch of it and put it in my pocket. And one idea begets another idea." He also suggests exposure to art in all forms. Most of all, he recommends designing and making lots of pieces. To those who admire his work but are afraid to design their own, he says, "You just have to try; you have to use your imagination.

"You have to ask yourself, 'Do I just want to work in wood and copy beautiful objects?' I see nothing wrong with copying, but how much more satisfaction do you get when you know you designed that piece, when it is your piece?"

On Timeless Beauty

"Elizabeth Gordon, who was the editor of *House Beautiful* for many years, called me one day. She said, 'Mr. Maloof, I saw your (curved bench) in New York and I'd like to feature it in the magazine.' This was the first time anything like this had ever happened to me. And she said, 'Are you Egyptian?'

"I said, 'No.'

"'Have you ever been to Egypt?'

"'No.'

"'Have you ever studied Egyptian history?'

"I said, 'No, why do you ask?'

"She said, 'Your pieces have a feeling of old Egyptian furniture.'"

On Nature

"I remember about 1955 we had a horrible rainstorm, and this area was all groves. The water was 2-ft. high, torrents of water, raging rivers. Somebody had some eucalyptus trees, and their roots were showing after the waters had receded a little bit. We made a left turn and Freda said, 'Sam, there's your table legs.' The roots came up like that (he gestures), just absolutely beautiful. And I reeled back and thought, 'Gosh, it does look like one of my pieces.'"

STRAIGHT FROM THE SHOP FLOOR. To preview the final shape of a table pedestal, Maloof traces a half-template on the floor near his bandsaw, trusting his eye as always.

On Design That Spans Oceans

"**I**'d never been to Japan, and I didn't have any books on Japanese architecture. I came from a small family, from a small farm town, and we never traveled or went on vacation to any exotic places. And then when I went to Japan—I've been there four times now—I began to notice things that I do that were done in ancient times. It was the same way when I was in the Middle East."

WIDE OVERHANGS. On cabinets, chairs, and window trim, Maloof often favors a long projection, reminiscent of Japanese architecture.

500 Pieces, One Perfected

"I can't say that I've done a piece that is absolutely complete, that I don't want to make a change on it at all. But I must say that my little low-back chair—I think I perfected it. I can't do anything else to it. I think it looks well, it sits well, it's built well.

"Those arms aren't really arms. When you sit down in a chair, there's nothing to reach for. These are handles. You can raise yourself up, instead of putting your hands on the sides of the chair. And then they are stretchers. Instead of having the stretchers below the seat, I have the stretchers up here. They give it strength, but you don't have to have any stretchers down at the bottom. As for a high arm, well, a lot of times I've seen chairs where the arm hits the edge of a dining table."

IN HIS 80s, MALOOF
REBUILT HIS LIFE. The new
property at the foot of the
San Gabriel Mountains
holds his new lumber
sheds, his old house and
workshops, and the new
house (facing page) he
recently designed. The
new home meant a second
chance to design and build
a spiral stairway (left).
He keeps a carving gouge
nearby to work on the
surface detailing when he
has time.

Maloof also values the experience that blossoming woodworkers can have at schools or in other communities of peers. "I find that students are not selfish; they help one another and critique each other's work. They feed on one another."

However, he warns against domineering teachers: "Some instructors demand that you work the way they work, and so there become just many little followers of this person or that person. I see a lot of work where I can tell where that person went to school right off the bat.

"I think a good teacher gives the whole rope to the students and lets them do what they want to do. I don't think you should curtail the excitement or the invention or the new direction. Sometimes [the student] falls flat on his face; other times it's great."

Trust Your Instincts When Creating, but Put Function before Form

Maloof had no formal training in art or furniture making, so there is a completely personal quality to his work—polished yet unsophisticated—which strikes a chord in a wide range of people. Throughout his career, Maloof simply did what made sense to him, trusting his own eye and instincts at a time when the concept of the studio furniture maker didn't exist.

Maloof's design philosophy is deceptively simple: to make pieces that function well and are beautiful—or "byoodeeful," as he says—referring to anything from a tree to a pottery vessel to a joinery detail. But function comes first. "I've seen tables that you couldn't eat off of, chairs you couldn't sit on, cabinets that were so shallow you couldn't put a pair of socks in them," Maloof says. "They were beautifully made and nice to look at, but I felt a piece could be very beautiful and very functional at the same time, and that is really the center of what I do. I want my chairs to invite people to sit on them. This has been my objective since my first commission."

As for designers who consider sculpture or art first and function second, Maloof says, "It's art furniture, and I think some of it is very interesting. I take my hat off to them. But to be different just to be different, though, is just a lot of poppycock.

"Some potters, they have a style and they stay to it. Other potters will continue changing—this direction, that direction. I heard a very well-known potter say, 'I've got to figure out what's going to sell good this next year.' That is for the birds. I've chosen to do what I do and I try to do the best work I can. And every year I add two or three pieces to what I've done."

ASA CHRISTIANA is the editor of *Fine Woodworking* magazine.

9 Tips for Better Design

BY MICHAEL FORTUNE

Several times a year I have the opportunity to teach a two-week class in furniture design and construction. I enjoy the challenge of working with people who think they are incapable of designing their own furniture. Most of my students are mystified about where design ideas come from and how they are developed.

Most articles about furniture design begin with the classical orders—golden mean, Fibonacci series, etc.—and end with well-known period pieces. My broader approach to design was distilled from my training at a commercial furniture-design school in the early 1970s, and refined over my 30-year career as a furniture designer and maker. I've found that great design ideas can come from anywhere, and the standard rules can choke inspiration rather than free it. For example, look to other cultures and you'll find ideas

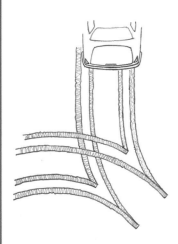

FROM TIRE TRACKS TO A TABLE. In the interplay of curves on a snow-covered driveway, Fortune found the base of this hall table.

Avoid Factory Dimensions

Mass-produced furniture is characterized by a limited number of thicknesses. These endlessly repeated dimensions are everywhere—in chairs, tables, and cabinet frames. This is because it is much cheaper for lumber mills to work in huge quantities, taking all 1-in. lumber to a uniform ¾-in. thickness. Fine furniture is not made with the same expediency, so we can successfully mill 1-in.-thick stock to ⅞ in. or thicker. Avoid common cross sections such as ¾ in. by 1¾ in. or ¾ in. by 2 in.; basically, avoid any common premilled dimension found at large lumber retailers.

NONSTANDARD THICK-NESSES. The thick, solid-wood top on this nightstand helps to distinguish it from factory furniture.

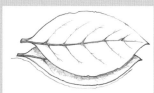

ORGANIC CURVES. The leaves of a backyard ash inspired this pivoting side table (above). The stalks and leaves of the daylilies in Fortune's backyard inspired this table base (far right).

HIS SIGNATURE CHAIR. **Fortune's No. 1 chair was inspired by a piece of rusty garden furniture. He refined the design with the influence of several past furniture designers.**

MESOPOTAMIAN LINES. **An 8,000-year-old vase in a museum inspired this table's leg and apron profile. Fortune reversed the lower curve to avoid a pigeon-toed look.**

that will appear brand-new in your own. Some of the most obscure corners of history are hiding beautiful ideas that you can borrow and adapt.

After you find a rough idea that resonates with you, you'll need to work out the overall proportions, lines, and details, guiding the design toward a successful conclusion. I'll share my primary sources of inspiration, and some visual dos and don'ts that have worked for me.

How to Find Ideas

If you are receptive, ideas can come from almost anywhere. In design school, my instructor's interest in three-dimensional puzzles spilled into his furniture. I admired the unusual origin of his designs, and was inspired to look differently at objects around me.

Look around you Almost anything from any culture—bridges, buildings, fine art—can inspire a design. If it strikes you as beautiful, it probably will resonate with others. Better yet, they won't know exactly why. When walking through a museum with my children, I came across a vase made in Mesopotamia about 6000 B.C. Captivated by the simple elegance of the shape, I returned to my workshop and doodled casually in an effort to convert the profile of the vase into the profile of a table leg and apron.

If you like gardening or the outdoors, natural forms are worth exploring. Plant stalks can become table legs, and leaves might inspire shapes for tabletops. If you are intrigued by structures like bridges, dams, and buildings, they can inspire any number of table bases.

Look to history The history of furniture is wonderfully diverse and goes back about 6,000 years. It is a rich source for inspiration. It isn't necessary to copy what has been done before, but it is important to learn from it. Try as you might to be completely original, you can't escape being influenced. Your furniture-design preferences are shaped by the style of furniture that you grew up with and what is immediately around you. By browsing through historical texts, you can gain a much broader interpretation of what you like and of what furniture can be. For example, the Cubist painting style made famous by Picasso, circa 1920, also spawned a Czechoslovakian Cubist furniture style. If you are interested in furniture made entirely with angled shapes, then this era is worth further research.

Over the years I have collected many reference books on the history of furniture. I turn to a few of them again and again to develop the proportions or other details of my rough ideas. When I designed my No. 1 chair in 1979, I was initially inspired by a piece of old, rusted, metal garden furniture. I was fascinated by the unusual placement

of the various parts and how they intersected. I added the influence of several furniture designers, notably Charles Rennie Mackintosh (Scotland), Hans Wegner (Denmark), and Frank Lloyd Wright (United States). To blend all of these ideas successfully, I moved from numerous simple sketches to quarter-scale models and then to several rough, full-size mock-ups. I have sold 300 of these chairs.

Think of pieces as people Objects broadcast signals that we interpret according to our own likes and dislikes. I am attracted to objects that have a receptive, almost human quality. For example, when I walk into a room with several different chairs, I go to the chair that looks comfortable and appears to have its arms open, welcoming the viewer. I have designed many chairs over the years with this receptive quality in mind.

BOOKS ARE ANOTHER SOURCE.
To generate ideas, Fortune flips through *World Furniture*, edited by Helena Hayward. To refine his ideas, he consults the clear line drawings in *Classical European Furniture Design*, by Jose Claret Rubira. He also looks at *Classic Chinese Furniture*, by Wang Shixiang, which has clear photographs of spare yet beautifully proportioned furniture dating back to 1400.

A BALLERINA'S STANCE. Fortune prefers graceful forms to knotted, muscular shapes, and believes others feel the same way.

People are used to seeing bodies and evaluating posture, so pay attention to the stance of your pieces in a human sense. Just as someone standing with their feet pigeon-toed appears awkward, almost embarrassed, furniture with inward-pointing feet also will seem ungainly. The same goes for a bow-legged stance (knees out) or knock-kneed (knees in): Neither is seen in the enduring fine works of art. Curves are also an essential human quality (see "Curves Add Interest" on p. 29).

Similarly, I find the graceful form of a ballerina more attractive than the bulky, knotty shape of a wrestler. With this in mind, I am inclined to design furniture that is composed of lightweight linear elements rather than massive shapes. A boxy, heavy shape can be lightened simply by putting it on a pedestal that is set back from the leading edges (sometimes called a "toe kick").

A WELCOMING EMBRACE. **With arms open, Fortune's chairs invite the viewer to take a seat.**

Upward and Outward

Another way I try to make a connection with the person viewing my furniture is to have it connect to its surroundings. Most of my furniture consists of shapes and details that extend outward as they move upward, subliminally connecting them to their surroundings. Usually this means pieces are larger at the top than at the bottom, but sometimes a flaring cornice is enough. Furniture that has inward sloping lines may appear to be solitary, less engaging, and even heavier than it really is.

CONNECTED TO THE WORLD. **Fortune's pieces reach outward as they move up, tying them to the space and objects above and around them.**

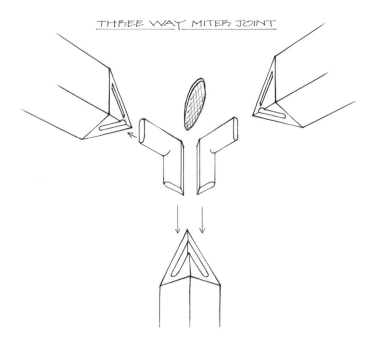

THREE WAY MITER JOINT

FIRST THE TABLE, THEN THE JOINT. Searching for an efficient way to build this clean-looking three-way miter joint, Fortune came up with a pair of L-shaped plywood tenons that fit into router-cut mortises. The joint, in turn, made dozens of other tables possible.

How to Transform Ideas into Design

Your creative process can be restrained by your existing knowledge of how to work with wood, so don't worry about those details during this time. Just keep in mind the bigger issues like structural integrity and wood movement. Before you think about joinery, brainstorm and develop the design.

Design first, engineer second Once you have a design you like, tackle the technical details. There is so much excellent reference material available these days, such as books, magazines, and DVDs, to assist us with resolving the construction details of furniture. Rarely will you invent a design that is completely new. More often than not you will find a joint or a woodworking technique that is close to what you need.

Simple is good It's easy to overdo things with ideas under the heading of "Wouldn't it look nice if I ..." Don't get too complicated

when developing your designs. I generally recommend working within a loose guideline I call "the rule of three." By that I mean that each piece of furniture should have no more than three strong design elements that work together to complete the whole.

Decide first on a focal point—the primary design element—and showcase it. Let the other two elements play a supporting role. The primary element is usually, but not always, the overall form or shape. The second may be the color and texture of the dominant wood. And the third element is usually any obvious detailing like inlay or knobs and pulls.

An accumulation of disparate shapes, woods, doors, drawers, and shelves easily can overpower an overall design. It very well could be that there is simply more than one piece of furniture on the drawing board and that they have to be separated. So build one, and just sketch the others to be built later as part of a series.

THE RULE OF THREE. Don't combine more than three strong design elements. The focal point of the cabinet (left) is its curved and stepped front. The bee's-wing mahogany is the second element, and the contrasting detail is the third. The dominant feature of the table (above) is the shape, low but with dramatically curved legs. The contrast between the Macassar ebony and the Australian lacewood is the second element, whereas the four-way matched grain is the third.

Evolution, not revolution Designing and building furniture as part of a series is a great way to completely explore and resolve an idea. You take what works best in each piece, and then apply it to the next. Your design and construction learning curve will shorten. You also may save time by reusing specialized jigs or bending forms. At the very least you will build confidence as you go. Remember, a design idea doesn't have to stay within one group of furniture, but can extend from tables to cabinets to chairs.

I call this an "evolutionary" approach rather than "revolutionary." I might work in

the same vein for months or even years until my designs evolve into something quite different. Along the way I am continually making design discoveries and recording them in a sketchbook for exploration someday. The great thing about revisiting an idea months or years later is that you come at it with experiences collected along the way.

MICHAEL FORTUNE is a furniture maker in Lakefield, Ontario, Canada, and teaches classes throughout North America. You can visit him on the web at www.michaelfortune.com.

FROM LAWN TO LIVING ROOM. Fortune's design for a simple garden chair led to a hardwood version. Aside from the dark wood and upholstery, he added a soft arch to the seat rail.

Curves Add Interest

A simple approach to making your work stand out is to use techniques that appear to be difficult to master. Curves are a good example. Keep in mind, though, that lots of curves on one piece of furniture can distract and ultimately tire the viewer.

Other woodworkers may be intrigued by the technical mastery involved in working with complex curves, but I don't think most viewers or buyers are knowledgeable enough to be sufficiently impressed. I rarely design furniture with compound curves, which move in two planes at once; I prefer to work with a few simple, single-plane curves in each piece.

On the other hand, try not to interrupt curved elements just to make joinery easier. For example, a graceful curve on a chair leg can be compromised by leaving a flat section to accommodate an intersecting stretcher. Similarly, a flat spot on a table leg where it meets the apron smacks of the expeditious joinery techniques found on mass-produced furniture.

DRAW A RADIUS OR BEND A BATTEN

While a simple radius curve will liven up a rectilinear piece of furniture, a stress curve is even more dynamic. Stress curves are more common in nature, and the straighter sections of the curve emphasize the curved parts. Make these even more interesting by tapering the batten, which creates an asymmetrical curve.

CURVES SOFTEN A BOXY DRESSER. Bent-laminated drawer fronts turn an ordinary chest of drawers into a more graceful and unique piece of furniture.

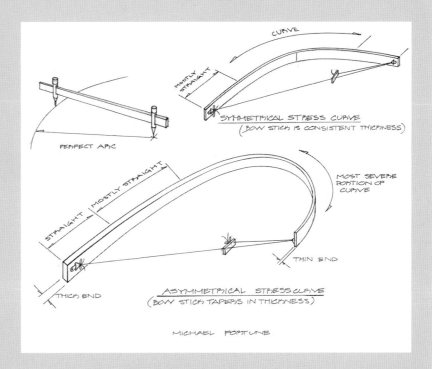

Drafting Basics

BY PHILIP C. LOWE

Many folks consider time spent at the drawing table to be time taken away from woodworking. They think that unless they're cutting wood, no progress is being made. Actually, both time and material are being saved, not to mention a lot of head-scratching. This principle holds true for many forms of furniture—from simple to complex, from reproductions to original designs.

The first of any piece of furniture is always the most labor-intensive. To be successful, both design and construction must be ironed out beforehand, so I do a full-size drawing for every new piece I build. By laying out a design at full scale, you get a better sense of its proportions and size. Also, patterns and templates for curved parts can be made directly from an accurate drawing, which means you don't have to redraw parts that were sketched out at a smaller scale.

Everything You Need in a Single Drawing

A full-size drawing helped Lowe determine critical design and construction aspects for this side table. Before putting tool to wood, he worked out the curves of the rails, the taper of the legs, the overhang of the top, the joinery, and a precise cut list.

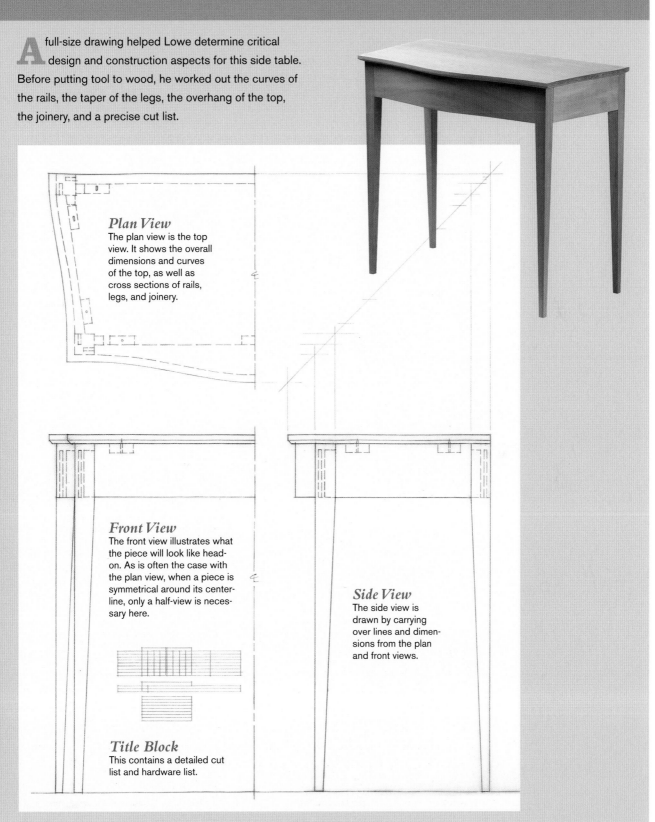

Plan View
The plan view is the top view. It shows the overall dimensions and curves of the top, as well as cross sections of rails, legs, and joinery.

Front View
The front view illustrates what the piece will look like head-on. As is often the case with the plan view, when a piece is symmetrical around its center-line, only a half-view is necessary here.

Side View
The side view is drawn by carrying over lines and dimensions from the plan and front views.

Title Block
This contains a detailed cut list and hardware list.

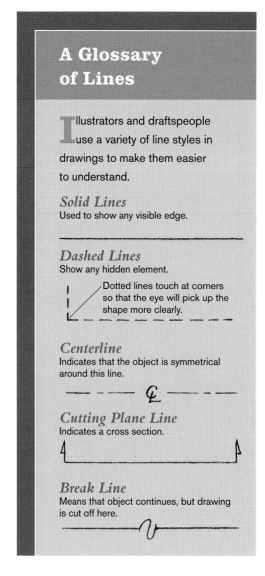

A Glossary of Lines

Illustrators and draftspeople use a variety of line styles in drawings to make them easier to understand.

Solid Lines
Used to show any visible edge.

Dashed Lines
Show any hidden element.

Dotted lines touch at corners so that the eye will pick up the shape more clearly.

Centerline
Indicates that the object is symmetrical around this line.

Ȼ

Cutting Plane Line
Indicates a cross section.

Break Line
Means that object continues, but drawing is cut off here.

The full-size drawing typically includes three views and a few other important details and sections. The number of views and sections needed is determined by the complexity of the design.

The Basic Tools for Drawing

My drawing table is a 4-ft. by 8-ft. angled surface covered with a vinyl mat and equipped with a cable-controlled parallel rule. But all you need to make accurate drawings is a large, smooth surface (like Baltic birch plywood or medium-density fiberboard) with two parallel edges to run a T-square against. Add a ruler, a set of triangles, a white plastic eraser, an erasing shield, and a dusting brush, and you're off.

For best results, I recommend hard pencil lead and special drafting paper. I use a mechanical pencil and drafting vellum called Charprint 916H, which I purchase in 42-in.-wide rolls.

The two tools used most often in drafting are designed to do the two most fundamental operations. The first tool, the T-square or parallel rule, is used to draw horizontal lines. Second is the triangle: Either the 30-60-90 or the 45-45-90 is used for drawing vertical lines perpendicular to the horizontals. These triangles also are used to draw common angles measuring 30 degrees, 45 degrees, and 60 degrees. A straightedge is important because it can be used to draw a straight line at any angle, such as the tapers on legs. A T-square flipped onto its back (so it will lie flat) makes a workable straightedge.

The compass is the tool of choice when a regular curve is needed. I draw irregular curves freehand, which can be more pleasing to the eye than a curve made using a compass or French curve. I smooth out these freehand lines with a long, flexible tool called an adjustable ship curve.

When drawing freehand curves, the lines tend to be a bit heavy. I clean them up using an erasing shield, a thin sheet of metal with various shapes cut into it. By covering the portion of the line that you want to save with the erasing shield, you can erase the exposed part and clean up unsightly stray lines with a white plastic eraser.

Then there is the pencil lead that you use. My mechanical pencil can hold any grade of lead. My choice is No. 4 hard lead, which is not likely to smear but still makes a clear line. If you use a pencil like this, you will need a lead pointer, which is a fancy term for a special sharpener.

If you happen to remove the drawing from the board and discover that you need to add something, you can place the paper back on the board, match any horizontal line with the T-square edge and tape the drawing back in place.

Designing a Side Table in Three Views

To help you understand the drawing process and its advantages, I'll draw (and design) a basic side table with a curved front and sides. There are many design and construction decisions to make on a table like this—overall proportions, curves, tapers, joinery—and all of these details can be drawn on paper before making the first cut in valuable stock.

Once I have the paper taped to the board, the best place to start is the floor. A simple horizontal line a couple of inches up from the bottom of the paper does the trick. From here, I think about the overall dimensions of the table: height, width, and depth. The height is based on the type of table it is. I draw a light, horizontal line at 29 in. to 30 in., the standard height for a side table, which most likely will have a vase or lamp on it. These two lines are the beginning of the front and side views.

Next, in the space above the front view, I draw a light rectangle that represents the size of the tabletop. This is the top, or plan, view. These few lines establish the overall size.

Half views are enough Once I am happy with the proportions, I pencil in the centerline on the plan view and carry it down to the front view. On most pieces of furniture, including this one, only a half view is necessary for the front and plan views. I draw everything to the left of the centerline. The side view will show the entire piece.

These half views have a few important advantages. They not only mean a smaller drawing and less work, but they also guarantee symmetry. I make a half template for the serpentine curve across the front, and simply flip it to lay out the other side. This is much easier than trying to draw the entire curve and match both sides. Also, the same curve is used on the sides.

I draw half of the serpentine curve across the front in the plan view. I draw this

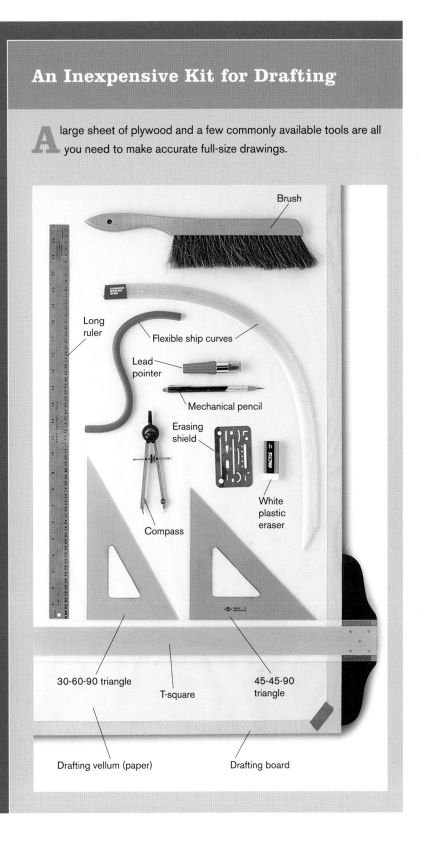

An Inexpensive Kit for Drafting

A large sheet of plywood and a few commonly available tools are all you need to make accurate full-size drawings.

Brush

Long ruler

Flexible ship curves

Lead pointer

Mechanical pencil

Erasing shield

White plastic eraser

Compass

30-60-90 triangle

T-square

45-45-90 triangle

Drafting vellum (paper)

Drafting board

Step 1: Draw Overall Dimensions and Curves

Determine the height of the tabletop and get an idea of its overall size. Then draw the actual curved edges on the left of the centerline. Only half of the table needs to be drawn in the front and plan views.

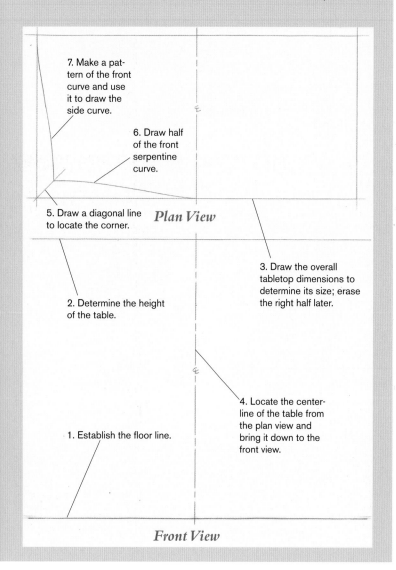

7. Make a pattern of the front curve and use it to draw the side curve.

6. Draw half of the front serpentine curve.

5. Draw a diagonal line to locate the corner.

Plan View

3. Draw the overall tabletop dimensions to determine its size; erase the right half later.

2. Determine the height of the table.

4. Locate the centerline of the table from the plan view and bring it down to the front view.

1. Establish the floor line.

Front View

Negotiating the Curves

DRAW HALF OF THE FRONT CURVE. Sketch it out freehand, trusting your eye.

SMOOTH THE CURVE. Use a flexible ship curve to create a fair, even profile.

MAKE A PLYWOOD PATTERN. Poke a series of holes through the paper to transfer the pattern to thin plywood.

DRAW SYMMETRICAL CURVES. Use the pattern to draw a matching serpentine curve on the side rail and to lay out the actual workpieces.

line freehand, working to get a curve that is pleasing to my eye. This curve can be subtle or extreme; it's a matter of taste.

I made this tabletop twice as wide as it is deep, allowing two important things to happen. One, the same half-serpentine curve pattern for the front can be used for the side. Two, the entire table can be doubled, turning it into a card table with an identical serpentine rail on all four sides.

After drawing the curve for the front, I use a piece of ⅛-in.-thick plywood to make a pattern of the curve by laying the plywood underneath the drawing and pricking holes along the line, through the

paper and into the plywood. I saw out the pattern and smooth it with a spokeshave and sandpaper. I can use it as a template for doing the rest of the drawing, and when building the table in the shop.

The overhang determines the table base Looking at the front and plan views, I decide the overhang of the tabletop. For this table, a slight overhang will keep the tabletop from hiding the rail and will accentuate the matching curves in both. At this point, I also determine the thickness of the tabletop and draw it into the front and plan views. A heavy chamfer under the edge lightens the look.

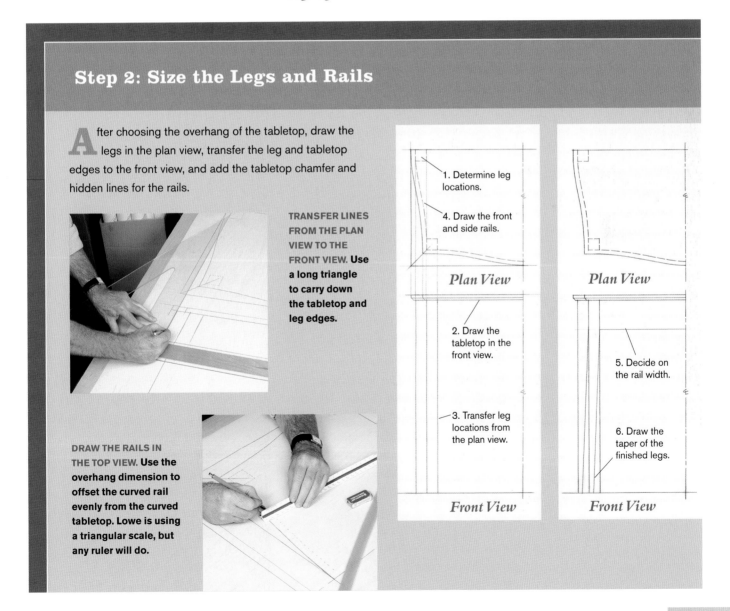

Step 2: Size the Legs and Rails

After choosing the overhang of the tabletop, draw the legs in the plan view, transfer the leg and tabletop edges to the front view, and add the tabletop chamfer and hidden lines for the rails.

TRANSFER LINES FROM THE PLAN VIEW TO THE FRONT VIEW. Use a long triangle to carry down the tabletop and leg edges.

DRAW THE RAILS IN THE TOP VIEW. Use the overhang dimension to offset the curved rail evenly from the curved tabletop. Lowe is using a triangular scale, but any ruler will do.

1. Determine leg locations.

4. Draw the front and side rails.

Plan View

Plan View

2. Draw the tabletop in the front view.

5. Decide on the rail width.

3. Transfer leg locations from the plan view.

6. Draw the taper of the finished legs.

Front View

Front View

Step 3: Draw the Side View

All of the information necessary to complete the side view is incorporated in the plan and front views.

To transfer dimensions from the plan view to the side view, draw a line at a 45-degree angle and project lines across and then down.

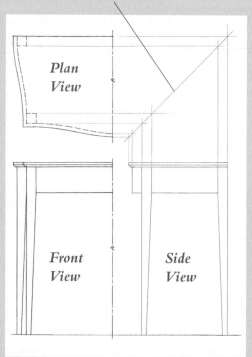

Plan View

Front View

Side View

NOW FILL IN THE SIDE VIEW. Carry over horizontal lines from the front view and transfer the other dimensions from the plan view using a 45-degree line or simply by measuring.

The overhang dimension is used to position the legs and rails in the plan view. At this point, I consider the width and thickness of the legs and draw them. Now, using a triangle, I project the dimensions of the legs down into the front view. I also continue these light lines to the floor, which end up forming the rectangles of stock from which the legs will be sawn.

On this traditional table, I keep the rails flush with the legs. It's easier to build an inset rail, but a flush rail creates a smooth flow around the corner for a more high-style look. To draw the curved rails in the plan view, you need a hidden line that is offset evenly from the curve of the top. The overhang of the tabletop is ⅝ in. I mark this offset from the tabletop edge in a dozen or so places and then use a ship curve to draw a smooth curve for the rail. Next, I pick a pleasing width for the front rail.

Jumping back to the legs, I consider how they should be tapered—on two sides or four? Having decided that a two-sided taper looks best on this table, I lay out the amount of taper at the floor line and locate one end of a long straightedge on the drawing at that point. The other end

Step 4: Add Joinery and Title Block

Design the joinery in the plan view, find the rail thicknesses, fill in the front and side views, and add the title block.

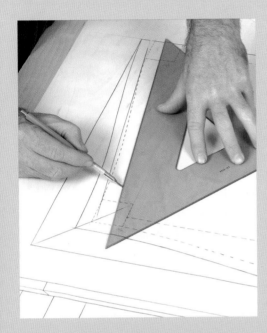

FIGURE OUT THE SIDE RAIL'S THICKNESS. Start with a construction line to determine the outside edge of the rail stock, then offset a parallel line from that to find the inside edge of the rail.

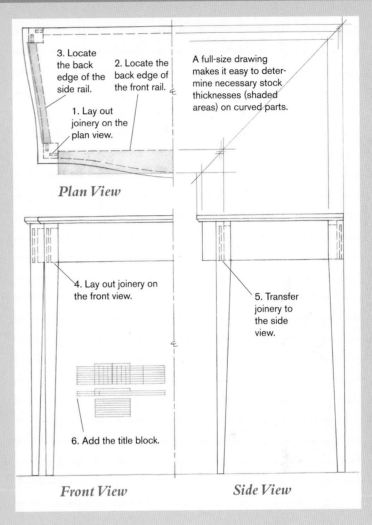

3. Locate the back edge of the side rail.

2. Locate the back edge of the front rail.

1. Lay out joinery on the plan view.

A full-size drawing makes it easy to determine necessary stock thicknesses (shaded areas) on curved parts.

Plan View

4. Lay out joinery on the front view.

5. Transfer joinery to the side view.

6. Add the title block.

Front View   *Side View*

goes on a point about ⅜ in. below the rail, where I generally start my tapers.

Develop the side view So far, I only have worked on the front and plan views. To create a side view, I project lines from the front view and take the horizontal dimensions from the plan view. Until now, only the external lines of the table have been addressed, so if any of the proportions need to be changed, this is the time to do it. The white eraser will make clean work of it. Once I'm satisfied, it's time to fill in the joinery.

Joinery determines the thickness of the rails First, in the plan view, I fill in the locations of the mortises and tenons. Then I can draw the back edge of the rail, determining its overall thickness.

On smaller tables like this, I keep the front cheeks of the tenons ¼ in. back from the outside of the leg and use a ¼-in.-thick tenon. These locations allow long mortises to fit inside the leg without touching one another and weakening the leg.

The first step on the plan view is to draw the back rail ¾ in. thick with the standard ¼-in.-thick tenon. Then, after drawing the joinery on the front rail in the plan view, I can draw the horizontal line indicating the back of that piece, and a clear view of the stock develops. I can determine easily that it must be 2⅜ in. thick to contain the curve.

The side rails can be taken from a thinner piece of stock by drawing a construction line from the outside edge of the curve to the rail's front shoulder, and then drawing a line parallel to that one to indicate the overall thickness of the part.

Project the joinery to the front and side views Now carry the tenon thicknesses and lengths down to the front view and in turn to the side view. One last decision that needs to be made regarding the tenons is their width and the size of any top or bottom shoulders to make the table resist racking. I think giving the tenons a

¼-in. shoulder at the top and no shoulder at the bottom is enough. I think it is easier to align the bottom edge of the rails to each other without a shoulder to deal with, making it easier to apply any banding that might run around the bottom edge of the rails and across the legs.

If there is no shoulder at the top, an open mortise is created and the strength of the leg is compromised. It wouldn't stand up to an accidental kick or a whack from a wayward vacuum cleaner.

The last element that I place on the drawing is the title block, which contains both a cut list and a hardware list. I refer to the drawing many times during construction, keeping myself organized and avoiding costly errors.

PHILIP C. LOWE owns and operates a wood-working school and makes period furniture at his shop in Beverly, Massachusetts.

What Information Goes into a Title Block?

The title block is an important last step. It contains rough and finished stock dimensions, listing wood species and comments for each part, as well as a hardware list, the date, and the maker's name and address.

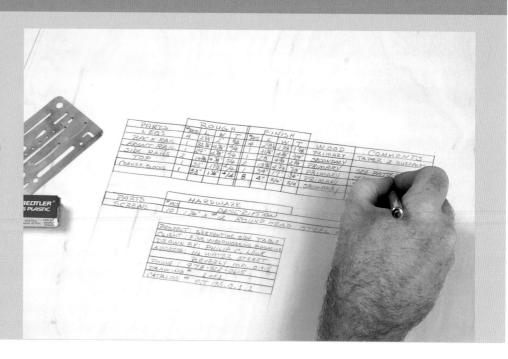

Mock-Ups Quicken the Design Process

BY KEITH ALLEN

Compared to any other furniture, chairs are more difficult to make. They're hard to design and hard to build. They need to be as lightweight as possible to make them easy to move around. Yet they also need to be strong to survive almost certain abuse. Most furniture designs begin with two-dimensional drawings, but drawings can fail to capture the complexities of a three-dimensional object such as a chair, and drawings are worthless for determining comfort.

To my mind, the chairmaker's ultimate challenge is psychological. After surmounting all of the obstacles to design and construction, the custom chairmaker is then called upon to produce precisely repeated multiples. I regard this boredom factor as the most difficult aspect of chairmaking.

For chairs, I usually dispense with drawings and begin instead with three-dimensional mock-ups. I can test-drive a good mock-up for comfort, and I can better assess how the chair is going to look. The mock-up can reveal any structural weakness early on as well as provide a convenient basis for precisely cloning multiples if I have more than one chair to make.

I make mock-ups of inexpensive, even junk, material. The parts are typically fastened together with butt joints, using a few toenailed screws per joint. I use #2 square-drive screws, 2 in. to 3 in. long, and predrill pilot holes and countersinks for the screw heads. Cutting a dry biscuit joint in the pieces being joined often makes it easier to align them during assembly.

You can easily change the dimensions and the joint geometry of mock-up parts by trial and error, as the chair design evolves

experimentally. A compound miter saw is a useful tool for this process. I record angle setups directly on the pieces as I cut them. The resulting mock-up is strong enough to test for comfort, and the temporary joinery gives me a good feel for whether permanent joinery will be strong enough to withstand likely abuse.

Make the Transitions in Stages

I've learned to make mock-ups in two stages. During the first stage, I determine the size and geometry of the parts and resolve ergonomic issues: how wide to make the front of the seat, for instance. In the second stage, I concentrate on form and aesthetic details: Should the top edge of the crest rail be rounded over or left square?

The first stage usually requires a minimal rough-shaping of relatively few pieces, such as the seat and back. When that's done, I'm almost ready for the transition from design to construction. I can simply disassemble the mock-up and use the sized pieces to produce blanks for however many chairs are needed. In making the actual chairs, I replace all of the screwed-together joints

in the mock-up with routed mortises and loose tenons.

In the second stage, I test aesthetic ideas directly on the mock-up by trying one design detail on the left-hand side and another detail on the right-hand side. Because making blanks for the final chairs from highly shaped pieces can be cumbersome, I usually clone the mock-up between the two stages. Design decisions made when working with the second-stage mock-up rarely require any change in the overall size of parts.

The two-stage mock-up process not only provides a natural transition between design and construction, but also helps me organize the process better and concentrate on one problem at a time. Also, construction of the actual chair is easier because the process roughly shadows the design process: Cut blanks, rout joints, shape parts, sand, assemble, and finish.

Experience Has Proved This Method Useful

I've used mock-ups to great advantage, as demonstrated with the two projects shown here. Both of these jobs called for making sets of eight upholstered dining chairs to go with dining tables that I had made for the clients. In each commission, building the mock-up took me about three days, and building a set of eight chairs from the mock-up took about two weeks, working alone.

I built the set of mahogany chairs (above right) in a style derived from traditional Queen Anne elements. The client handled the upholstering chores and experimented directly with the mock-up, attaching webbing and padding to it, to decide on the appropriate cushioning. With the finished chairs, I provided slip seats for the upholstery. The set of bird's-eye maple and cherry chairs is quite contemporary, what I call a "George Nakashima-meets-Gerrit Rietveld" sort of style (above left). Upon viewing the mock-up, and at my suggestion, the client decided to replace two front legs with a single, central, vertical support. Modifying the mock-up was painless.

Upholstery—foam and fabric on plywood inserts—was the client's responsibility. After using the mock-up to produce chair blanks, I reassembled it and delivered it to the client, along with the plywood inserts for all of the chairs. While I worked on the chairs, and with a deadline fast approaching, the client took the mock-up and inserts to the upholsterer for a test sitting to determine just the right cushioning. The upholstered inserts were ready by the time I completed the chairs. On delivery day, using four metal tabletop fasteners per chair, I installed all eight inserts within an hour. Having the mock-up available for the upholsterer's use probably saved the client a week or more in total project time.

An Efficient Chairmaker Is a Happy Chairmaker

Although no method can eliminate all of the tedium of some projects, the efficiency of my mock-up method has reduced the boredom factor for me to a tolerable level. I once either dreaded taking on chair commissions or simply rejected them. Now, the mock-up helps me solve design problems and communicate with clients better than drawings or full-blown prototypes ever did. This method makes me feel so efficient and organized that I'm planning to use it for a few speculative pieces of furniture.

KEITH ALLEN designs and builds custom furniture in his shop on a 50-acre farm near Raleigh-Durham, North Carolina.

DESIGNING IN THREE DIMENSIONS. **For both sets of completed chairs shown, the author cut to the chase in the design process by skipping the drawing stage.**

Fine-Tune Designs Before You Build

BY GARY ROGOWSKI

Woodworkers, as we all know, love to roar into a weekend project. They can then spend weeks or months on it, as we also know, only to find out one sad day that the finished piece doesn't look quite right. It may in fact be a bit homely or ungainly. But didn't those plans look promising? Didn't that drawing seem right? You can avoid this dilemma with a simple and rewarding exercise: Build a scale model first. This is the advice I give my students; those who latch on to this technique never again build without it.

Don't get me wrong: Drawings and plans, whether full- or partial-scale, are very useful. But adding a three-dimensional model made with ordinary shop tools and available materials will help you learn more. The model will show you form, help you fix proportions, balance, and symmetry, even help you think about the best way to build a piece. In the end, you can save a load of time and money building the right design instead of one that may never feel quite right.

See It before You Build It

Models can help you work out design ideas for all types of pieces. They don't require much time or material to build, but they can save a lot of both in the construction of your furniture.

A DRAWING IS ONLY THE START. A model lets you see a piece in three dimensions and answer questions about its form and proportions.

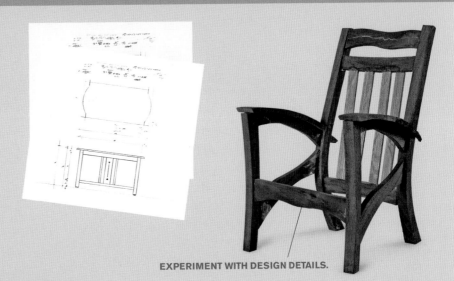

EXPERIMENT WITH DESIGN DETAILS.

PHOTOCOPIED CONTENTS CAN FILL OUT AN INTERIOR.

MODELS CAN BE AS DETAILED AS THE FINAL PIECE.

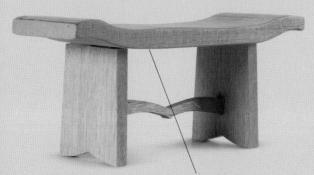

SOFTWOODS ARE EASY TO SHAPE AND CARVE.

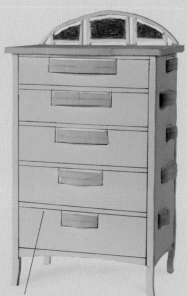

COMPONENTS CAN SIMPLY BE DRAWN IN PLACE.

Start by Drawing Ideas in a Sketchbook

Building a model will help you visualize and refine a new design, but it's best to launch the project on paper first. How do you get from an idea you saw once in a magazine or at someone's house to the point where you can build a model? I find it easiest to begin by sketching or doodling, without censoring my ideas. I do this in a notebook that I keep for future reference. You never know how the germ of one idea may give life to a totally new design later on.

This process usually yields several ideas that appeal to me for my current project. At this point, I establish basic outside dimensions and draw a box that represents the proportions of the piece. With this visual key, I now can sketch to general proportions so I don't end up with a great-looking cabinet design in my notebook and a squashed-looking shoebox in reality.

I narrow down my notebook sketches to three ideas and work up more detailed ideas on drawing paper. Then I let these ideas percolate for a while. Finally I boil down the best elements in each to a single design and do a final sketch.

Once a design is sketched and I like its elements, I make my elevation and plan drawings to scale. Afterward, if I'm confident about the elements of the piece, I can do full-scale drawings. But if I still have questions about the form or proportions, I might want another level of information. That's when I make a model.

FULL-SIZE OR SCALE MODEL?
Both are easy to make. Larger models give a greater sense of how the finished piece will occupy space; small mock-ups in wood can show remarkable detail while being portable and easy to store.

From Sketchbook to Model

First, decide on scale. Are your questions about the design primarily about the right-ness of its basic proportions? Do you need to transport the model and show it to clients? A small-scale model will probably answer. Or do you need to live with the piece for a while, to see how it casts shadows and fits into its intended space? If so, full-scale is probably your best bet.

When I built library tables for the Oregon State Archives project, I made a ⅛-scale model for several reasons. One was to impress the selection jury with my design, giving them something tangible to see and discuss. I built the model in cherry, the same as the tables would be, but I sketched in the inlay details with a pen. The other advantage? It forced me to walk through the stages of building the piece and led me to resolve key questions about construction. Which parts would I put together first? What steps had to be completed before moving to the next phase? Would this design hold up over time, or did I need to modify the structure?

At this point in the process, you can congratulate yourself for building the model, but then let it rest for a couple of days. Let it sit in a corner of your shop or in the place where the finished piece will finally live. Then come back to it and see how it feels. Your gut will tell you a lot about whether you got it right. If it's not right, then you'll need to start figuring out where to cut and where to add. I tell my students that planning at this stage may feel like it's slowing you down, but in the end it can save you time as you build with confidence, knowing you have a design that works, fits the space, and looks great.

GARY ROGOWSKI, a contributing editor to *Fine Woodworking* magazine, runs the Northwest Wood-working Studio in Portland, Oregon. Visit his studio on the web at www.northwestwoodworking.com.

Materials Are Inexpensive

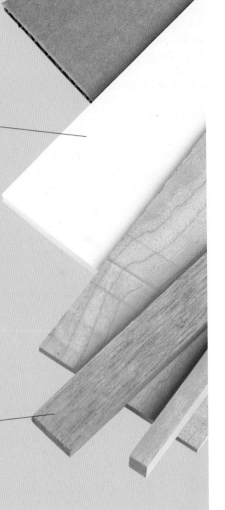

CARDBOARD

Commonly available and inex-pensive, it's best for full-scale or half-scale models, and great for modeling full-size table-tops. Cardboard cuts easily with a bandsaw, a tablesaw, or a knife and straightedge, holds with yellow glue or hot-melt glue, and is sturdy enough for simple tenon joints. Details can be drawn or painted on the surface.

FOAMCORE

Sold at art-supply houses in ⅛-in., ³⁄₁₆-in., and ½-in. thick-nesses, its higher price makes it a better choice for small-scale models or full-size mock-ups of small pieces. Any saw or sharp knife will cut it. Use pins, glue, or even packing tape to hold it together. Ad-vantages are its stiffness, light weight, and white color, which forces you to concentrate on the shape of the piece. Its sur-faces can be painted, inked, stenciled, you name it.

WOOD

Material can come from the shop scrap barrel, typically ⅛-in. or ¼-in. resawing offcuts or other scraps. Working in small scale makes parts easier to handle and the design easier to see. Wood scraps can be cut with saws and joined with a variety of glues.

Working Small

Small-scale models are easy to build and transport, and they take up little space. They also can be made from the same stock as the full-scale piece. Nothing beats a wooden model for selling a furniture design to a client or spouse.

First, mill the stock to whatever thickness you need. Cut lengths using a tablesaw crosscut sled or chopsaw. Be cautious in cutting these smaller parts. Sometimes a pencil eraser end is a better and safer grip than your fingertip for holding things in place. Simple joints can be made on this scale, but most pieces are just butt-jointed together and glued. Strengthen where needed with gussets and corner blocks.

THE PROCESS STARTS WITH A SKETCH. Rogowski keeps his design doodles in a notebook for future reference. That way, the germ of one idea can give life to a totally new one later on.

GLUE-UP IS EASY. Be sure to reinforce joinery. Hot-melt glue works, but it can be messy with a lot of squeeze-out. Yellow glue works if your gluing surfaces are clean and flat. Cyanoacrylate works well, too.

SAFETY FIRST. For safety, use a zero-clearance insert when cutting small parts at the tablesaw. A piece of scrap (right) can be fashioned as a tapering jig for bandsawing model table legs.

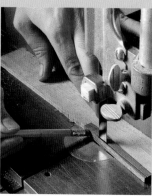

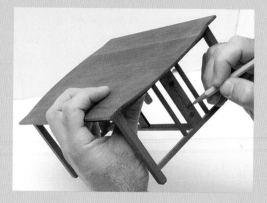

TRY OUT INLAY IDEAS. Working in small scale makes it convenient to draw—and erase—decorative details directly on the model's surface.

Working Big

When you want to see how a piece will take up space and work with other furniture around it, build a full-scale model. Cardboard works best for full-scale or half-scale models. In just a few hours, Rogowski can create models as large as 2 ft. by 7 ft. with moving parts to help clients see how something might fit or look. Draw in door stiles and rails, or stack one layer of cardboard on another to create depth and texture. Use a sheet of single-wall cardboard and glue on an edge to give it thickness. Spray-paint the cardboard if you want to look at another color besides tan. Use white if you simply want to concentrate on the form of the piece.

THE MATERIAL CUTS EASILY. Components for a full-scale table model can be made in minutes. Just slice up cardboard parts on the tablesaw and glue them together.

HOT-MELT GLUE WORKS GREAT ON CARDBOARD. With the base constructed, it's easy to experiment with a variety of tabletop sizes and designs.

CARDBOARD IS STURDY ENOUGH FOR MOCKED-UP JOINERY. Rogowski glues a loose tenon to the inside of a rail and knifes a mortise into a cardboard leg.

Scaling Furniture from Photos

BY MIGUEL
GOMEZ-IBAÑEZ

Thumbing through magazines and books, you may see furniture that you would like to make. But to do that, you need a set of working drawings. To evaluate proportions and details accurately, you need to draw the piece to scale.

Published photos usually provide overall dimensions: depth, width, and height. Although helpful, they do not provide enough information on which to base a detailed drawing.

Using a copy of the photo of the furniture piece, string, a straightedge, an architect's scale, a sharp pencil, a bench or table with a sheet of plywood, and a T-square, it's possible to generate lines on each plane of the image beginning with one known dimension. Then you can break down the overall dimensions into smaller increments within that framework. This technique opens up a lot of opportunity to build projects without plans, yet remain faithful to the originals.

Perspective-Drawing Basics

During the 15th century, artists in Florence, Italy, developed a process for perspective drawing that allowed them to accurately depict three-dimensional objects on a two-dimensional canvas using simple principles. These artists realized that objects that are closer to you appear larger than those that are farther away. In addition, parallel lines on each face appear to converge as they recede into the distance, and ultimately appear to vanish altogether at a single point on the horizon. The viewer's eye level then is denoted by a horizon line. Finally, lines constructed to form (or partially form) an image will converge to a point on the horizon line—known as the vanishing point.

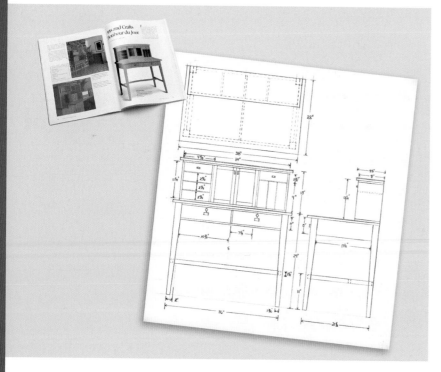

Locate the Vanishing Points

Take the time to locate the vanishing points accurately. Hurrying at this stage will result in many inaccuracies down the line. Begin by taping a photocopy of the piece to the drawing paper, making sure that it is plumb to the baseline. The front and side both have vanishing points.

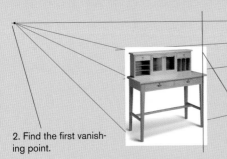

2. Find the first vanishing point.

1. Align the photo plumb on the paper.

3. Starting from the first vanishing point, draw the horizon line perpendicular to the vertical (or plumb) line.

5. Draw additional vanishing lines.

4. Find the second vanishing point.

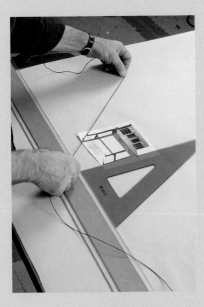

LOCATE THE FIRST VANISHING POINT. Pivot a taut string from your thumb until it aligns with the top and bottom of the piece.

FIND THE SECOND VANISHING POINT. Once the horizon line has been drawn from the first vanishing point, use the string method to find the second vanishing point upon the horizon line.

PUSH-PIN PIVOT. Stick a push pin into each vanishing point and use it to pivot a straightedge to draw accurate vanishing lines.

Construct a Vertical Scale

Because the upper case holds crucial information to be measured, it's best to strike the vertical measuring line on the front corner of that plane.

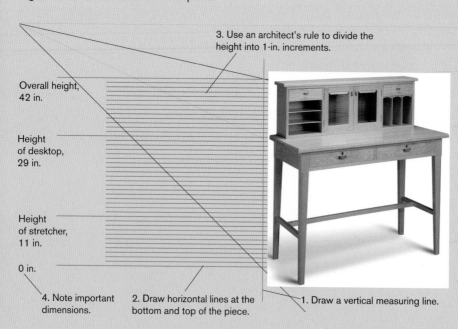

3. Use an architect's rule to divide the height into 1-in. increments.

Overall height, 42 in.

Height of desktop, 29 in.

Height of stretcher, 11 in.

0 in.

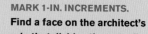

4. Note important dimensions.

2. Draw horizontal lines at the bottom and top of the piece.

1. Draw a vertical measuring line.

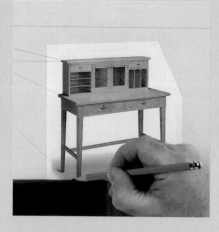

MARK THE TOP AND BOTTOM OF THE PIECE. Draw horizontal lines outward from where the vertical measuring line intersects with the top and bottom vanishing lines.

MARK 1-IN. INCREMENTS.
Find a face on the architect's rule that divides the overall height of the piece into the same number of increments as its height in inches. You will need to skew the rule to do so.

COMPLETE THE VERTICAL SCALE.
Use a T-square to draw horizontal lines from each mark back to the vertical measuring line to complete the vertical scale.

Applying perspective-drawing principles to photographs is perspective drawing in reverse. Here, you begin with a completed drawing (the photocopy of your photo), and the task is to determine the horizon line and vanishing points.

Draw the Vanishing Points Based on the Photograph

Start by taping paper onto your drafting table, making sure the paper extends to both ends of the table. You'll need the room because the vanishing points of the perspective drawing will carry well beyond the photograph on each side.

Next, think about where the vanishing points will land. Usually, one will be close by, and the other much farther away. If the vanishing points are too far apart to fit on the drafting table, bring them closer together by reducing the scale of the photocopied image. Then, situate the photocopy so that the vertical lines that define the sides of the piece are perpendicular to the parallel rule or T-square, and tape the photocopy to the paper.

Establish the first vanishing point To the front and sides of the piece of furniture are planes that recede to a vanishing point in the distance—one to the right and one to the left.

A string is a handy tool for finding a vanishing point. Hold down one end of the string with your thumb, pull it taut, and then pivot from that point. Move the string across the photocopy until it lines up with the top and bottom planes of the piece of furniture. The point at which the string aligns with the top and bottom of the piece, as well as with the other horizontal planes in the piece, is the vanishing point. Stick a push pin in that spot.

Draw the horizon line Now draw a horizontal line through the first vanishing point to represent the horizon. The horizon is eye level—the point of view of the photocopy.

The line drawn from the first vanishing point will be perpendicular to the vertical lines that describe the sides of the piece of furniture.

Find the second vanishing point Once the horizon line has been established, finding the next vanishing point is easy because you already know it has to occur at some point along that line. Use the string and your thumb to find the second vanishing point, just as you did to find the first one. Place a push pin at that point.

Once you have established both vanishing points, draw lines from each one across the photocopy to define the top and bottom of the image. Use the push pin placed in each vanishing point to serve as a pivot for the straightedge. Maintaining contact with the pin as you swing the straightedge will keep the vanishing lines accurate as you draw. Once you've drawn the vanishing lines around the perimeter of the image, you are ready to determine the vertical dimensions of the piece.

Scale for the Vertical Dimensions

Establish a vertical measuring line on one of the corners of the piece of furniture in the photo. The line should extend beyond the top and bottom of the photo.

Draw perpendicular lines off to one side both from the top and bottom of the measuring line that establishes the height of the piece. These two lines will be parallel to each other. Now divide the measuring line into 1-in. increments. In this example, the height is 42 in. Use the architect's rule to find a scale in which the distance from 0 in. to 42 in. is somewhat longer than the distance between the two parallel lines. Lay the scale at an angle so that the 0 point is on one line and the 42-in. point is on the other. In this case, a scale of ⅛ in. = 1 ft. worked well. Mark the 1-in. increments along the scale on your drawing. Then

Create Width and Depth Scales

Width and depth are trickier to visualize because they are created in perspective. Still, there is an accurate graphic solution for plotting both views.

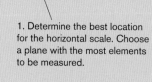

4. Use a series of diagonals to bisect the box and create a graduated scale.

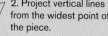

3. Project two lines from the vanishing point to create a box in perspective.

2. Project vertical lines from the widest point of the piece.

RECTANGLE REPRESENTS THE WIDTH SCALE. Draw a measuring line to the vanishing point along the width of the desk where it meets the upper case. Then draw vertical lines at each end. Draw lines from one vanishing point (above) to mark off a grid space in perspective.

1. Determine the best location for the horizontal scale. Choose a plane with the most elements to be measured.

5. Repeat the process to create a depth scale.

BISECT THE WIDTH-SCALE RECTANGLE. Draw diagonals from opposite corners of the rectangle to locate its center. Next, strike a vertical line at the intersection point to divide the area in two.

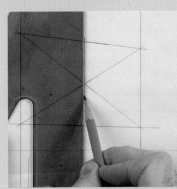

CONTINUE TO DIVIDE INTO SMALLER INCREMENTS. Bisect each grid area. Divisions appear to get smaller as they approach the vanishing point because they are in perspective.

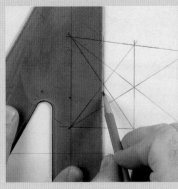

DRAW A SCALED PLAN. From the three scales you now can determine any dimension you need to draw an accurate measured plan.

extend each mark back to the measuring line on the corner of the piece of furniture. You now have a ruler than can be used to measure 1-in. increments on any vertical dimension on the piece.

Determine Horizontal Dimensions

Horizontal measurements are a bit harder to determine. The process is similar to laying out the vertical dimensions in that you take a known dimension—usually the width at the top—draw parallel lines up from the two ends, then divide this distance into smaller, more useful increments. However, the width dimension that is provided with the photograph applies to a line that is receding into the background, so the increments on this line recede as well, getting smaller from foreground to background.

Dividing a receding line into accurate dimensions is done using the diagonals of a rectangle to divide the distance in half, and doing that as many times as necessary to reach a useful set of increments. The rectangle is formed by the two vertical lines extended from points that describe the width of the image, and another pair of lines that meet at a vanishing point. The four lines form a rectangle that recedes into the background.

Bisect rectangles to find useful increments for measuring When you connect the opposite corners of this receding rectangle with diagonals, you have found its center. Drawing a vertical line from the center point onto the photocopy divides

the distance between the two sides in half, according to the rules of perspective. Because the distance you are bisecting is receding, the two halves are not equal lengths, but they are accurate to the image in the photocopy.

This process of bisecting the width using diagonals is done as many times as necessary until you arrive at a set of useful increments. In the example, the known width is 38 in. Bisecting this dimension gives you two increments of 19 in. Do this four more times, and you have increments of $^{13}/_{16}$ in., which is fine enough for most measuring and similar to the 1-in. increments of the vertical scale.

Finally, create a depth scale, using the same procedure you used in developing the width scale. When you connect the sets of points and extend those lines across the face, sides, and top of the piece of furniture, you will establish a complete and detailed grid. The grid will enable you to read any element on each of these defined planes. With this information, you will be able to draw your piece full scale and create an accurate working drawing from which to build.

MIGUEL GOMEZ-IBANNEZ is an architect and furniture maker in Boston, Massachusetts.

Building Without Plans

BY CRAIG VANDALL
STEVENS

Most of us who work with wood began by making at least some things from plans. I was no exception. But working from plans can begin to feel restrictive. At some point we all wonder, "What if I designed it myself?"

Making a standing screen presents a wonderful chance to explore the design aspect of woodworking. With its straight lines and straightforward joinery, a screen presents a minimum of construction challenges, opening the way for thoughts of design. The length of the project usually can be measured in days rather than in weeks, and that can reduce the pressure of working

with your own design. Still, although I've chosen to illustrate the process of design by following the development of a standing screen, the techniques I outline in this chapter apply not just to screens but also to any type of furniture. If you take the leap into designing your own work, I think you'll see it's a very rewarding process.

Rough Sketching is Fine

I develop furniture ideas by sketching. I tend to make small sketches and make them quickly, especially early in the design process. I don't want to get hung up on a lot of detail early on, when I'm trying to

From Quick Sketches . . .

You don't need finely detailed drawings to design a good piece of furniture. Small drawings without much detail provide a good way to explore overall proportions.

THE PROPER PROPORTIONS. Early on, while he's searching for an overall shape he likes, the author draws quickly, placing a handful of drawings on a page to make comparing them easier.

TRACING REFINES THE SKETCH. Once he's picked a drawing he likes, the author uses tracing paper to refine some details. Here, he traced the proportions of the frame but experimented with different ways of dividing the panels.

establish the overall form of a piece. Finding attractive proportions is one of the most challenging aspects of designing furniture, and sketching quickly enables me to explore proportions effectively. I don't think you need to be talented at drawing to design good furniture, and drawing small and quickly reduces the artistic burden.

I have a number of sketchbooks, large ones that I use in the shop and small ones that go on the road. I typically use a soft pencil, but in a pinch I'll use anything handy. I have a 9mm mechanical pencil that makes clean lines and doesn't arouse suspicion at church in my choir folder. I also have some fat drawing pencils that are great for putting the first idea for a piece down on paper. The line they leave is wide enough that I'm not tempted to draw a lot of detail, just shapes and proportions.

Whatever pencil I use, I resist the temptation to erase—I just live with errant lines or work them into the drawing. The main idea is to get some ideas down, not to make the drawing perfect. If you can't keep your fingers off the eraser, try drawing with ink.

When one of these sketches strikes an idea I like, I usually draw a number of variations of it. I'll often sketch out half a dozen or more takes on it in a sketchbook or on a large sheet of paper. Then I choose the one I like best and refine it further. I often use tracing paper to duplicate the basic shape of the piece a number of times, and then I sketch in variations on the details. Aside from saving time, tracing ensures that the part of the original drawing I like—the overall proportions, say—remains constant while I play with various details I'm less certain about.

To a Simple Scale . . .

An easily made paper scale enables you to assign dimensions to your drawing and make the leap from a small, freehand sketch to a full-scale mock-up.

1. THE FIRST DIMENSION. Assign a measurement to one dimension; the author decided the screen would be 60 in. tall. Tick off the top and bottom of the piece, and the distance between them will represent 60 in.

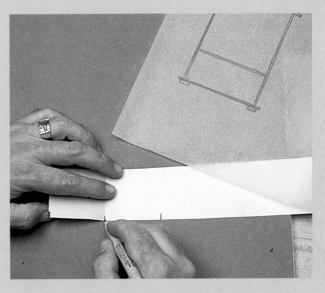

2. FOLD, CREASE, MARK. Fold the scale so that the first two tick marks meet. Then tick the crease halfway between them—it will equal 30 in.

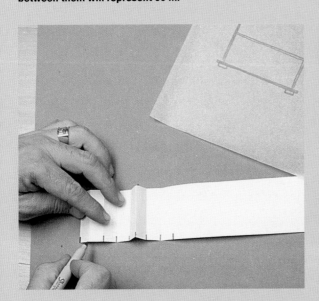

3. KEEP ON TICKING. Continue folding the scale in half and marking the creases.

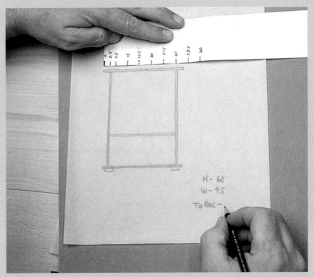

4. ROUGH SKETCH GETS REAL DIMENSIONS. Once the scale has been marked, it can be used to measure any part of the screen.

Homemade Scale Provides Dimensions

The freehand concept drawings I've described are a great way to arrive at shapes and proportions you find pleasing. But if you don't draw to scale or in accurate perspective, how do you turn a small, rough sketch into something you can build from? While a student of James Krenov at the College of the Redwoods, I learned to use a simple homemade scale to assign dimensions to a concept sketch.

To make the scale (see the photos on p. 57) you need to assign a value to one dimension of the piece you've drawn. The measurements of all other parts will be derived from that first one. For example, in the case of my standing screen, I decided its overall height should be 60 in. On a piece of scrap paper slightly longer than my sketch of the screen, I made pencil marks that corresponded to the top and bottom of the screen. That gave me my scale: For this sketch, the distance between the two marks would equal 60 in. I folded the paper in half with the pencil marks touching, creating a crease halfway between the marks that equaled 30 in. I made a tick mark at the crease. I folded the scale in half again and again until it was folded up like a Japanese fan. I put tick marks and the appropriate number of inches at each of the folds, and the scale was ready to use. Holding the scale horizontally across the sketch, I used it to measure the width of the screen. Such a scale can be used to determine almost all the dimensions of a sketch.

Mock-Ups Let You See the Piece Before Building It

Once I have dimensions on my drawing, you might expect that I'd make a dimensioned shop drawing. Instead, I move at this point directly to making a mock-up of the piece. Making a mock-up is one of the most helpful steps along the path of building a piece of furniture. A full-size mock-up allows me to see the object in three dimensions and to make informed decisions regarding proportions and size. A full-size drawing of a piece doesn't give me anything like the impact of a mock-up. It also locks me into decisions on detailing before I'm ready. I generally don't make a scale model, either, because it doesn't provide the sense of physical presence that a mock-up does.

My mock-ups aren't built to last. I use common materials (for the screen I used 2× stock for the frame and kraft paper for the panels) and the quickest possible joinery (drywall screws, brads). I want a mock-up to be as simple as possible to make and easily modified again and again until I'm comfortable with the design. I probably spent about an hour and a half building the screen mock-up. The less time it takes to build one, the more inclined I'll be to alter something I don't like. And that's the whole point of a mock-up.

I use my first mock-up, like my first sketches, to determine the overall shape and proportions of a piece. When I had the first mock-up of the screen in front of me, I saw that it was far wider than it appeared in the sketch. What had looked nicely balanced on paper was somewhat clumsy in three dimensions and full size. I made decisions regarding the overall width of the screen (I decided it needed narrowing), the thickness of the lower rail (it needed thinning), and the way the feet relate to the rest of the screen (they needed to be less clunky).

Implementing such changes is easy. I don't need a second mock-up; I simply unscrew the first one (or unclamp it if I haven't yet driven the screws) and use the chopsaw to shorten some members and the bandsaw to shave a bit off the elements that look too heavy. With the bandsaw, I'm not measuring and taking off specific amounts, just taking off enough to make a difference visually. I generally start with all of the parts a little oversized and work down from there. I had roughed out a few extra blanks for feet, and I quickly cut out a couple of new possibilities on the bandsaw.

To a Full-Scale Mock-Up . . .

Many details can be worked out at the mock-up stage. Built with 2× stock, drywall screws, and kraft paper, this mock-up is quick to make and easy to revise.

SIZING UP THE FRAME. Before determining any of the details, the author considers the overall proportions of the screen and the placement of the crossbar.

GET ME OUT OF THE SHOP. Placing a mock-up in a room for a few days can help clarify the design's strengths and weaknesses (left).

TO THE BIG BOARD. A piece of plywood propped on a chair (another old mock-up) serves as an easel for sketching the carving design. The author uses a fat pencil to produce a flowing line (right).

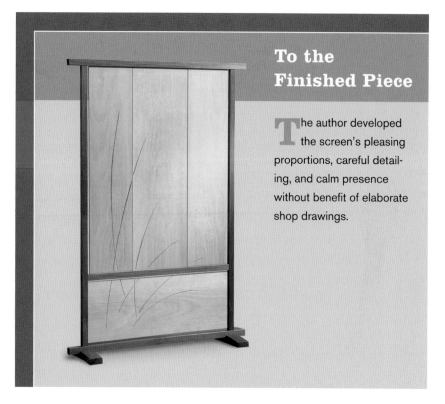

To the Finished Piece

The author developed the screen's pleasing proportions, careful detailing, and calm presence without benefit of elaborate shop drawings.

I put two different feet on the mock-up to compare likely candidates.

When I finish a mock-up, I take it into the house and live with it a while. I place it so it's the first thing I see when I walk into the room. Over the next few days, I try to let it surprise me when I enter the room. The first impression I have of the proportions is telling. It's not a life-changing moment of clarity. It's usually just a quick thought like, "It's too tall," or "The feet are too fat." I pay attention to these impressions, because they are uncluttered by logic, analysis, formulas, and so on. Everyone has such responses, but it may take some coaxing to get yourself to trust them.

With this new input, I take apart the mock-up, make the changes, reassemble it, and take another look. At this stage, I might also add some fine detailing to the mock-up. (Before this, I have avoided including details such as subtle textures and reveals because I find them distracting early on.) The new proportions may result in the need to fiddle with the dimensions of other parts, but the mock-up is definitely making headway. Overall, I find that a mock-up provides an enjoyable and reassuring way to develop and refine a design.

How I Design a Carving

The screen's panels provide a wonderful canvas for the free-flowing type of carving I do. To design a carving, I use sketching techniques very similar to those used to design the screen itself. I start small, drawing on the panels of my thumbnail sketch of the screen. Working small helps me see the carving design as a whole and keeps me from getting bogged down in details.

Once I have an idea that works well with the screen design, I begin sketching full scale. I use kraft or butcher paper from a wide roll to make the drawing. I'll prop up a piece of plywood and tape the paper to it so that I can draw while standing. I keep the small sketch nearby for reference as I work full size.

I use a soft pencil, and often instead of holding it the way I would to write, I hold it almost flat under my palm. This produces a wider, bolder line and permits my arm and hand to move in comfortable arcs, creating graceful lines more easily.

I pin the finished sketch to the mock-up so I can stand back and see it framed in the screen. Sometimes after seeing it in place, I make changes to the drawing to create a better sense of balance with the screen.

Once I'm satisfied with the sketch, I'll lay out the real panels in the order they'll take in the screen and transfer the design to the panels with carbon paper. Then the carving can begin.

One important general tip on carving design: Resist the urge to fill the whole space. Leaving some space uncarved can significantly increase the impact of the carving. Particularly when you are working a large surface in this style of chip carving, the old maxim applies: Less really is more.

CRAIG VANDALL STEVENS studied furniture making at the College of the Redwoods' fine woodworking program in California. He currently designs and builds one-of-a-kind furniture for exhibition and commission. You may visit him on the web at www.cvstevens.com.

A Short History of Design

BY GRAHAM BLACKBURN

Since its inception almost 35 years ago, a vast range of furniture from various periods has appeared in *Fine Woodworking* magazine. What follows is a condensed overview describing many of these various styles. I've tried to put them into a historical perspective based on their defining characteristics, but the process of design is continual and unending. Hepplewhite and Sheraton styles, for instance, were made during the Mahogany Period in England but weren't prevalent in the United States until after the Revolution, during the Federal Period.

Any attempt to categorize definitively the products of a given period is bound to be inexact. It is in the very nature of furniture design to evolve, often haphazardly, taking a little from here and a little from there, sometimes making a large leap with the invention of a new technique or a new material.

British furniture is most often described in terms of the various monarchs during whose reigns it was made, but for a more familiar division of furniture design in America, I've chosen more local names. Nevertheless, it remains true that most American furniture is very similar to the contemporaneous British styles. A great deal of furniture from the early periods

made in the United States was built by craftsmen either trained in Britain or who used British patterns. By the 20th century the differences had more to do with individual makers than with national styles.

GRAHAM BLACKBURN is a furniture maker, author, illustrator, and the publisher of Blackburn Books (www. blackburnbooks.com) in Bearsville, New York.

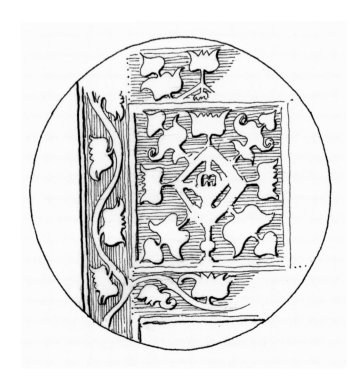

The Pilgrim Century, 1620–1750

Much early American furniture came here with the first immigrants, including, most famously, the Pilgrims. They brought—and then made—oak pieces typical of the Jacobean, William and Mary, and Carolean periods in Britain; pieces that retained a strong Gothic influence, sturdy pieces, heavily carved pieces, pieces with cup-turned legs and bun feet. Much of the work from this Early Colonial Period is representative of a utilitarian life.

"BIBLE" BOX, 1670

• As with most boxes of the period, this one is nailed together

• Oak throughout, but many boxes were made of pine or with top and bottom of pine

• Lunette and flute carvings were simple and geometrically based

• Overhanging, cleated top

THE ELDER BREWSTER CHAIR, CA. 1650

• Wainscot constructed oak (wainscot means "wagon oak" and refers to the paneling)

• Joiner's work

• Framed construction, pinned for strength

• Bold turnings

• Heavily carved

• Stout stretchers

• Less-heavily carved chairs of the same construction are common

• Reminiscent of earlier British chairs in the Gothic style

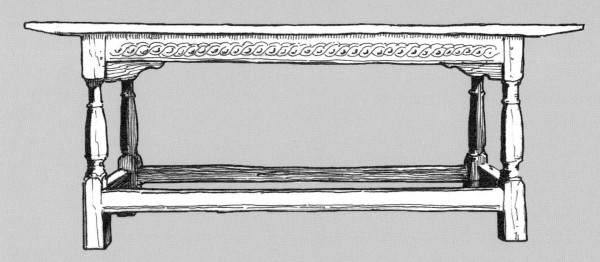

DINING TABLE, CA. 1700

- Oak

- Strap carving on front apron

- Simple turning with square ends on legs

- Stout stretchers

- Edge-joined top

- Pinned mortise-and-tenon construction

- Bracketed legs

- Post-assembly carving (as on old chests)

THE NICHOLAS DISBROWE CHEST, 1660

- Nicholas Disbrowe is the first known American maker

- Oak, frame-and-panel construction

- Uncompromisingly rectangular

- Similar to earlier English oak styles, but distinctive Connecticut Valley, Hadley style

- This piece shows the chest becoming a chest of drawers

- Tulip motif carved over entire foot

The Mahogany Period, 1702–1780

The Mahogany Period (late Colonial), covering the first half of the 18th century, roughly parallels the periods known in Britain as Queen Anne and Georgian. Walnut gave way to mahogany as the predominant wood, and the beginning of the period saw a sudden simplification of style into a less ornamented and more severely elegant aesthetic. Perhaps the most typical element is the cabriole leg, at first plain and finished with a simple turned pad foot, and later developing into a highly carved element complete with ball-and-claw, hairy-paw, or lion's foot. Furniture was made by cabinetmakers rather than joiners, and the list of American Chippendales is long (Thomas Chippendale was the most famous English cabinetmaker of the period and by whose name furniture of the middle of the period is often known). It includes the Goddards and Townsends of Newport, Rhode Island, and many notable Philadelphia makers, including William Savery, Thomas Affleck, and Benjamin Randolph.

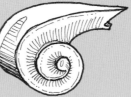

ARM TERMINAL VOLUTE.

KNEEHOLE DESK (BUREAU), CA. 1765

• Made by John Townsend of Newport, Rhode Island

• Mahogany, with poplar as a secondary wood

• Block and shell front

• Shell-carved kneehole door

• Bracket feet

• Solid top

• Single, wide drawer

• Two tiers of narrow drawers

• Closely related to the highboy on the facing page, this is essentially the lower half of a chest on chest with a kneehole cupboard

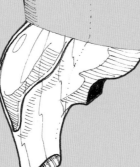

SAVERY-STYLE "TONGUE" CARVING ON KNEE.

SIDE CHAIR, CA. 1780

• Typical Chippendale style

• Mahogany

• Square back

• Cupid-bow crest rail

• Pierced and carved splat

• Highly carved, squared-off cabriole front legs

• Ball-and-claw feet

• Stump rear legs

• Rectilinear seat

WILLIAM SAVERY ARMCHAIR, CA. 1750

- Typical Queen Anne style

- Mahogany

- Rounded back

- Plain, profiled splat

- Not much carving, except for volutes and shells

- Cabriole front legs

- Simple trifid feet

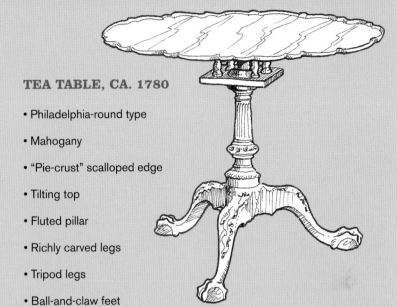

TEA TABLE, CA. 1780

- Philadelphia-round type

- Mahogany

- "Pie-crust" scalloped edge

- Tilting top

- Fluted pillar

- Richly carved legs

- Tripod legs

- Ball-and-claw feet

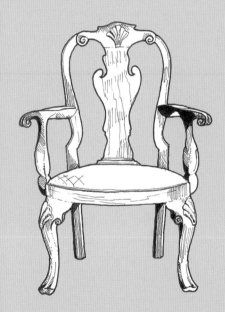

HIGH CHEST OF DRAWERS (HIGHBOY), CA. 1770

- High-style work typical of Philadelphia cabinetmakers

- Chest-on-chest, double-case construction

- Richly carved, broken scroll bonnet

- Carved corners

- Carved cabriole legs with ball-and-claw feet at front and back

- Sophisticated proportions, progressively graduated drawers

- Veneered casework

TEA TABLE, CA. 1750

- New England-rectangular style

- Maple; originally painted red

- Markedly slender cabriole legs

- Pad feet

- Deeply scalloped apron

Federal Period, 1780–1840

After the Revolution, American tastes and sympathies transferred from Britain to France, especially with regard to furniture styles. The French Empire style planned and fostered by Napoleon was adopted and distinctively modified by American cabinetmakers and is typically known as Federal style. In comparison to the light and well-proportioned furniture typified by the Hepplewhite- and Sheraton-style pieces of the end of the Mahogany Period and the early days of the Federal Period, much Federal furniture is dark, heavy, and vulgar. The finest, however, is often superb and owes much to one of the most famous of all American cabinetmakers, Duncan Phyfe, a New York woodworker possessed of great taste and a wonderful eye for proportion.

TYPICAL HEPPLEWHITE PULL.

LYRE-BACK SIDE CHAIR, CA. 1815

- Klismos-type chair with classical details, made by Duncan Phyfe

- Mahogany

- Shaggy front legs

- Hairy-paw feet

- Lyre splat

- Heavily reeded

- Graceful curves

- Light, stretcherless construction

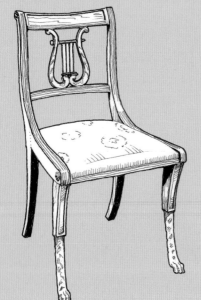

TABLE, CA. 1810–1820

- Reminiscent of the Sheraton style

- Pier-type table with ovolo corners

- Mahogany and maple painted black with gilt and polychrome

- Harbor view painted on center of apron

- Typical of Baltimore Federal-style painted furniture

- No stretchers, Sheraton-style tapered and fluted legs

- Inlay and banding

- Tapered feet

SECRETARY, CA. 1820

- Highly varnished

- Veneered construction

- Massive in scale and proportion

- High-style Philadelphia Federal bureau, French Empire inspired

- Mahogany and bird's-eye maple

The mid-19th century saw mass-production become the norm in all areas of American life—from farming to high-end furniture making. Some furniture historians refer to this as the era of the "degraded style," and though commercialism certainly resulted in a lot of cheap, shoddy, and undistinguished work, there also was a remarkable burgeoning of vigorous new styles, some unabashedly derivative, including Rococo Revival, Egyptian Revival, Gothic Revival, and Italian Revival.

Nineteenth-century furniture (which is often referred to as Victorian, after the reigning British monarch) tends to be thought of as extremely ornamented, overstuffed, and often in terrible taste, but it also includes much innovative elegance, typified by pieces from makers such as Emile Gallé, Louis Majorelle, Michael Thonet, Charles Voysey, and Charles Eastlake. There is, in fact, no one common characteristic of the period other than that of diversity.

LIBRARY TABLE, CA. 1880

- Typical of the Modern Gothic style

- Ebonized cherry

- Inspired by the craft traditions of the Middle Ages

- Supposed honesty of construction and materials

- No applied ornamentation

SIDE CHAIR, CA. 1880

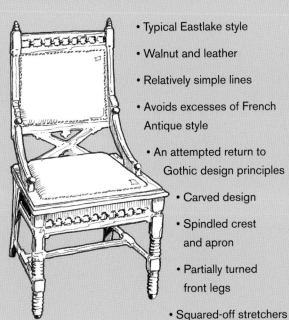

- Typical Eastlake style

- Walnut and leather

- Relatively simple lines

- Avoids excesses of French Antique style

- An attempted return to Gothic design principles

- Carved design

- Spindled crest and apron

- Partially turned front legs

- Squared-off stretchers

CABINET, CA. 1876

- Classical motifs

- Elaborate marquetry panels

- Typical of Renaissance Revival style

- Carved, curved, and applied gilt ornamentation

- Maximum opulence

- Rosewood

Shaker, 1800–1900

Throughout the 19th century, the Shaker communities were producing furniture so different from everything else being made that the furniture is now recognized as a major American style. Its essential quality is simplicity. Eschewing ornamentation, the Shakers made furniture that not only was eminently practical and honest but also possessed a restrained elegance. Often giving the appearance of great delicacy, Shaker pieces are nonetheless constructed on sound and sturdy principles and have been the original inspiration for many a woodworker attracted by their straight lines and lack of ornamentation.

SIDE TABLE, CA. 1830

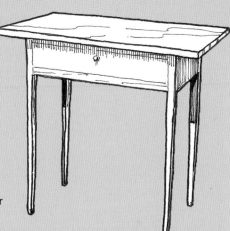

- The quintessential Shaker table
- Cherry, with pine interiors
- Tapered legs, turned at feet
- Large top with wide overhang
- No molding, carving, or inlay
- Fully dovetailed, flush-front drawer

CUPBOARD-CHEST, CA. 1830

- Pine; originally painted red
- Simplicity of form offset by sophisticated joinery
- Raised panels
- Pinned mortise and tenons
- Turned pulls and pegs
- Molded-lip drawer fronts
- Fully dovetailed drawers

SIDE CHAIR, CA. 1840

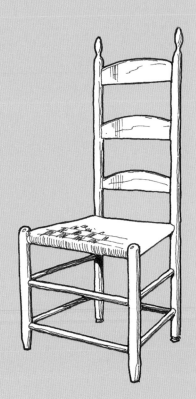

- Woven tape seat
- Seemingly simple, but thoughtfully designed and carefully constructed
- Slats graduated to become wider from bottom to top
- Tops of slats are beveled
- Back legs outfitted with "tilters" for greater comfort (tilters allow you to lean back in the chair without damaging it)

Arts and Crafts, 1890–1920

Reacting against the fashionable excesses and often shoddy work of mass production, the English designer William Morris inspired a generation of American furniture designers dedicated to honesty, utility, and, above all, good-quality workmanship. Charles and Henry Greene, Gustav Stickley, Ralph Whitehead (who founded the Byrdcliffe Arts Colony), and the anonymous craftsmen of the Roycroft Community in East Aurora, New York, produced a body of furniture variously known as Mission, Arts and Crafts, and Craftsman furniture, which has remained popular—and distinct in style—to the present, taking its place as a legitimate major American style.

SIGNATURE ROYCROFT BULBOUS FOOT ON TAPERED LEG.

ROYCROFT LOGO, STAMPED ON MOST PIECES.

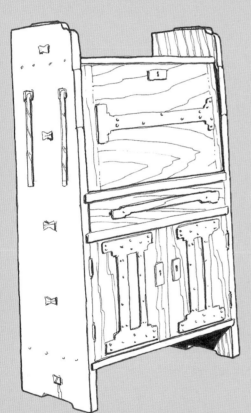

DINING CHAIR, CA. 1910

- White oak, leather seat
- Plain, Mission-style joinery with distinctive Roycroft tapered legs
- Bulbous feet
- Well-finished surfaces, with design emphasizing workmanship

LIBRARY TABLE, CA. 1910

- Fumed white oak typical of Stickley furniture
- Rectilinear, with reverse flying-buttress corbels
- Exposed mortise-and-tenon joinery
- Structural integrity embodied by post-and-lintel design system
- Handwrought hardware

DESK, 1904

- Design by Greene and Greene
- Structural elements emphasized as design features
- White oak
- Protruding dowel ends
- Through-tenons
- Oversized battens
- Locking escutcheons
- Butterfly keys
- Proud partition edges

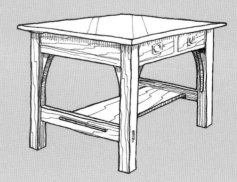

Quintessential Arts and Crafts

BY GRAHAM BLACKBURN

The Arts and Crafts style—a perennial favorite with woodworkers—has been popular for over a hundred years. There are examples in every antique and secondhand furniture store and reproductions abound, but what exactly defines Arts and Crafts? Ask anyone familiar with the style—also known as Mission, Craftsman, Crafts, Cloister, or even Quaint—how they identify it, and you'll get answers that typically contain words such as "foursquare," "straightforward construction," "exposed joinery," and "quartersawn oak." Such elements make the Arts and Crafts style inviting to many woodworkers who are new to the craft and who are less intimidated by Arts and Crafts furniture than they are by other, more sophisticated styles. Despite its apparent simplicity, however, it's just as easy to get a piece of Arts and Crafts furniture wrong as it is to fail at your first attempt at constructing a Chippendale piece that features cabriole legs—unless you have a full understanding of what the essential design details are and how they work together.

It's true that the Arts and Crafts style originated partly in response to overdecorated and directionless 19th-century furniture, but equally important were concerns about the shoddy quality of mass-produced factory furniture and its effect not only on the consumer but also on the people who made it. Arts and Crafts was conceived as an essentially utilitarian style affordable by all; the idea that its manufacture should be something in which the maker could take pride was central to the philosophy underlying what became known as the Arts and Crafts movement.

A piece of furniture built in the genuine Arts and Crafts style is therefore first and foremost completely functional. The furniture is solidly constructed with a minimum of superfluous ornament, unashamed yet not boastful of its joinery, and, more often than not, made of oak. Oak is a supremely appropriate wood for hard-wearing furniture and a species that harks back to the period in furniture-making history when craftsmanship was valued more than commercial success.

The movement embodied the writings of a variety of influential 19th-century art critics, philosophers, architects, and designers, such as John Ruskin and William Morris, as well as the work of 20th-century furniture makers Gustav Stickley (and his brothers), Elbert Hubbard, and the Roycrofters. Other seminal figures included the noted California architects Charles and Henry Greene; Frank Lloyd Wright; and internationally known and influential designers and furniture makers Charles Voysey, Ernest Gimson, and the Barnsley brothers.

Because the movement that resulted in this style of furniture began as far back as the middle of the 19th century, the range of design elements that belong to this style is, in fact, much broader than many people realize.

Six Quintessential Elements

Material Quartersawn oak has much to recommend it: strength, durability, relative stability, and an attractive figure characterized by the medullary rays not visible in flatsawn stock. Although a hardwood, oak is not excessively difficult to work—it is easier, in fact, to produce a crisp surface with a less than perfectly sharp tools on a piece of oak than on a piece of softwood. Oak is not toxic and may have a wide range of color—red, white, or brown—depending on the species. The wood also takes stain well and can be fumed, a technique that can produce a wonderful aged look. Although most factory-built Arts and Crafts furniture was made of oak, many well-known designers have used other species, such as walnut, mahogany, and cherry.

Construction techniques Although cabinet construction with veneered surfaces is occasionally used for the body of an Arts and Crafts piece, the majority of authentic pieces are made using solid wood and frame-and-panel construction.

Consistent with the directness and honesty that are the hallmarks of this style is the use of slats where a solid piece or a frame-and-panel section would be overkill. Unlike the furniture of the Gothic Period, turned elements are rare in Arts and Crafts designs. All of this is in keeping with the principle of using the simplest possible methods of work for the most honest and unpretentious result.

Simple does not, however, mean sloppy, especially in terms of the construction of a piece. In fact, because the aim of the Arts

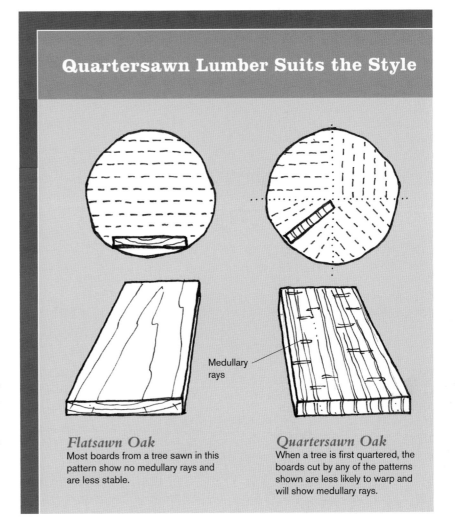

Quartersawn Lumber Suits the Style

Flatsawn Oak
Most boards from a tree sawn in this pattern show no medullary rays and are less stable.

Medullary rays

Quartersawn Oak
When a tree is first quartered, the boards cut by any of the patterns shown are less likely to warp and will show medullary rays.

and Crafts movement was to design furniture that the maker could be proud of, a nice execution, particularly of exposed joinery, is essential when building a genuine Arts and Crafts piece.

Joinery Without a doubt, the mortise and tenon is the king of Arts and Crafts joints (see the drawings on p. 77). Dovetailing, doweling, and lapped and housed joinery also are used where appropriate, but in keeping with the demands of strength and honesty, the mortise-and-tenon joint plays a major role in the majority of Arts and Crafts pieces.

Several varieties of tenons are used, including stub, blind, through, and tusk, but each is used only when and where necessary for maximum strength without

Influential Makers of the Era

By the late 1800s, the Industrial Revolution was changing the world of furniture: The individual craftsman was being supplanted by factory production as the leading influence on style. Driven strictly by commercial concerns, mechanization was overtaking what had been a craft with an aesthetic founded on tradition, training, and individual craftsmanship. The result was an abuse of style and an excess of indiscriminate decoration that took the form of a series of "revivals" produced primarily for the sake of novelty in an attempt to capture the market. The Arts and Crafts movement developed primarily in opposition to this trend, as designers, architects, and furniture makers strove to produce items that placed a greater value on purer ideals of artistic honesty and craftsmanship. Initially, at least, the Arts and Crafts movement was more about what not to do than it was about a clearly defined new style. This is why there is such a broad range of pieces—spanning a long period—that can be identified as belonging to the Arts and Crafts style.

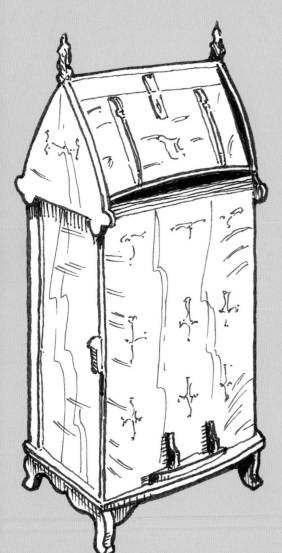

CHARLES ROHLFS

Drop-Front Desk, 1883

Heavily influenced by the Gothic style, Rohlfs was a leading figure in the American Arts and Crafts movement and was a friend of Elbert Hubbard (founder of the Roycroft Community at East Aurora, New York). Rohlfs was influenced by modern designers such as Charles Rennie Macintosh and, as many other Arts and Crafts designers did, looked back to the Gothic Period in his use of oak, as exemplified by this desk.

GUSTAV STICKLEY

Armchair, 1902

Regarded by many as defining the style, Stickley's mass-produced pieces made of oak were the most commercially successful manifestation of Arts and Crafts furniture. Although his are among the most simple examples of the style, Stickley drew his inspiration from more sophisticated designers, such as Charles Voysey and William Lethaby in England.

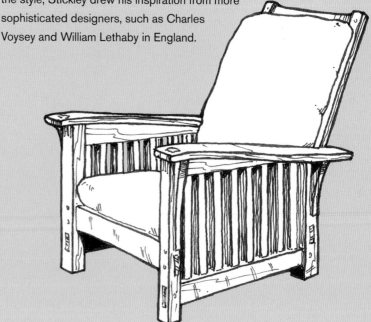

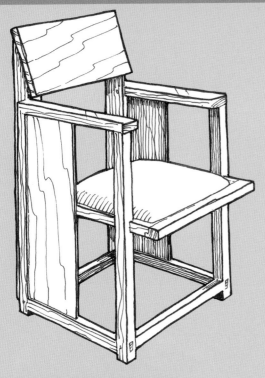

BYRDCLIFFE ARTS COLONY

Wall Cabinet, 1904

This stained poplar cabinet, with a carved and polychromed door panel, was a typical product of the Byrdcliffe workshops in Woodstock, New York, founded by the wealthy Englishman Ralph Whitehead, who had been a student of the eminent Victorian art critic John Ruskin—the generally acknowledged father of the Arts and Crafts movement. Simplicity of design as well as individual craftsmanship in a communal environment inform this version of Arts and Crafts style.

FRANK LLOYD WRIGHT

Armchair, 1904

Although not an avowed member of the movement, the architect Wright, like the Greene brothers, designed furniture for his houses—such as this extremely rectilinear pine chair with exposed joinery—which, although typically "Wrightian," is also distinctly in the Arts and Crafts style.

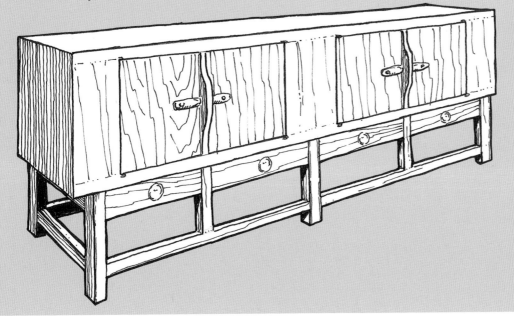

ERNEST GIMSON

Sideboard, 1905

Gimson was one of the chief figures of the Arts and Crafts movement. His sideboard, with its rectilinearity, simple lines, use of native wood (chestnut), and restrained use of minor ovolo molding on the legs, is an expression both of the values of the movement as directly expounded by William Morris and of the related attempt to reintroduce traditional country crafts to high-quality furniture.

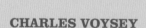

ROYCROFT COMMUNITY

Magazine Rack, 1910

In contrast to the previous one-of-a kind pieces by Charles Voysey, the Roycrofters, founded by Elbert Hubbard—an ardent believer in many aspects of the Arts and Crafts movement not limited to furniture alone—produced extremely simple and unsophisticated "factory-made" pieces in white oak.

CHARLES VOYSEY

Dining Chair, 1907

Voysey was another admirer of William Morris and a leading exponent of the British Arts and Crafts movement. His particularly spare style—a Shaker-like simplicity complemented by more flowing and elegant details, such as the heart-shaped cutout and square legs that taper to octagonal feet—was the precursor to the American Mission style popularized by makers such as Gustav Stickley.

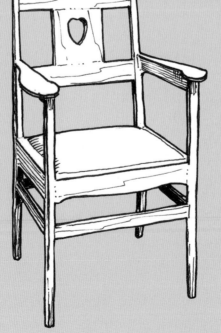

SIDNEY BARNSLEY

Cabinet-on-Stand, 1914

This walnut cabinet-on-stand (with holly and ebony stringing) is in many ways far removed from the output of the Roycrofters and the Stickley shops, but owes its essential design to the same principles of honesty of purpose and design shorn of superfluous decoration. Barnsley, his son Edward, and Ernest Gimson constitute the "grand old men" of the Arts and Crafts movement and were the leading influences.

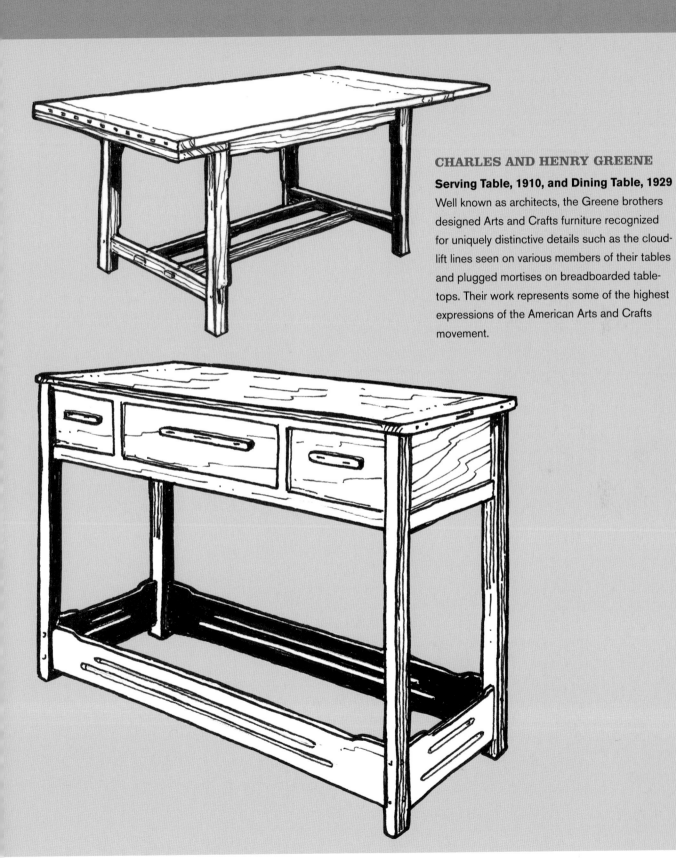

CHARLES AND HENRY GREENE

Serving Table, 1910, and Dining Table, 1929

Well known as architects, the Greene brothers designed Arts and Crafts furniture recognized for uniquely distinctive details such as the cloud-lift lines seen on various members of their tables and plugged mortises on breadboarded table-tops. Their work represents some of the highest expressions of the American Arts and Crafts movement.

Paneling

Paneling from the 18th- and 19th-centuries typically has a frame consisting of stiles and rails of different widths, invariably molded on the inner edges, surrounding a fielded or raised panel.

Arts and Crafts paneling is typically square, with equal-width rails and stiles. Panels are sometimes carved, but more often than not they are plain and flat in unmolded frames.

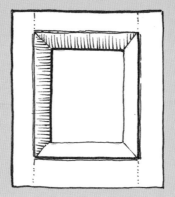 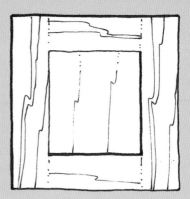

compromise. This means that if, for example, a through-tenon is the strongest possible form in a given situation, the design will make a virtue of the necessity by not attempting to hide or disguise the joint. This results in the ends of through-tenons being finished a little proud of the surface, often nicely chamfered and with any wedges thoughtfully arranged for a pleasing visual pattern and the most efficient use.

Design paradigms In American Arts and Crafts pieces, whether of the mass-produced variety typified by Gustav Stickley's Craftsman furniture or the higher-end custom designs of the Greene brothers, there is an immediate impression of squareness. This is most evident in the profiles of tops, edges, and other flat surfaces, such as broad chair arms. Molding is almost completely absent, sharp edges are gently relieved but not rounded, and overhangs are kept to a minimum.

Although many details are, in fact, square—such as in paneled framing, where a bottom rail wider than other frame members is rare (see above), and in the design of glazed doors, where all panes are equally square—absolute squareness is largely illusory, and slopes and curves are common. It is not that the style is inelegant—many pieces can be found based on elegant design paradigms, such as the golden rectangle—but the strength and utility of a piece always dominate.

Both gently and boldly formed curves are common in skirts, chair rails, and the lower edges of cabinet sides, but they are invariably simple and rarely compound, except for occasional tight cutouts on stool bases. Such shapes, including ogees and intersecting arcs, are nods to the influence of medieval Gothic oak furniture, much valued by leaders of the Arts and Crafts style for its craftsmanship and honesty. Curved yet square-edged brackets are another common feature of many pieces.

One other detail that would seem to belie an apparent squareness and angularity is the frequent use of tapered legs. The tapers, however, are usually limited to a short section near the base. Tapering legs like this prevents the piece from appearing too heavy, but because the tapers are equally formed on all four sides of the leg, a general feeling of squareness persists.

Decoration Despite a superficial plainness characterized by square edges, the lack of molding, the use of a relatively homogenous material, and the flatness of panels, Arts and Crafts furniture often is decorated with a variety of techniques ranging from simple curved cutouts to delicate floral inlays. Reflecting a continuing sensitivity to other styles and fashion on the part of designers such as Harvey Ellis or Charles Rennie Macintosh, who are perhaps better known for their Art Nouveau styles, the influence of the more flowing, nature-based Art Nouveau style is felt in many Arts and Crafts pieces—for example, in the products of various "utopian" workshops such as the Byrdcliffe Arts Colony in Woodstock, New York—in the form of pastel-colored painted sections, tulip inlays, and lily patterns.

Central to the principle of craftsmanship in this style of furniture is the use of other natural materials, such as reed and rush for seats, leather upholstery, and hand-wrought hardware made from iron or hammered brass. The hardware often is as square and sturdy as the furniture it serves and stands in complete contrast to the elegant and finely wrought shapes found on 18th-century pieces or the overworked fantastic shapes common on much 19th-century furniture. A gratuitous form of decoration in terms of structural

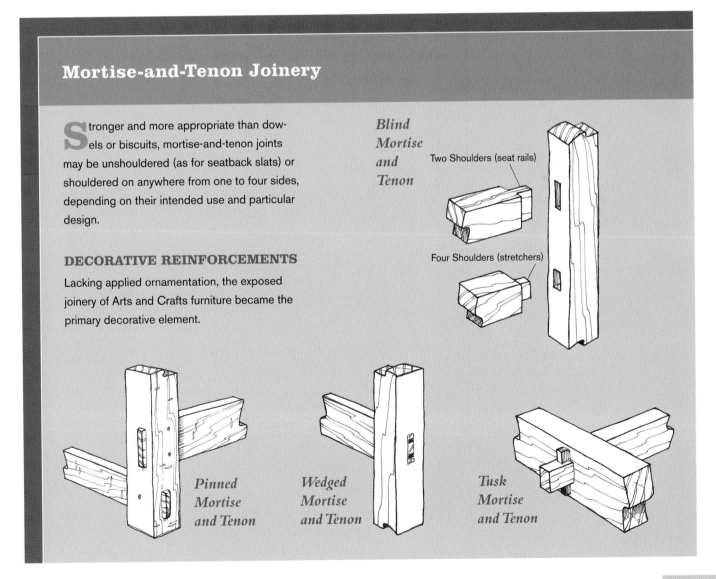

Mortise-and-Tenon Joinery

Stronger and more appropriate than dowels or biscuits, mortise-and-tenon joints may be unshouldered (as for seatback slats) or shouldered on anywhere from one to four sides, depending on their intended use and particular design.

DECORATIVE REINFORCEMENTS

Lacking applied ornamentation, the exposed joinery of Arts and Crafts furniture became the primary decorative element.

Blind Mortise and Tenon

Two Shoulders (seat rails)

Four Shoulders (stretchers)

Pinned Mortise and Tenon

Wedged Mortise and Tenon

Tusk Mortise and Tenon

Brackets and Cutouts

Not all details are perfectly rectilinear. Small accents, many in the form of brackets or cutouts, enliven otherwise straightforward designs.

Brackets, though square-edged, unmolded, and flat, often are given a gently curved profile.

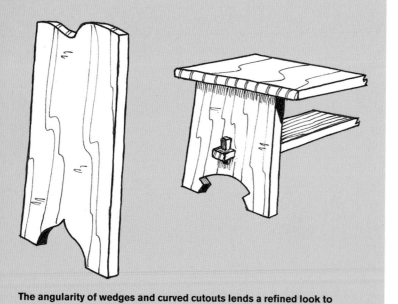

The angularity of wedges and curved cutouts lends a refined look to Arts and Crafts pieces.

function, but one that is consistent with the incorporation of natural materials, is the frequent use of a row of hand-wrought nails as an edge decoration.

Finish It would be inappropriate to finish an Arts and Crafts piece with a glossy lacquer. But although natural finishes like simple oiling and waxing may predominate, other processes, such as filling, staining, and fuming, are common.

Careful surface preparation is most important. In the case of an open-grained wood like oak, a matching wood filler should be used. If oak is filled first, it then may be waxed or perhaps lightly oiled and then waxed. If wax alone is used, it should be colored so that the wax-filled pores in the wood do not show white.

Fuming, the process of exposing oak to the fumes of ammonia, is a common method of turning oak darker without producing the irregular color that can result from careless staining. The popularity of fuming, especially among early proponents of Arts and Crafts furniture, resulted from the misconception that genuine Gothic furniture was extremely dark. That darkness, in fact, came from centuries of exposure to smoky atmospheres. When new, however, most Gothic furniture was brightly painted or valued precisely for its light golden color.

GRAHAM BLACKBURN is a furniture maker, author, illustrator, and the publisher of Blackburn Books (www.blackburnbooks.com) in Bearsville, New York.

Building in the Language of Greene and Greene

I have made a roomful of furniture in the style of Charles and Henry Greene, brothers who designed houses and furniture in California in the first decades of the 20th century. One of the most difficult aspects of making this furniture was finding ways to produce the details, the little touches that define the Greenes' work and make it so appealing to the hand and eye. The square black pegs, which are left slightly proud of the mahogany surface; the exposed splines, also proud and gently radiused back to the surrounding wood; the rounded double-L brackets—these and other signatures of the Greenes' furniture are all deceptively tricky to make well. Once mastered, though, they provide the basic vocabulary for building furniture in the language of Greene and Greene.

The dining chair in the photo on p. 80, one of a set of eight I built, is a straight reproduction of a chair designed by the Greenes in 1908. Working from photographs, I followed their example as closely as I could. The only concession the client and I made to cost was to leave out a subtle carving detail at the base of the legs. I took a more interpretive approach when I made the sideboard in the photo below and the writing table in the photo above. For each of these, I used a Greene and Greene piece as a starting point but redesigned the original to satisfy the client's needs, the demands of function, and my own sense of proportion.

BY THOMAS HUGH STANGELAND

SWEET DETAILS DEFINE THE FURNITURE OF GREENE AND GREENE. Learning to produce them is key to making furniture that compares to the originals. The author's sideboard (above) and writing desk (top) are fresh designs, but their superbly made and marshalled details give them the ring of the real thing. Both are made of sustained-yield mahogany and Ebon-X, an ebony substitute.

saw ways to soften a composition of straight lines and solids by rounding edges and introducing gentle curves. There's an Eastern overtone as well in the balanced but slightly asymmetrical patterns of the Greenes' detailing.

It's in the Material

The impact of the details in the Greenes' furniture is partly a function of the materials they used. Combining ebony and mahogany gives the furniture warmth as well as a strong visual contrast. I wanted to achieve the same effects but without using endangered woods. I considered using maple with walnut accents, but I finally chose sustained-yield mahogany and Ebon-X, an ebony substitute made of chemically altered walnut. The chemical treatment gives the Ebon-X a rich black color and working properties that aren't that far from ebony's.

Square Pegs

Glinting, square ebony pegs are a hallmark of Greene and Greene furniture. The pegs rise above the mahogany, and each little edge is gently radiused back to the surrounding wood, providing a reflective surface and a tactile message of hand craftsmanship. The pegs emphasize the joints in the furniture and many are caps for counterbored screws. But as I laid out the mortises for them on the crest rails of the chairs, I realized that some of the pegs are purely decorative. I followed the Greenes' example in making the pegs in a variety of sizes, from $\frac{3}{16}$-in. sq. to $\frac{1}{2}$-in. sq. As far as I could tell, the variation in size was a matter of aesthetics. I found, too, that their placement was not exactly symmetrical. Rather than being lined up in rows, the pegs were arranged in subsets slightly offset from each other to add visual interest (see the photo at left).

I made $\frac{1}{4}$-in.-deep mortises for the dozens of pegs with my hollow-chisel mortiser. It makes the job quick; the little tearout is not

REPRODUCING DETAILS. Square black pegs left proud convey the Greenes' message of hand craftsmanship in the author's reproduction chair.

EBONY SUBSTITUTE. To substitute for ebony, the author used Ebon-X (chemically altered walnut) for black details.

Springs of Inspiration

The Greenes' system of detailing did not develop all at once. It grew gradually as they were exposed to a variety of influences and ideas. Like many craftsmen of their day, Greene and Greene were deeply influenced by the Arts and Crafts movement. Arising in 19th-century England in reaction to the mechanization and shoddy goods of the Industrial Revolution, the movement was a call for honest hand craftsmanship. The Greenes were particularly influenced by Gustav Stickley and other proponents of Arts and Crafts who emphasized openly expressed joinery and function before frippery— features also evident in all the Greenes' work.

What sets the Greenes' work apart is the blending of an Oriental aesthetic with Arts and Crafts. In Japanese temple architecture and Chinese furniture, the Greenes

CHINESE BRACKETS FOR STRENGTH AND A SINUOUS LINE. Drawn from Chinese furniture, curved brackets tie Greene and Greene pieces together visually as well as structurally.

BRACKET ALIGNMENT IS TRICKY. The author locates a dowel hole on his table by sliding the bracket along a guide board clamped to the apron and marking with a dowel center.

noticeable after I drive in the slightly over-sized pegs. You could also use a drill and chisels or chop the mortises by hand.

To make the pegs, I ripped 8-in.- or 10-in.-long sticks of Ebon-X so they were exactly square in section and fractionally larger than the corresponding mortises. I squared up both ends of each stick on the disc sander with the stick held against the miter gauge. I sanded out the disc scratches with 150-grit paper on my handheld orbital sander. These sanded ends would eventually be the exposed surface of the pegs: Achieving a totally smooth surface was essential.

It would be murder to make the tiny radiused edges with the pegs already in their mortises, so I did my shaping ahead of time. I rounded down slightly on each edge at the end of the stick with an orbital sander, keeping the roundovers equal. To get the gleam of polished ebony, I took the sticks to my grinder and burnished the ends with red rouge on a cotton buff wheel.

When I was satisfied with the finish, I bandsawed about ⅜ in. off each end of all the sticks and repeated the process until I had a good supply of pegs. The bandsawn face would be hidden in the mortise, so I didn't

BRACKET JOINERY

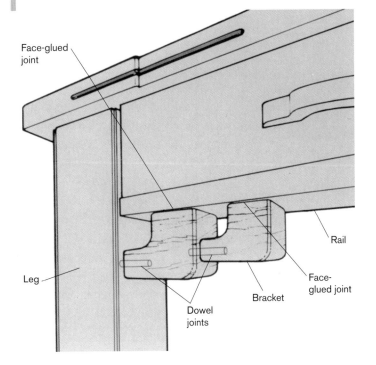

Face-glued joint

Leg

Dowel joints

Bracket

Rail

Face-glued joint

have to clean it up. But I did chamfer the four bottom edges, so they wouldn't hang up or cause tearout when I drove the peg into the mortise. I did the chamfering on my stationary belt sander, holding the little pegs by hand (leave your fingernails a little long for this chore). Or you could do the chamfering against a stationary piece of sandpaper on a flat surface. I put a little glue in the mortise and drove the pegs with a rubber mallet.

Curved Brackets

Those little double-L brackets below the seat of the chair and the cases of the sideboard and writing table are derived from Chinese furniture. In addition to tying parts together visually and adding a curve, they provide some resistance to racking forces (see the top left photo on p. 81). Although they may look innocent, they're quite a challenge to make.

I made the brackets in bunches. I made a Masonite® template for each size L and traced it over and over on a board machined to the correct width and thickness. Because the wide end of the L would be face glued, I put it on the edge of the board to give it a long grain surface. I cut the brackets out on the bandsaw and then sanded their outside curves on my stationary disc sander and their inside curves with a sanding drum chucked into my drill press. To be sure I had flat, square glue surfaces, I touched them up using the miter gauge with my stationary disc sander.

All the curved edges on the fronts of the brackets are rounded over, and I did the work with a router inverted in a vise. If you make a small push block with a foam or rubber bottom surface, you'll be able to get your hands away from the action while keeping good pressure on the little workpiece. Because the grain changed direction as I routed around the bend, I found it was important to go fairly quickly and maintain even pressure.

I doweled pairs of L's together and then doweled and face-glued them to the furni-

ture, as shown in the drawing on p. 81. To drill the dowel holes in the L's, I clamped them in my drill-press vise with stop blocks set up to keep them oriented properly as I tightened the vise.

Gluing up the brackets was a two-stage operation. First I joined the two L's. I laid them on the tablesaw (any reliably flat surface will do) and pushed the dowel joint together by hand. I found if I held them for 30 or 40 seconds I could leave them and they'd stay tight. When they were dry, I gave them a quick hit on the belt sander to make sure the glue surfaces were flat and square.

The second stage was gluing the brackets in place. To locate the dowel hole in the leg, I put a dowel center in the bracket and slid the bracket along a guide board to mark the spot (see the top right photo on p. 81). After I'd drilled the dowel hole, I clamped the bracket in place using one small quick-release clamp to pull the dowel joint tight and another to keep pressure on the face joint.

Exposed Splines

The arms on the chairs I made are joined to the front legs with large splines shaped in a shallow S. Like the square pegs, the splines are left proud of the surrounding wood and gently radiused back to meet it. The sinuous black line of the Ebon-X in the mahogany arm emphasizes the joint and underscores its double curve. Here the spline is structural, but where a similar element appears in the breadboard ends of the sideboard and writing table, it is purely decorative.

I made the loose splines for the chair by temporarily screwing a rough-cut dummy spline in the joint and flush-trimming it to the shape of the arm with a router. I removed it and used it as a template with a straight router bit and an oversize bearing wheel to turn out Ebon-X splines ⅛ in. proud of the arm. As with the pegs, I did the sanding, radiusing, and burnishing on the exposed edges of the splines before screwing and gluing them in place.

EXPOSED SPLINES. Exposed splines masked movement of solid panels in the Greene's work. But the plywood top (left) won't move. So the spline (below) is glued to both the panel and breadboard end.

Breadboard on the Sideboard

I made the tops of my sideboard and desk breadboard style, as the Greenes did. The breadboard ends are decorative in my piece because I used a veneered plywood panel and didn't have to accommodate seasonal movement. The ends are solid mahogany, biscuited and glued to the panel. At the front, I inserted false loose splines of Ebon-X. Because the breadboard ends extend beyond the panel, the splines had to follow in a shallow S-shape, as shown at right.

I routed mortises for the splines with a slot cutter fitted with a bearing wheel. After chiseling out the ends of the mortises, I cut Ebon-X splines to length and rough cut their back edges to the shallow S-shape on the bandsaw. Like the square pegs, the false splines stand proud of the surface, so I put them in temporarily and scribed a line following the contour on the edge but spaced away ⅛ in. Then I removed the splines and bandsawed to the line. I gently radiused the edges that would be exposed, sanded and burnished them, and glued them in place.

EXPOSED SPLINE FOR BREADBOARD ENDS

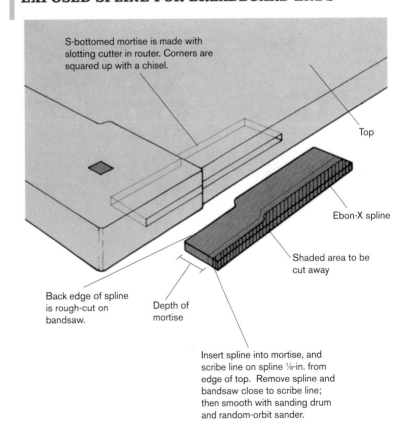

S-bottomed mortise is made with slotting cutter in router. Corners are squared up with a chisel.

Top

Ebon-X spline

Shaded area to be cut away

Back edge of spline is rough-cut on bandsaw.

Depth of mortise

Insert spline into mortise, and scribe line on spline ⅛-in. from edge of top. Remove spline and bandsaw close to scribe line; then smooth with sanding drum and random-orbit sander.

A New Greene and Greene Sideboard

With my reproduction Greene and Greene chairs around his dining table, my client asked if I would make a sideboard to go with them. I quickly agreed, but soon found it to be an entirely different undertaking. Reproducing the chairs had been a matter of mechanics: I had to figure out how to do what the Greenes had done. But making something in their style to fit a specific site would be a matter of interpretation.

My starting point for the commission was a sideboard the Greenes made in 1909. But I would have had to contort the original to make it fit the site. The three drawings at right show the development of my sideboard: the Greene's original (top), a drawing midway in the adaptation (middle), and the final version (bottom).

SITE SPECIFICS

The client intended the sideboard to be a visual anchor at the end of the room, so it had to be visible above the backs of the dining chairs. And it had to fill a long alcove. These requirements brought the sideboard's overall dimensions to 7 ft. long and 42 in. high, quite a bit longer and higher than a typical sideboard. I would have to do all I could to keep the piece from looking abnormally high.

REAPPORTIONMENT

The Greenes' sideboard has doors at each end and a bank of wide drawers in between. I decided to change this arrangement for several reasons. First, because the sideboard had to be so long, drawers located in the center would wind up being far larger from side to side than they were from front to back: a recipe for drawers that bind. I also thought wide, central drawers would emphasize the length of the piece. And my client, who entertains on a large scale, was concerned that the cabinets in the original were on the small side. I solved all these problems by moving the doors together into the middle, so they would open on one large cabinet, and by splitting the drawers into two banks, one on either side of the doors, as shown in the middle drawing.

To help mask the height of the sideboard, I resorted to unusual proportioning on the drawers. Where a normal silverware drawer is 3 in. high, I made these 6 in. It would have been possible to stay closer to normal sizes if I had added

EVOLUTION OF A SIDEBOARD

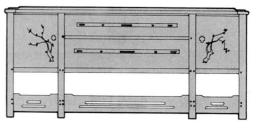

Sketch for Thorsen House sideboard, Greene and Greene, 1909

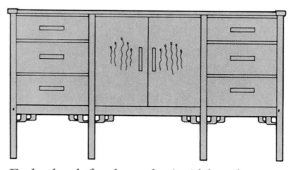

Early sketch for the author's sideboard
Doors have been moved to the middle to make the cabinet more spacious. The wide stretchers have been removed in favor of brackets.

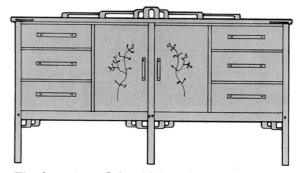

Final version of the sideboard
Two legs have been eliminated, giving the piece a more horizontal appearance. Bracket form has been adapted to make an open plate rail. Drawer handles have been elongated. The stylized tulip inlay of the earlier version, drawn from the chair splats, has been replaced with a more naturalistic composition.

a fourth drawer, but having more drawers in a stack emphasizes the vertical lines. I also preferred the appearance of three drawers. Call it mystic balance if you will, but an odd number of drawers always looks better to me.

HOW MANY LEGS?

The Greenes' sideboard has eight legs joined by wide stretchers. I decided to omit the stretchers and adopted the bracket detail from the chair to add decoration and a bit more strength below the case. But the number of legs didn't seem right. I did a sketch of a sideboard with four legs, but I thought such a long sideboard would appear ill-supported on four legs even if it could have been made soundly. I drew a version with eight legs (see the middle drawing), but that tended to emphasize the height of the piece and made for a clutter of brackets. So I drew a version with six legs; that immediately looked right to me.

PLATE RAIL

With the placement of the legs, doors, and drawers determined, I turned to the plate rail. The Greenes' sideboard has a low, solid plate rail. I wanted something that would lighten the sideboard and relate to the brackets, so I designed a low, open plate rail by adapting the bracket shape, stretching it out horizontally. I also took the opportunity to make a visual link to the legs. By creating a vertical center point in the plate rail, I carried through the line of the middle leg.

I used my bracket-making techniques to produce the parts of the plate rail. I doweled the parts together as before, but because the assembled rail was somewhat delicate, I screwed it into the sideboard's top from below rather than gluing it. This way, I could transport it separately and then attach it on site.

Pulls

If a door or a drawer front could be compared to clothing on a person, then knobs and pulls would be like neckties, pins, and earrings—finishing touches that are key to the overall impact of a piece. I used the same type of pull on the table drawers as I made for the sideboard. I tried a number of different sizes before settling on the right one for each piece, as shown in the bottom photo. The pulls are a variation on the Asian "cloud lift," an abstract representation of clouds found throughout the Greenes' work. I bandsawed the pulls and filed and sanded them to finished shape; then I radiused the edges with a router. I had to scale them down considerably from the ones used on the sideboard. For the sideboard, I decorated them with square pegs, but on the smaller pulls for the writing desk, I found they looked cramped so I left them off.

A Fitting Finish

I wanted the pieces I made to have an immediate presence, a feeling of having been around for a long time: In a sense, they had been. To achieve this, I treated the wood with potassium dichromate, an oxidizing agent borrowed from photographic processing. It comes in powder form and is mixed with water and sponged on. Before applying it, I wet-sanded every surface to raise the grain and knock it back down. While applying the potassium dichromate, I kept an air hose handy to disperse the puddles that formed in the inside corners. If they are left to stand and soak in, the color will be uneven. I then sprayed three coats of catalyzed lacquer, sanding between coats with 320-grit paper.

THOMAS HUGH STANGELAND is a professional furniture maker in Seattle, Washington.

Elements of the Shaker Style

BY CHRIS BECKSVOORT

Woodworking masters Jere Osgood, Sam Maloof, and George Nakashima each evolved a style and explored it to its ultimate conclusion, and to hell with what was in vogue. The Shakers did the same thing, continually refining their idiom until they approached perfection, without regard to the latest trend. They developed a style of furniture that blends well and fits comfortably in any type of house. The Shakers went out of their way to eschew fashion: The result is timelessness.

I grew up in a house full of Danish modern furniture, which was, it turns out, heavily influenced by Shaker designs. Like the Danish furniture makers, I fell under the sway of Shaker furniture the moment I discovered it—in my case, during a slide lecture in an architecture appreciation course I took in college. The simplicity and utility of the furniture I saw in the slides stunned me. In the late 1970s, I began restoring Shaker furniture, and much of my own work has been in the Shaker vein ever since. I very seldom reproduce slavishly, but you can look at my work and without batting an eye see its derivation is Shaker.

To make a Shaker-looking piece, adopt a Shaker attitude: Keep it simple in design and materials, make it functional, and incorporate authentic details. The details shown on these pages were commonly used by the Shakers until about 1860, after which their furniture began to show the worldly influence of the Victorian style.

The Shakers believed, "That which has in itself the highest use possesses the greatest beauty." It took the rest of the world nearly a century to come to the same conclusion, when, in the early 20th century, Louis Sullivan declared, "Form follows function." But these dictums alone do not lead inevitably to a particular style, much less to a specific set of elements and details. In addition to being inspired by their beliefs, the Shakers and the furniture they made were influenced by their historical context.

In short, the Shakers took the furniture they were familiar with, the local styles from New England to Kentucky, and stripped it of superfluous ornamentation. The Shaker craftsman Orren Haskins (1815–1892) perhaps said it best: "Why patronize the outside world? . . . We want a good plain substantial Shaker article, yea, one that bears credit to our profession & tells who and what we are, true and honest before the world, without hypocrisy or any false covering. The world at large can scarcely keep pace with it self in its stiles and fassions which last but a short time, when something still more worthless or absurd takes its place. Let good enough alone, and take good common sense for our guide in all our pursuits, and we are safe within and without."

Shaker furniture, especially from the classic period of 1820 to 1850, contains little in the way of excessive moldings and virtually no carving or veneer.

The Shakers favored native materials and were dead set against materials they felt were decadent, such as brass. The Western communities tended to follow the local vernacular style to a much greater degree than their Eastern counterparts. So the Shaker furniture from Ohio and Kentucky appears more ornate.

Some forms of furniture were never built by the Shakers. You will never see Shaker coffee tables, for example, nor tea tables, highboys, pencil-post beds, or uphol-stered pieces. Some furniture companies market these items "in the Shaker style," including improbable pieces such as enter-tainment centers.

Certain elements appear over and over in Shaker furniture and make sense within the idiom. In striving for a design that remains faithful to the Shaker style, be mindful of their approach: Just as you wouldn't build Queen Anne out of poplar, you wouldn't build Shaker out of rosewood. And pay close attention to the details.

CHRIS BECKSVOORT builds custom furniture in New Gloucester, Maine, and is a contributing editor to *Fine Woodworking*. He is also the author of *The Shaker Legacy* (The Taunton Press, 1999). Visit him online at www.chbecksvoort.com.

CROWN MOLDINGS

Moldings along the tops of Shaker case pieces are hard to justify as anything but decorative. Most styles of furniture (and architecture) incorporate moldings or some type of overhang at the top. To the eye, a crown molding or overhang denotes an ending; it is much like a period at the end of a sentence. The Shakers, presumably, were not immune to this near-universal need for closure.

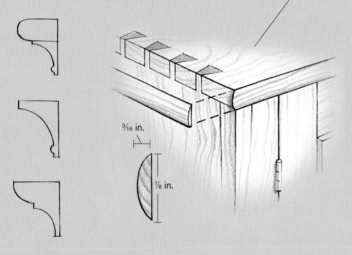

BASE MOLDINGS

Shaker craftsmen used base moldings and profiled bracket bases for protection, not decoration. A rounded or shaped edge is far less prone to splintering or chipping than is a sharp, square corner. This is especially true near the floor, where base molds and brackets are likely to encounter brooms and mops or shoes and boots.

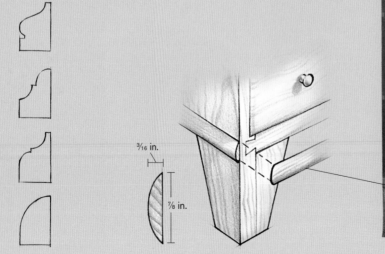

CHERRY CUPBOARD
80 in. by 44 in. by 19 in.
Canterbury, New Hampshire
Circa 1850–1900

DOOR FRAMES AND PANELS

The doors on early Shaker pieces usually had raised, fielded panels. Over time, however, the raised panel fell out of favor, perhaps because it appeared too decorative or possibly because the shoulder was seen as just another dust collector. In any event, the flat panel ultimately replaced the more traditional raised panel as the first choice of Shaker cabinetmakers. In the transition, the pillow panel, as I call it, was sometimes used. Instead of having a well-defined, shouldered field, the panel was planed on all four edges to fit the groove in the frame. The result was a field that was barely noticeable. Although square-shouldered door frames were used on occasion, more often than not the frames featured a quarter-round thumbnail profile along their inside edges. To me, this represents a perfect example of a utilitarian, as opposed to a strictly decorative, molding. Rounded edges along the inside of the door frame are much easier to keep clean than straight, square shoulders.

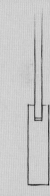

¼ in.

3 in.

¾ in.

Flat panel with
thumbnail frame

Raised, fielded panel
with thumbnail and
square frame

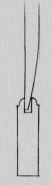

"Pillow" panel
with thumbnail
frame

Flat panel
with square
frame

DRAWERS

Shaker craftsmen built both flush and lipped drawers. Flush drawers had square edges and fit fully into their openings. Lipped drawers, although more difficult to make, covered the gap around the drawer front to keep out dust. The lips, however, were usually on the top and two sides only. A lip on the bottom was considered too fragile, should the drawer have to be set on the ground. The quarter-round and thumbnail profiles were commonly used on all four edges of lipped drawers. Neither the Shakers nor their worldly contemporaries used the bevel-edged, raised door panel as a drawer front. That design fiasco was perpetrated on consumers by the kitchen-cabinet industry.

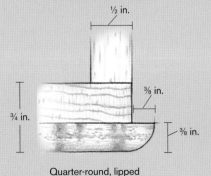

½ in.

¾ in.

⅜ in.

⅜ in.

Quarter-round, lipped

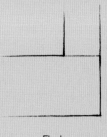

Thumbnail, lipped

Flush

KNOBS

Shaker craftsmen continued the theme of simplicity right down to the knobs. Prior to the 1850s, most Shaker knobs were shopmade, although some early pieces had commercially manufactured porcelain knobs in either white or agate, a marbled brown color. After 1860, manufactured knobs became more and more common.

The typical Shaker knob was a variation of the mushroom form. Sizes ranged from ⅜-in. dia. on tiny desk drawers to 2¼-in. dia. on large built-ins. Knobs up to 1½-in. dia. were typically spindle turned, with either a plain tenon (glued and wedged through the door or drawer front) or a threaded tenon. Larger knobs were usually face turned and attached with steel screws from the inside. Shop-built Shaker knobs were always made of hardwoods, often of a contrasting species to the rest of the piece.

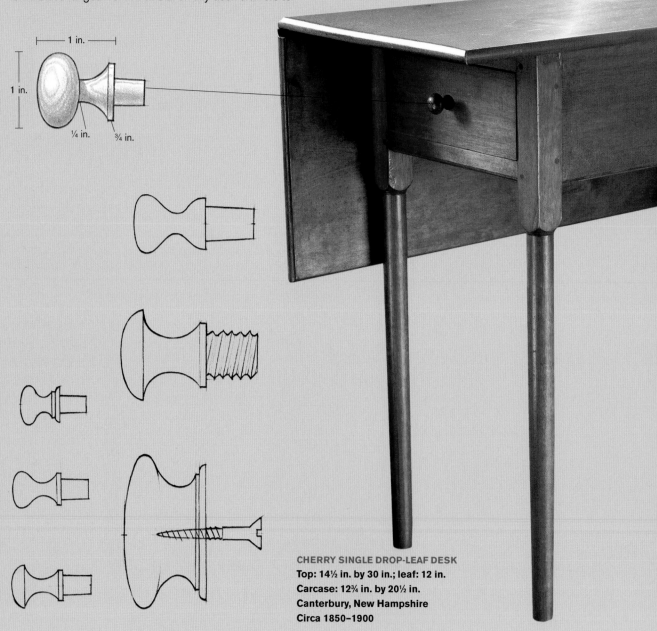

CHERRY SINGLE DROP-LEAF DESK
Top: 14½ in. by 30 in.; leaf: 12 in.
Carcase: 12¾ in. by 20½ in.
Canterbury, New Hampshire
Circa 1850–1900

TABLETOP EDGES

A fair number of Shaker tabletop edges were square or only slightly eased. A square edge, however, was by no means the only profile used. Shaker craftsmen realized that a simple, shaped profile was not only less prone to damage than a square edge but also less painful when bumped.

Rule joints were used on drop-leaf tables. The joint looked crisp and was less likely to lodge crumbs or pinch items hanging over the edges.

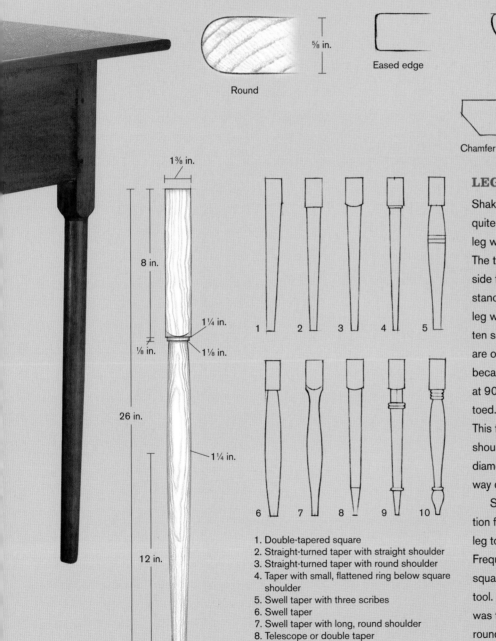

⅝ in.

Round

Eased edge

Ovolo

Bull nose

Chamfer

Double chamfer

1⅜ in.

8 in.

1¼ in.

1⅛ in.

⅛ in.

26 in.

1¼ in.

12 in.

1 in.

1. Double-tapered square
2. Straight-turned taper with straight shoulder
3. Straight-turned taper with round shoulder
4. Taper with small, flattened ring below square shoulder
5. Swell taper with three scribes
6. Swell taper
7. Swell taper with long, round shoulder
8. Telescope or double taper
9. Straight taper with rings
10. Swell taper with rings and pear foot

LEGS AND TURNINGS

Shaker table legs were, for the most part, quite simple. The double-tapered square leg was by far the most common form. The tapers were cut only on the two inside faces to give the leg a wider, sturdier stance and appearance. Another favorite leg was the straight-turned taper, most often seen on drop-leaf tables. These legs are often splayed a few degrees, because turned tapered legs attached at 90 degrees to the top appear pigeon-toed. Swell tapers were also popular. This form started a bit narrow under the shoulder, then swelled to a maximum diameter at one-quarter to one-half of the way down.

Shaker craftsmen handled the transition from the square area at the top of the leg to the turned portion in several ways. Frequently, they cut the shoulder perfectly square, a 90-degree cut with a parting tool. An easier, more common transition was the 45-degree cut, resulting in a rounded shoulder.

Edge Treatments Make a Difference

BY WILL NEPTUNE

op edges are an opportunity, a chance for a furniture maker to reinforce and enhance the overall design of a piece: to emphasize the horizontal or vertical aspect, to draw attention away from the base and toward the top or vice versa, to repeat an element or quality of the base, or to take the piece in a new direction. But a top edge, whether on a table, a desk, or a case piece, is not experienced in isolation. Rather, the edge affects you in concert with the rest of the piece.

An edge is a kind of hot spot, a place where the top and the base come together. An edge is also just one part of the top. When you design an edge, you must consider the size and the shape of the top, as well as the edge profile itself.

I'm going to look at 18th-century edges because they're the ones I'm most familiar with and because the 18th-century furniture makers worked out most of the moldings and edge profiles we're still working with today. If edges themselves are an opportunity, so too is the study of edges. Whether you build 18th-century reproductions or your own contemporary creations, a close look at edge treatments offers you a chance to add another set of options to your designer's tool kit.

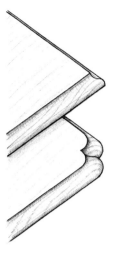

EDGE IGNORES BASE. The shaped top of this Connecticut lowboy is a bold design (imagine the lowboy with a rectangular top), but there is little relationship between the top and the base.

The game of edge design is one in which little moves often have big consequences. Imagine two Queen Anne lowboys, similar in size and overall design. Both have rectangular tops with simple ogee moldings, but one has dimpled corners (see the drawing at top right). In the latter, the small, curved creases in the molding soften the edge and lessen the severity of the otherwise rectilinear top. Or imagine that the top of a table you've made looks too thin once the edge has been molded. Should the top have been thicker or would a different molding have looked better? Either way, the slightest of alterations might have made all the difference.

Sizing the Top

When designing a tabletop, you should consider the size of the top before the shape of the top or the treatment of its edge. This is because you first take in the overall stance of a piece. You register the thickness of the top and the degree of its overhang long before you take in small-scale details such as the profile of the edge. From a distance, the elevation (front) view dominates the plan (top) view. A thin top tends to make the entire piece seem more delicate; a thick top tends to have the opposite effect. Large overhangs emphasize the horizontal; small overhangs allow you to grasp the relationship between the top and the base.

But the interaction of overhang and base is rarely so simple. As you come closer, a large overhang will block the view of the base. This limits opportunities for small edge details to tie the base and top together. So large overhangs tend to put a premium on plan-view design ideas. It may be enough for a large rectangular top to be made of beautiful wood: a single wide board or well-matched, figured wood. On such a table, a simple edge treatment will

EDGE AMPLIFIES TOP. In this pie-crust table, the top is intricately shaped in both plan view and in elevation. The concentric curves of the concave and convex edge carvings produce a pattern of inside and outside corners, enhancing the effect of the top's shape.

up close, the scrolled apron of the lowboy shows as well as the top. With the bureau, the focus on the stack of shaped drawers is reinforced by having a shallow front overhang shaped to match the curving pattern of the drawers.

If the overhang is kept small on all sides, a curious thing happens. The horizontal quality of the top is suppressed, and the overall visual effect is one of compactness, which can be seen in the Newport block-front desk (see the top right photo on the facing page). A small overhang on the desk contributes to a compact stance and places the emphasis on the elevation.

Shaping the Top

In addition to the size of a top, the shape of a top in plan view provides another level of information to read along with the edge treatment. A top with a visually active shape leads the eye around its edge. If the edge itself has an interesting profile, the shape of the top can intensify the effect of the profile. Tripod pie-crust tables (see the photo at left) are a perfect example of this phenomenon.

Historically, shaping the tops of tables and case pieces was an expensive and desirable alternative to the more common rectangular top: embellishment equaled sophistication. However, I believe shaped tops proliferated due, as much as anything, to their dramatic visual effect. In many instances, a simple four-legged rectangular base would receive a shaped top to dress it up. Another approach was to have the base and top share a common form. The top becomes an extension of the base: The shaped edge functions as one more layer of concentric information.

By itself, a shaped top shows only in plan view; it essentially disappears in true elevation. But when moldings are introduced to the edge, a new effect develops. Patterns of shaped miters occur at every break from flat to flat, curve to curve, or

hold the viewer's gaze to the center of the top, emphasizing the wood itself.

Now consider a table or case piece for which you want to emphasize one elevation over the others, say a chest of drawers that will be viewed mostly from the front. The side overhang can be large, creating a strong horizontal effect from the front, and the front overhang can be small. The benefit of the small front overhang is that, as you come closer, your view of the base isn't cut off. Lowboys (see the photo on p. 93) and block-front bureaus (see the bottom right photo on the facing page) are both good examples of this design idea. Even curve to flat. Often a shaped top develops a rhythm of inside and outside corners. This rhythm has a powerful visual effect on the edge. The more complex the molding, the more complex the intersections, and the more powerful the effect. If either the top or the molding was square, the effect would be lost.

Molding the Edge

Once you've looked at the way the size and shape of the top interact with both the top edge and the overall piece, you are ready to consider the edge itself. The design of an edge profile is all about curves or the lack of them. When it comes to designing curves (whether they're an aspect of an edge or of some other furniture element), there are those who prefer freehand curves and those who prefer compass-based constructions.

EDGE EMPHASIZES ELEVATION. The molded top edge and submolding on this Newport knee-hole desk read as one wide molding. The vertical quality of the wide molding emphasizes front elevation over plan view, directing the eye to the shells, which terminate the blocked design.

EDGE REPEATS BASE. The carefully matched veneer pattern on this Biedermeier tripod table leads the eye around the edge, making a direct visual connection between top and apron.

EDGE REINFORCES BASE. The blocking in this Boston block-front bureau is worked out through the entire elevation. The top edge is molded following a pattern of curves concentric to the drawer-front plan. The blocking design is reinforced by the top-to-base relationship.

A Glossary of Edge Profiles

SQUARE

This most basic edge shape is bold and simple. The single vertical surface will light up as a uniform plane or be uniformly in shadow.

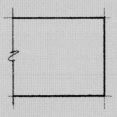

HALF-ROUND

The curve of the half-round (or bullnose) flows smoothly into the flat surfaces, softening the appearance of the edge. There are no hard surfaces or corners to interrupt the flow, but the price is the lack of clear boundaries. Though still a simple shape, the half-round seems more complex than the square edge because as you move around it, bars of light travel across its curved surface.

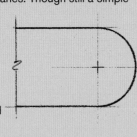

ASTRAGAL

The astragal begins as a soft half-round, but adds fillets to both sides. The combination of flats and a curve creates a bolder and more severe border than that of the segmental (below). The added complexity of the flats makes the top appear thinner.

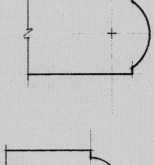

SEGMENTAL

The segmental produces the same softness and sense of movement in light as the half-round, but the corners formed where the curve breaks at the flat win back some hardness and provide a definite border. Moving the compass point inward makes the edge a smaller piece of a larger circle; if the circle gets too large, the segmental appears as a square edge. But if the circle gets too small, the edge becomes, in effect, a half-round because the corners are less distinct.

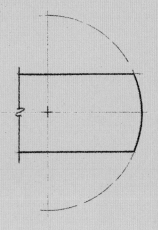

I certainly work with freehand curves, but I find myself reaching for a compass more often than not. I typically begin with either a tracing of an edge profile from a period piece or a rough freehand sketch of an edge profile I like. Then, by careful observation and some guesswork, I try to find compass settings that will pass a line along the original. Many times two or three compass points will get me very close.

A curve that is pleasing to the eye is said to be fair. I've found that experimenting with a compass gives me a good sense of the character of fair curves. You can't kid yourself with a compass: Either the radius lines of the two arcs share a common line or they don't. Flats or dead spots on a curve show up quickly with a compass because you can't get the curves to meet.

As a practical matter, designing edge profiles by using sections of circles enables you to use common, in-stock cutters to mold the edge. For short runs, I often find it quicker to cut an ogee with two router bits rather than to grind a large cutter. Using part of the curve of a core-box bit

THUMBNAIL

In a thumbnail edge, the curved surface is tipped, blurring the distinction between vertical and horizontal, yet the small top fillet provides a crisp border. Moving the compass point down and to the left, as in the thumbnail below, generates a larger curve, flattening the edge profile.

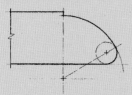

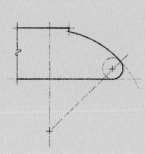

OGEE

The reverse curve of the ogee breaks the thickness of a top into several horizontal bands. This layered effect makes the top look thinner and more delicate. The concave and convex parts of the curve are perceived as separate elements, but because the transition is fair, there is no hard line to interfere with the feeling of softness. Yet the crisp top corner provides a distinct border.

Ogees 1 to 3 have similar curves but different proportions. Increasing the radius of the upper, concave curve changes the overall proportions of the profile, making the half-circle nose appear pointier.

In ogees 4 to 6, the compass point for the concave curve moves upward. As the compass point moves up, the arc becomes less than a quarter-circle, and the top corner becomes more obtuse, making it softer and less defined.

A more subtle effect occurs where the concave and convex curves meet. If the convex curve completes a half-round, as in ogees 1 to 4, you sense the horizontal tangent line at the top of the curve. This comes across as a shelf, and gives the edge a harder, even harsh, look. Moving the compass point both upward and to the right, as in ogees 5 and 6, allows you to begin the upper, concave curve before completing the half-circle of the nose curve. This tips the tangent line away from horizontal and gives the resulting S-curve a more gentle feel.

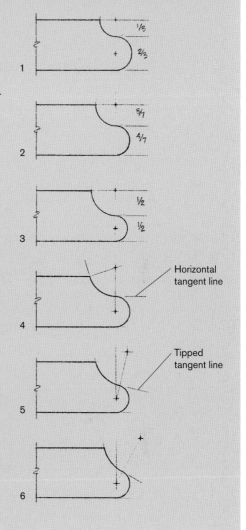

and shortening the wings of a quarter-round bit will allow you to mold ogees with little cleanup.

Over the years, I've observed a few fundamental principles for designing edge profiles: Round surfaces are softer looking than flat surfaces; vertical lines and horizontal lines have a more severe effect than angled lines; 90-degree corners have a harder look than obtuse corners; and the viewer of an edge reacts to shadow and light as much as to volume and shape.

In the glossary shown above, I look at six basic edge profiles. The trick for the designer is to manage all the variables of the edge treatment while keeping an eye on the rest of the piece as well. A hands-on approach is the only way, ultimately, to discover the edge treatments that make sense for your work.

WILL NEPTUNE is a furniture maker and former woodworking instructor at the North Bennet Street School in Boston, Massachusetts.

Designing Along the Grain

BY PAUL HARRELL

GRAIN CONTROL. The wood for this desk was cut so that the grain follows and accentuates its concave front, convex sides, and flared legs.

I
f someone remarks on the grain in a piece of furniture, they are usually responding to something exotic: wood with wild quilted figure or vibrant bands of color, perhaps a piece of quarter-sawn oak with a sunrise of medullary rays streaming across it. Most furniture does without such arresting patterns, but the visual power of the grain is still at work. Even in furniture made with the plainest wood, the grain pattern can have a profound impact on the success of the design.

On the drawing board, a design is all outlines. When you build the piece in wood, in effect you draw a lot more lines on it. Selecting and orienting the wood to control those new lines is a key part of the design process. Often, the difference between enhancing and undermining a design is just a matter of rotating a leg blank 90 degrees before you saw it, or spending a minute or two laying out a group of stretchers before cutting them out. Selecting and sawing wood with care is like good joinery: Neither will rescue a bad design, but they are both necessary to turn a good idea into fine furniture.

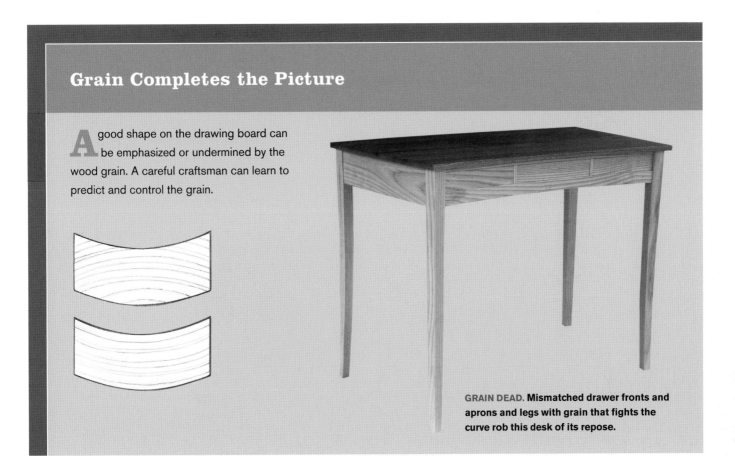

Grain Completes the Picture

A good shape on the drawing board can be emphasized or undermined by the wood grain. A careful craftsman can learn to predict and control the grain.

GRAIN DEAD. Mismatched drawer fronts and aprons and legs with grain that fights the curve rob this desk of its repose.

Same Dimensions, Different Design

I made the two tables shown here to demonstrate how deeply a few small changes in the selection and sawing of wood can affect a design. The tables have the same materials, the same details, and the same dimensions. But they are not the same design.

In the table on the facing page, the three drawer fronts are cut from the same piece of wood, and as the face grain flows across them it curves upward in the middle, accentuating the concave shape. The stretcher below the drawers is sawn so that its face grain also picks up this inward bow. The grain of the convex side apron is continuous with the front, having been cut from the same board. But it was sawn so that its face grain curves downward, to emphasize the apron's outward bow. In the legs, the grain sweeps out at the bottom to follow their flare.

But in the table above, two of the drawers match fairly well, whereas the

third is from a different plank. The face grain on the side apron goes any which way. As the legs curve outward, the grain sweeps inward.

If I've succeeded, nothing in the first table calls attention to itself. All the shapes seem clear; it has what English furniture maker Edward Barnsley called repose. In the second table, the haphazard choice of wood makes the piece seem at odds with itself.

I've presented a few techniques for predicting and controlling grain. I don't think there is always one right way to have the grain flow across a piece of furniture. The point is not to let it be an accident.

Arranging the grain for wooden legs

Because legs are seen from all sides, it is important that the grain on adjacent faces be compatible. For a straight or tapered leg, you can get the same grain pattern on all four faces by cutting the leg blank so that the grain (as viewed on the end) runs diagonally from one corner to the other.

ORIENTING THE GRAIN FOR LEG BLANKS

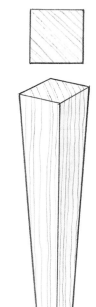

Parallel end grain results in a leg with two straight-grained faces and two wavy-grained faces.

Diagonal end grain results in a leg with straight grain on all four faces.

ORIENTING THE GRAIN TO FOLLOW A CURVED LEG

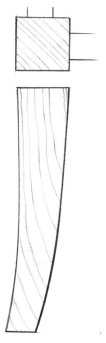
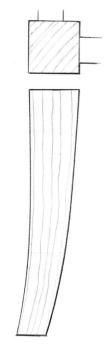

With end grain diagonal but running side to side, the face grain fights the curve of the leg.

With diagonal end grain running outward, the face grain will follow the curve of the leg.

FINDING LEGS IN LUMBER

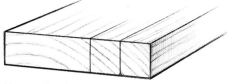

You can often find leg stock at the edges of flatsawn planks.

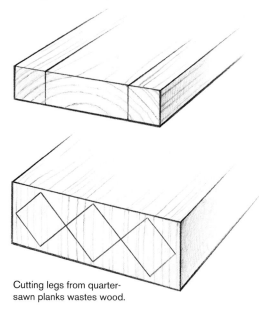

Cutting legs from quarter-sawn planks wastes wood.

Cutting the leg with the end grain parallel instead of diagonal results in two faces with straight grain and two with curving grain.

If the legs will be curved, the diagonal pattern of the end grain should run toward the outside corners of the legs. This allows the grain lines to follow the shape of the legs instead of running counter to it. If the legs are oriented incorrectly, the grain lines will be cut as the curve is sawn. The grain will appear to fight the curve of the leg, and in addition, the grain will be shorter, and the legs weaker.

When I want to cut blanks for legs, I try to find planks that have diagonal grain at one or both edges. It's possible to get legs with the right grain from a thick quartersawn plank, but you have to make a lot of sawdust to do it, and you lose a board better suited as a tabletop, cabinet case, or veneer.

PAUL HARRELL studied under James Krenov at the College of the Redwoods in Fort Bragg, California.

Grain Design for Doors

When I'm building frame-and-panel doors, I want wood for the stiles and rails that will frame the panel, not compete with it. I try to keep the pieces as uniform as possible, never mixing flat and quartersawn pieces.

Just as with curved aprons and stretchers (see p.102), doors that curve inward or outward across their faces will benefit from having rails whose grain accentuates the curve.

After cutting out pieces for a door or doors, I always experiment with different arrangements of the parts. The same pieces turned a different way will often have very different appearances.

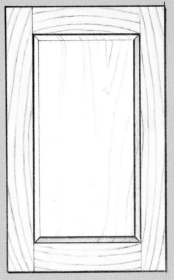

Curved grain creating a circular pattern gives a frame unity.

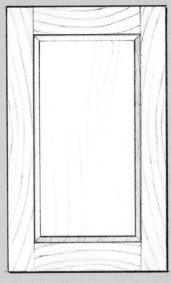

Turned outward, curved grain fights a frame's shape.

Dealing with Drawers

I often resaw thick veneers for drawer fronts from a single plank, but even these will vary subtly in grain and color. The thick veneers sawn from the top of the plank have tighter face grain than the ones toward the bottom, which have a wide flat-sawn section in the center. If the color is consistent, putting the fronts with the tighter grain at the bottom of the bureau should give the piece a solid, grounded feeling. If the flat-sawn center section is darker, as it will be in some woods, these fronts might look better at the bottom.

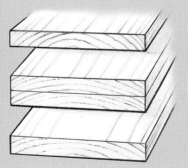

Resawing veneer from a single plank for drawer fronts ensures a good color match.

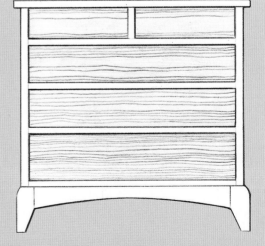

Using tighter-grained veneers for lower drawers can give a chest a harmonious rootedness.

Sawing Wood for Aprons and Stretchers

I look for mild, fairly straight-grained stock for straight aprons and stretchers. The various pieces don't have to be identical, but I avoid mixing widely different grain patterns. If the wood has a strong pattern of bands or streaks of color running through it, it's worth the effort to match the aprons end-to-end so that the pattern is continuous.

For curved aprons and stretchers, it's important that the face grain accentuate the shape. On a concave apron, face grain that curves upward in the middle like a frown will reinforce the curve of the piece; face grain that runs perfectly horizontal will reduce the apparent curve; face grain that curves downward in the middle like a smile will fight the curve.

When sawing a curved part, pick a blank with diagonal end grain. If you cut it with the end grain running up from front to back, the face grain will accentuate the sweep of the curve, whether convex or concave. If the end grain slopes the wrong way, the face grain will work against the curve.

The amount of curve in the face grain can be predicted by the amount of slope in the end grain. A steep upward slope in the end grain will yield an exaggerated curve in the face grain.

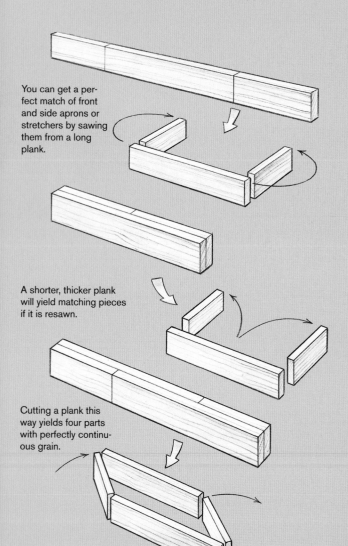

You can get a perfect match of front and side aprons or stretchers by sawing them from a long plank.

A shorter, thicker plank will yield matching pieces if it is resawn.

Cutting a plank this way yields four parts with perfectly continuous grain.

Accentuating a Bow
When cutting a concave or convex piece, choose a blank with diagonal end grain and orient it so that the end grain slopes up from front to back. The face grain will accentuate the curve of the cut.

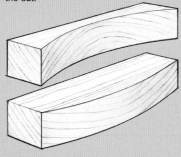

Undermining a Bow
The same part oriented with the end grain sloping the other way produces face grain that runs counter to the curve.

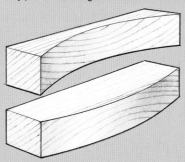

Stronger Curves
Steeply sloped end grain produces an exaggerated curve in the face grain.

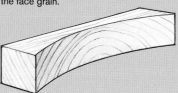

Understanding Wood Movement

BY CHRIS
BECKSVOORT

For centuries, granite has been quarried along the Maine coast. Way back in the woods behind my shop, on a granite outcropping, sit a few leftover slabs 10 in. thick by 2 ft. wide by 12 ft. long. The granite faces show a series of ½-in. holes drilled 12 in. to 18 in. apart. The old-timers would have driven dried wood into these holes, then walked down the row pouring water onto the wood. Eventually, the granite slabs would split apart. When wood cells absorb water, they swell and expand, and not even granite can stop it. So forget about pins, glue, screws, or fancy joinery; wood will move and break apart your work if you don't follow the rules.

The exact amount of wood movement depends on any combination of several factors, including the environment (the degree to which humidity fluctuates) and how the lumber has been sawn (see p. 104).

The amount of movement also varies among wood species, particularly among the hardwoods. For example, beech, hickory, oak, and hard maple move substantially more than cherry, walnut, and butternut.

Last, the type of finish you apply to a piece affects wood movement. Because

How Wood Moves

GRAIN ORIENTATION DETERMINES THE AMOUNT OF MOVEMENT

You can predict how lumber will behave by looking at the growth rings. Flatsawn boards revealing long ring sections that are parallel to the pith of the log will move the greatest amount.

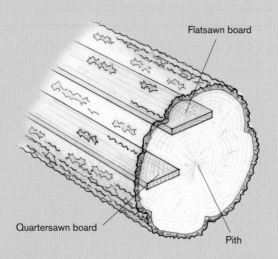

Flatsawn board

Quartersawn board

Pith

Flatsawn Board

Most seasonal movement in a board is along the rings. With annual rings nearly parallel to the surface, flatsawn boards exhibit more seasonal movement and are prone to cupping.

Quartersawn Board

A quartersawn board has annual rings running perpendicular to the surface, so the board will experience far less seasonal movement and will be less likely to cup.

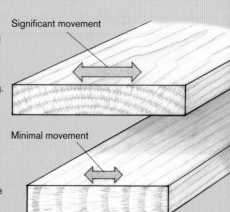

Significant movement

Minimal movement

FRAME-AND-PANEL CONSTRUCTION ISOLATES MOVEMENT

Your approach to controlling wood movement will depend a lot on whether the piece is made using slab or frame-and-panel construction.

Slab construction is typical in chests, tabletops, and headboards and consists of single, wide boards or narrow boards glued up edge to edge. With solid-wood slabs, you have to worry about cross-grain movement, which can be significant with large widths.

Frame-and-panel construction, on the other hand, minimizes the effects of wood movement by isolating large areas (the panel) and restricting movement to relatively small areas (the frame). The panel is set into grooves of the appropriate depth, but it is not glued in place. Instead, this "floating" panel is free to expand and contract within the frame.

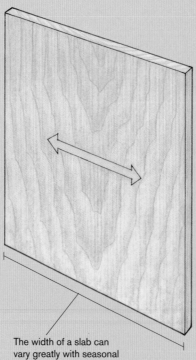

Frame-and-panel construction allows the panel to move within the stable frame.

The width of a slab can vary greatly with seasonal changes in humidity.

The width of a frame is relatively stable.

light skin finishes such as wax and oil allow greater moisture absorption, wood that has been coated with either of them moves more than wood that has been finished with deeper-penetrating sealants such as urethane and lacquer.

As a professional woodworker, I can't afford to cut corners when it comes to wood movement. So I devote my energy to building furniture right the first time—whether it's a chest, a case, a bed, or a table.

Blanket Chests

A blanket chest, in which the grain runs in a band around the entire box, is an example of slab construction. The depth and width of the chest remain constant, because the wood does not move lengthwise. But the wood does change in height in response to changes in humidity. The blanket chest gets slightly taller in summer and shorter in winter. Because movement in the top is from front to back, the hasps of the lock don't always fit. The solution is to use quartersawn wood for the top, file the hasp parts to increase clearance, and use a good sealing finish.

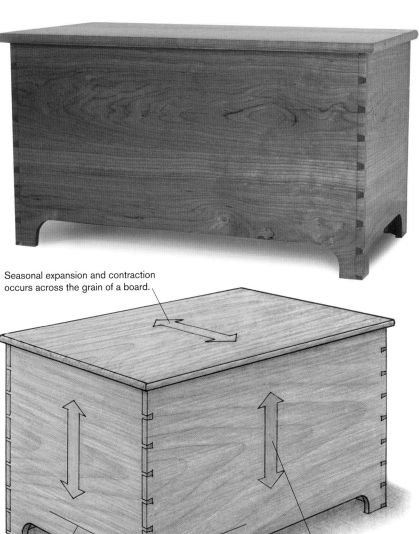

Seasonal expansion and contraction occurs across the grain of a board.

Grain direction

Grain direction

With the grain running in the same direction all the way around the case, all four sides will move in the same direction.

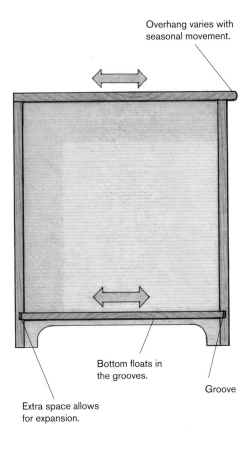

Bottom Floats in Grooves
Grooves are cut into the four sides of the chest to hold the bottom. The bottom is sized so that there's enough space in the grooves to allow for seasonal movement.

Overhang varies with seasonal movement.

Bottom floats in the grooves.

Extra space allows for expansion.

Groove

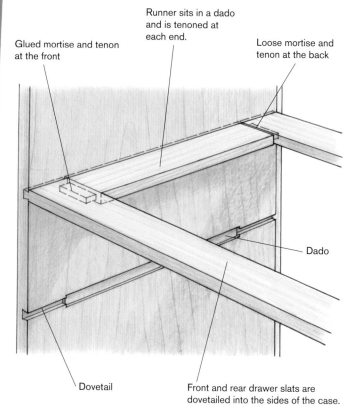

Glued mortise and tenon at the front

Runner sits in a dado and is tenoned at each end.

Loose mortise and tenon at the back

Dado

Dovetail

Front and rear drawer slats are dovetailed into the sides of the case.

Case Pieces

Web frames provide lightweight, low-movement alternatives to solid drawer dividers. For frame-and-panel cases, web frames are merely four slats—mortised and tenoned and then glued. For slab-constructed cases, web frames become a bit more involved. I start with four slats. Two are dovetailed into the sides of the case; one slat in the front, and one in the back (flush with the back rabbet). Before gluing, I rout a dado to connect the front and back dovetails. Then I cut a mortise into each end of both dovetailed slats. I measure the length of the drawer runners and add the depth of the two mortises, minus 1/16 in. for dry wood or minus 3/8 in. for damp wood. I glue the front slat into the dovetailed slots and then cut the tenons on the front-to-back runners. The front tenon is glued into the mortise, and the runner is forced into the connecting dado. The back slat is then glued into its dovetail slot, but the back mortise and tenon is not glued.

Fitting doors and drawers The issue of wood movement in doors and drawers must be taken into account. Because they will change in width over the course of a year, I install slab doors only in narrower case openings using quartersawn wood and then stabilize the door with battens.

Frame-and-panel doors are much less of a headache. For quartersawn cherry, I aim for a gap at the lock side of the door that is between the thickness of a nickel ($\frac{5}{64}$ in.) and a dime ($\frac{3}{64}$ in.). The hinge-side gap is constant year-round, the top gap is a dime fit, and the bottom gap is a nickel fit.

Fitting drawers is bit more involved. Again, I prefer to use quartersawn stock to minimize wood movement. I start by making drawers the same size as the opening, side to side. When assembled, I trim them to fit, with a $\frac{1}{64}$-in. (minimum) to $\frac{1}{16}$-in. (maximum) total side clearance.

The top-to-bottom dimension is another story. The opening is constant, but the drawer front changes in height. I also make my front about $\frac{1}{32}$-in. narrower than the sides by planing that amount off the bottom (after cutting the grooves for the drawer bottom).

A frame-and-panel back accommodates movement Building high-end furniture and having a preference for solid wood, I make my backs as frame-and-panel units, set into rabbets and glued into place. This method creates a totally sealed back, which allows for movement yet provides racking resistance.

The success of this method depends on the width and grain orientation of the outside frame members. Because the frame is glued into the rabbets, any excess wood movement will break out the lips of the side and top rabbets. I have determined that by using quartersawn cherry no wider than $1\frac{3}{4}$ in. for the sides and top of the frame members, there is enough give in the wood to accommodate any potential movement. Less well-behaved woods require correspondingly narrower stock. In any event, the stock must be quartersawn.

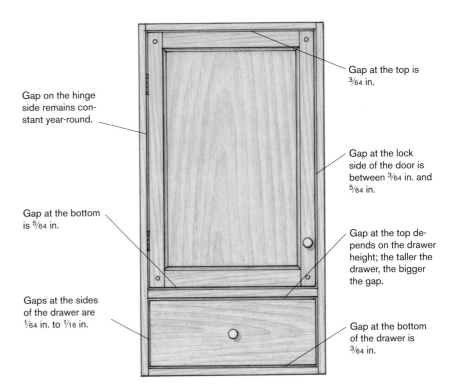

Gap on the hinge side remains constant year-round.

Gap at the top is $\frac{3}{64}$ in.

Gap at the lock side of the door is between $\frac{3}{64}$ in. and $\frac{5}{64}$ in.

Gap at the bottom is $\frac{5}{64}$ in.

Gap at the top depends on the drawer height; the taller the drawer, the bigger the gap.

Gaps at the sides of the drawer are $\frac{1}{64}$ in. to $\frac{1}{16}$ in.

Gap at the bottom of the drawer is $\frac{3}{64}$ in.

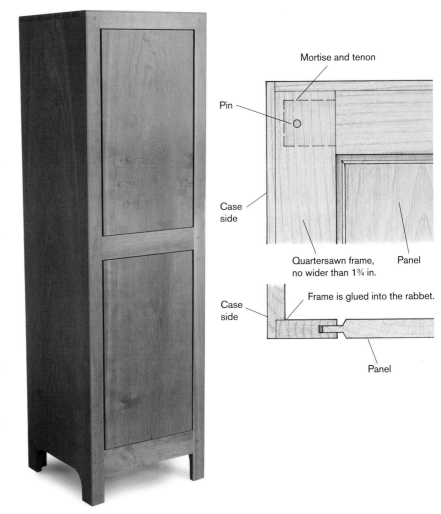

Mortise and tenon

Pin

Case side

Quartersawn frame, no wider than $1\frac{3}{4}$ in.

Panel

Case side

Frame is glued into the rabbet.

Panel

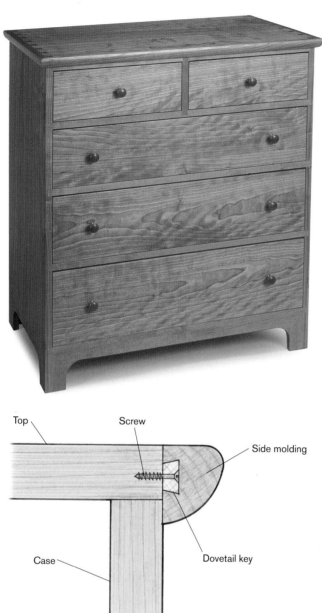

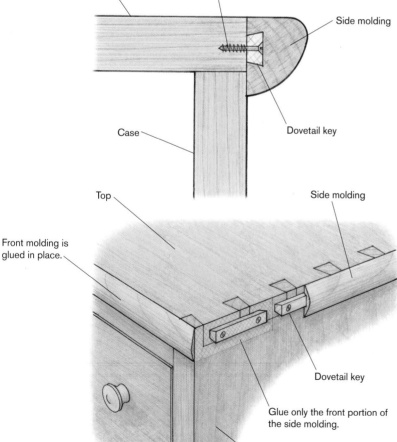

Top

Screw

Side molding

Case

Dovetail key

Top

Side molding

Front molding is glued in place.

Dovetail key

Glue only the front portion of the side molding.

Case side

Side moldings that hold Most antiques that I've looked at have the side molding glued (and/or screwed) at the miter and nailed the rest of the way back. As the case side moves over the years, the nail holes widen and the nails lose their grip. The long-lasting solution is to use dovetailed keys and slots. I cut my molding and miter the corners to fit. The side molding receives a dovetail slot that runs its full length, in the meatiest portion of the molding, not necessarily its center.

To locate the dovetail keys, I hold the molding in position, then make knife marks on the case side at the top and bottom of the slot at both the forward miter and at the back. I connect these tick marks, then cut a dovetail key the length of the cabinet side. Ideally, you want it to be 0.003-in. to 0.005-in. thinner than the depth of the slot to draw the molding tight. Then I mark the strip into five or six equal parts. Into each segment I drill and countersink two holes to accept #4 flathead screws, 1 in. apart. Between these holes, I drill for a 20-ga. brad, apply a drop of glue around the underside of the brad hole, and position the strip between scribe lines. I nail the brads, then sink the screws. Once the long length of the dovetail key has been installed, I chisel out a ⅜-in. section at each pencil mark, leaving five or six perfectly aligned dovetail keys.

Beds and Headboards

A slab headboard that's 12-in. to 14-in. wide may move up to ¼ in., which means the mortise into which it fits needs to be that much wider. If the headboard is to be pinned and glued in the middle (fixed), leave an ⅛-in. space at the top and bottom of the mortise. But the headboards on some beds, such as pencil posts, sit loosely in the mortises on the posts. The unit is held together by bolts in the rails. Extratall headboards (as in old Victorian styles or sleigh beds) require extradeep grooves or large shoulders and mortises.

Attaching a Fixed Headboard

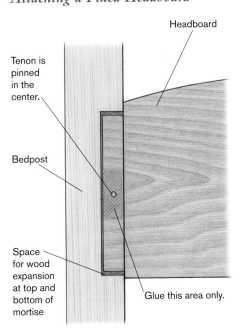

Tenon is pinned in the center.

Headboard

Bedpost

Space for wood expansion at top and bottom of mortise

Glue this area only.

Attaching Loose Headboards

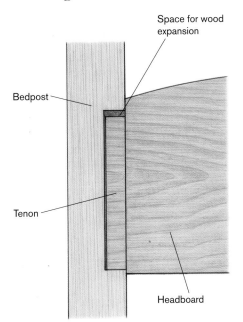

Space for wood expansion

Bedpost

Tenon

Headboard

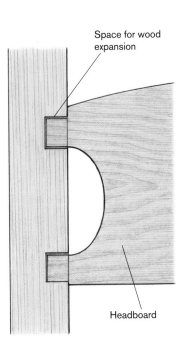

Space for wood expansion

Headboard

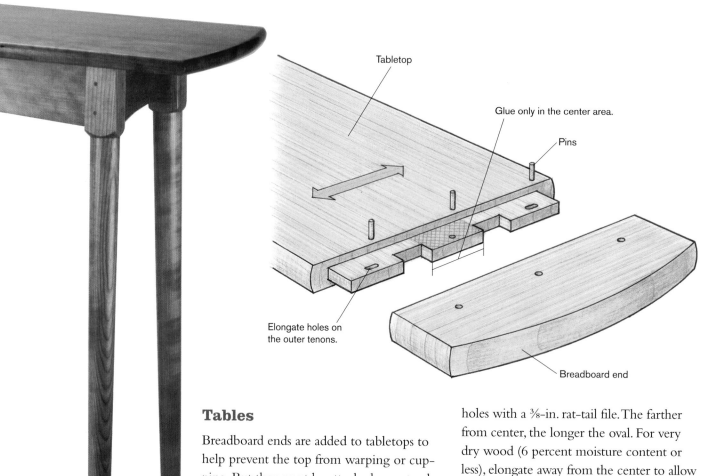

Tabletop

Glue only in the center area.

Pins

Elongate holes on
the outer tenons.

Breadboard end

Tables

Breadboard ends are added to tabletops to
help prevent the top from warping or cupping. But they must be attached so as to allow the top to expand and contract.

The preferred method for making
breadboards is a single tongue with cutouts.
For a stronger joint, parts of the tongue
are cut out to within ¼ in. to ½ in. of the
shoulder, and the corresponding areas of
the mortise are left in place to hold the
weak faces of the breadboard together.

The trickiest part of construction is
pinning and gluing the breadboard ends. I
like to plane a slight (¹⁄₁₆ in.) concave bow
into the breadboard to keep the ends tight
against the table. I make the mortise longer
than the tongue, center the breadboard, and
clamp both ends onto the table. I drill a
⅜-in.-dia. hole in the center and then one
(for narrow tabletops) or two holes (for
wider ones) on either side of center.

I remove the breadboard end and scribe
a line along the edge of the holes closest to
the end. Next, I elongate all but the center

holes with a ⅜-in. rat-tail file. The farther
from center, the longer the oval. For very
dry wood (6 percent moisture content or
less), elongate away from the center to allow
the top to expand. For wet wood (12 percent moisture content or more), elongate
toward the center to allow for shrinkage. Do
not file beyond the scribe lines; doing so will
relieve the pressure holding the breadboard
to the table shoulder.

Mortises and tenons that breathe You
may have surmised that cross-grain gluing
is a no-no. That is correct up to a point.
Wood has a small amount of give to it, and
aliphatic resin (yellow) glue is slightly elas-
tic. So you can feel relatively safe making
cross-grain joints, such as mortises and tenons, as long as the tenons aren't too wide.
With cherry, for example, I limit cross-grain
joints to a width of 5 in. As a precaution, I
glue only the top half of the joint. Theo-
retically, the top of the rail will stay flush
and the bottom will move ever so slightly.
That also should work for hardwoods that
are less well-behaved than cherry.

Narrow Aprons Can Be Glued and Pinned

In general, tenons for aprons that are less than 5 in. wide can be glued and pinned, but glue only the top portion of the joint.

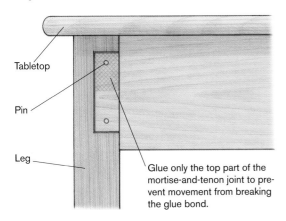

Tabletop

Pin

Leg

Glue only the top part of the mortise-and-tenon joint to prevent movement from breaking the glue bond.

Wide aprons use floating pins

The tenon of a wide apron requires space at the bottom for expansion. A fixed pin at the top forces movement downward.

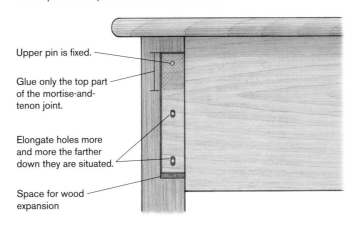

Upper pin is fixed.

Glue only the top part of the mortise-and-tenon joint.

Elongate holes more and more the farther down they are situated.

Space for wood expansion

Tabletops need room to move No matter how I go about attaching a top to its base, I anchor it firmly in the middle, ensuring that both halves are free to move equally. As a matter of course, I orient the grain in the long direction to minimize the amount of movement.

A good way to attach tops is to make ¼-in. grooves, or a series of ¼-in. slots, ½ in. below the inside top of the rail. I then install shopmade wood buttons, which grip the grooves and screw to the underside of the top. The buttons at the ends of the tabletop can go to the full depth of the groove, whereas the buttons along the sides must be placed according to the wood's moisture content and the time of year. (Fit them tighter in summer, looser in winter.)

For a table with rails substantially thicker than ¾ in., I countersink ½-in.-dia. holes from the bottom of the rails. Then I drill ¼-in. holes all the way through. I use a rat-tail file to elongate holes away from the center. Holes in the center of the end rails stay as they are. Because the wood movement is side to side, the ovals in the long rails run across the thickness of the rail. That's why I don't recommend this method for thin rails.

CHRIS BECKSVOORT builds custom furniture in New Gloucester, Maine, and is a contributing editor to *Fine Woodworking*. He is also the author of *The Shaker Legacy* (The Taunton Press, 1999). Visit him online at www.chbecksvoort.com.

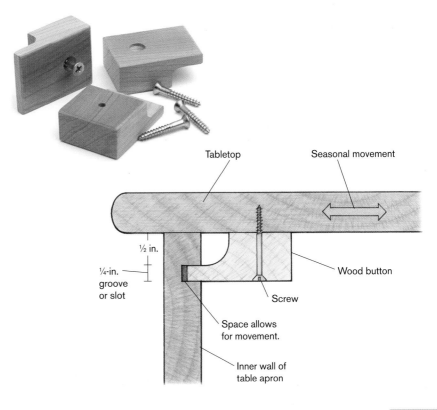

Tabletop

Seasonal movement

½ in.

¼-in. groove or slot

Wood button

Screw

Space allows for movement.

Inner wall of table apron

Supporting
Drop Leaves

BY CHRIS
BECKSVOORT

A sagging leaf on a drop-leaf table can be a chronic nuisance, to say nothing of the Christmas turkey that could end up in your lap. I've come to rely on six different support systems to keep leaves solidly in place. My favorite is a smooth-acting, pull-out slide that can be sized appropriately for end tables or dining tables. The pull-out slide's simple appearance and operation complements the Shaker-style furniture that I prefer. But no matter what system you choose to support table leaves, you have to hinge the leaves to the table. Let's take a look at the best way to accomplish that.

THERE'S MORE THAN ONE WAY TO SUPPORT A DROP LEAF. This table uses sliding supports, the author's favorite option, but there are other choices.

Drop Leaves Require a Special Joint and Hinge

The earliest examples of drop-leaf tables tended to be rather sturdy and often had but one leaf. These primitive tables had butt joints between the top and leaf and used plain butt hinges, as shown at top right, p. 115. A better way is to cut a rule joint where the leaf meets the tabletop, and use a special hinge made specifically for the job.

Drop-leaf hinges, as shown below have the barrel on one side and the screw countersinks on the other. One leaf of the hinge is longer than the other to span the gap at the edge of the leaf created by the rule joint.

The rule joint consists of a quarter-round with a fillet along the edge of the top and a cove along the edge of the leaf. The rule joint provides a smooth transition from top to leaf, whether the leaf is in the up or down position. It also discourages crumbs, tablecloths, and fingers from becoming caught in the closing joint.

DROP-LEAF HINGE

For best appearance, drop leaves use a rule joint and a special hinge made specifically for this joint.

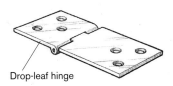

Drop-leaf hinge

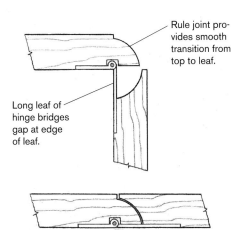

Rule joint provides smooth transition from top to leaf.

Long leaf of hinge bridges gap at edge of leaf.

Six Different Support Systems

Each of the six support systems has advantages for particular applications. Spinners (see pp. 113-114) are compact, uncomplicated, and work well with smaller leaves, such as those on side tables. Swing arms (see p. 114) also are best for small, light leaves. Swing legs and gate legs (see pp. 114-116) can be used for smaller leaves but are best for heavy loads, such as dining table extensions, because they transfer loads directly to the floor.

Swing and crane supports (see drawings p. 115) are a compromise between swing arms and swing legs. Because the load of the leaf is distributed between the table's rail and stretcher, these supports will hold more weight than swing arms. But swing and crane supports lack the solid support gained by the swing legs' contact with the floor.

Sliding supports (see pp. 116-117) can be proportioned to work well with small, light leaves or leaves that must support heavier loads, as long as the leaf is restricted to half the width of the tabletop.

Spinners A spinner is basically a stick that pivots on top of the table's side rail to support the leaf. Because only half the overall length of a spinner supports the leaf, it should be as close to twice the width of the leaf as table width and rail length permit. For example, a 10-in. leaf should have about an 18-in. spinner. Half the spinner supports the leaf, whereas the other bears against the underside of the tabletop.

You make spinners right along with the rails. Just start with stock that's a little longer and a little wider than the finished rail. Rip a 1-in.- to 1½-in.-wide strip from the top edge. Then crosscut the strip at 45 degrees to create the spinners, as shown on p. 114. The 45-degree cuts let the spinners rotate in only one direction and create positive stops when the spinners are closed.

Glue the pieces that were between and

on the ends of the spinners back onto the rail, using the spinners as spacers. On the drill press, drill a ¼-in.-dia. hole through the center of each spinner. Then clamp the spinners into position on top of the rail, and drill through the spinners and into the rail about 1 in. Remove the spinners, and glue a ¼-in.-dia. dowel about 2 in. long into the rail. Redrill the spinners' holes about ¹⁄₆₄ in. larger than the dowel, so the spinners will rotate freely on the dowel. After the rails are cut to length and width, tenoned, and sanded, slide the spinners over the dowels and trim off any excess dowel length. After the table is completed, glue a small block to the underside of the tabletop to stop the spinners at 90 degrees to the rail in the open position.

Swing arm Swing arms are braces attached to a table's rail that pivot 90 degrees to the rail to support leaves. Swing arms are usually built as part of a secondary rail assembly that is applied to the outside face of the table's side rails. Swing arms are fastened to the secondary rail with either finger joints or knuckle joints, as shown on right.

Finger joints are probably more common because they are easier to cut. Their interlocking parts are square-cornered like a box joint instead of rounded as in a knuckle joint. If you use a finger joint, undercut between the fingers and round off the inside corner of each finger for clearance. After cutting the joint, slide the pieces together and drill a hole for a pivot pin. The end of the support can be shaped as desired, but traditionally it has an ogee shape.

Swing legs A variation of the swing arm is the swing leg. As with the swing arm, one end of the support arm is joined to a secondary rail by finger joints or knuckle joints. However, the arm portion of the support is usually longer, and rather than being free, the opposite end of the arm is tenoned into its own leg. A variety of leg configurations is possible with swing legs,

SPINNER LEAF SUPPORTS

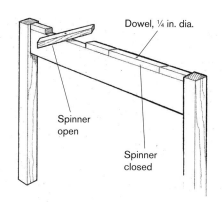

Spinner supports are quick to make and easy to install on table rails without a lot of extra work.

Dowel, ¼ in. dia.

Spinner open

Spinner closed

SWING ARMS

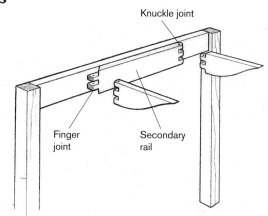

Swing arms usually are joined to a secondary rail by finger or knuckle joints. These joints require more work than spinners but will hold more weight. And swing arms don't interfere with drawers.

Knuckle joint

Finger joint

Secondary rail

SWING LEGS

By transferring the load directly to the floor, swing legs can handle more weight than swing supports.

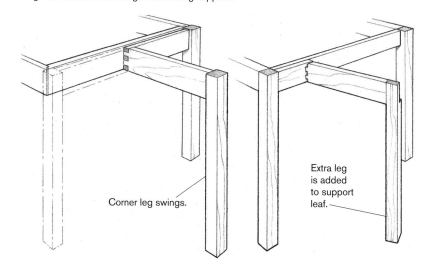

Corner leg swings.

Extra leg is added to support leaf.

GATE LEG

The lower stretcher creates a secondary point of contact for a sturdy gate-like structure that will handle large, heavy leaves.

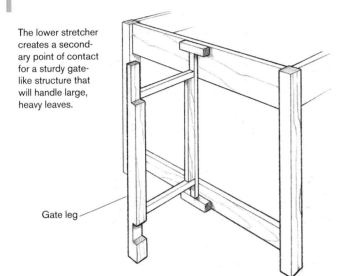

Gate leg

STANDARD HINGE

A standard hinge leaves an awkward stepped gap between table and leaf when leaf is in the down position.

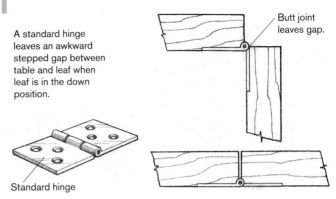

Butt joint leaves gap.

Standard hinge

SWING AND CRANE SUPPORTS

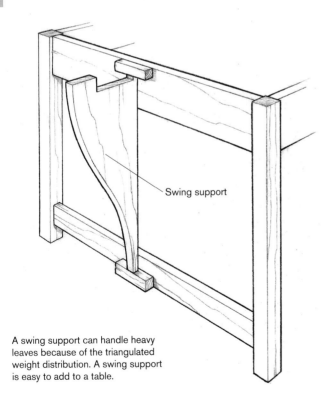

Swing support

A swing support can handle heavy leaves because of the triangulated weight distribution. A swing support is easy to add to a table.

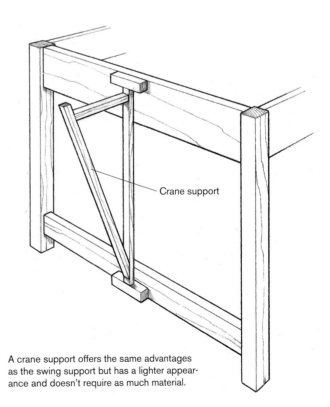

Crane support

A crane support offers the same advantages as the swing support but has a lighter appearance and doesn't require as much material.

as shown on p. 114. Because of their direct contact to the floor, swing legs can handle heavier leaves than swing arms.

Gate legs A permutation of the swing leg is the gate leg. If the drop-leaf table has lower stretchers between the legs, then the swinging legs also can include a lower stretcher for a two-point attachment at the top rail and at the bottom stretcher. This gate-like assembly, as shown on p. 115, is a sturdy support that can handle large, heavy leaves without racking. A gate leg can be attached to the primary rail and stretcher or to a secondary rail and stretcher, as was done with the swing leg.

Swing and crane supports A swing support is a vertical brace, roughly triangular in shape, that pivots between the table's top rail and a lower stretcher to support a leaf. If, instead of a single vertical piece, the support is made of three separate pieces, as shown on p. 115, it is called a crane support.

Like the gate-leg table, swing and crane supports rely on the extra strength of two pivot points for greater strength and stability. The pivot points could be built into the top rail or stretcher, but frequently they are added to the face. Swing and crane supports are sturdier than apron-mounted swing arms, but not as strong as swing legs, which distribute the load directly to the floor. The size of the stretcher will ultimately determine the strength of a swing or crane support.

Slides are less likely to sag Of all the methods for supporting a drop leaf, my favorite one is the sliding support. It's a neat, clean installation and provides firm support that is less likely to sag than other options.

Sliding supports, as shown in the top photo, are relatively easy to make. In just a couple of hours I can make efficient wooden slides that are a real complement to a drop-leaf table. And if you are not a purist or are pressed for time, you can buy pressed metal hardware that accomplishes nearly the same thing.

Hidden supports slide smoothly My approach is to build a U-shaped channel or housing that holds two sliding supports, one for a leaf on each side of the table, as shown in the bottom photo on p. 118. The design easily could be modified for tables with one leaf. The housing fits between the aprons of the table, and each support slides through a slot cut into the apron. Because this table includes a drawer, the housings also pass through the drawer kickers, which are support rails above the drawer that keep it from drooping when opened.

To create mortises in the kickers in this table, I glued 1-in.-thick stock onto ⅛-in.-thick strips, leaving two 3-in.-wide gaps in each kicker to hold the support housings (see below). The glued-up construction let me cut all the parts to size on the tablesaw. This construction eliminated the need for a special process to cut out the mortises. I temporarily clamped the kickers in place at the top of the table's side rails while I fitted the slide housings.

SLIDING DROP-LEAF SUPPORTS

Slides that support table leaves fit together in a housing when not in use. Supports should be sized according to the size and weight of the leaves. These are suitable for leaves measuring 10 in. by 32 in.

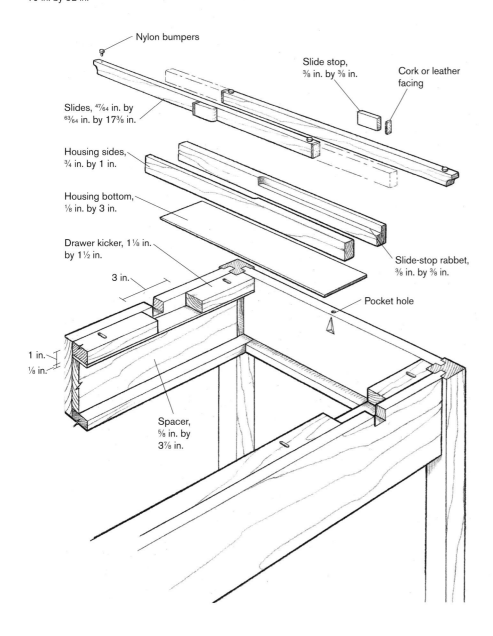

Nylon bumpers

Slide stop, ⅜ in. by ⅜ in.

Cork or leather facing

Slides, ⁴⁷⁄₆₄ in. by ⁶³⁄₆₄ in. by 17⅜ in.

Housing sides, ¾ in. by 1 in.

Housing bottom, ⅛ in. by 3 in.

Drawer kicker, 1⅛ in. by 1½ in.

3 in.

1 in.

⅛ in.

Slide-stop rabbet, ⅜ in. by ⅜ in.

Pocket hole

Spacer, ⅝ in. by 3⅞ in.

HOUSINGS PROTECT THE SLIDING SUPPORTS FROM DAMAGE OR INTERFERENCE BY THE DRAWER'S CONTENTS. The housings drop into mortises in the drawer kickers. Nylon bumpers make for smooth sliding action.

I also made the U-shaped housings by gluing the sides onto ⅛-in.-thick bottoms, leaving enough space between the sides for the slides to bypass each other smoothly. I routed rabbets for the slider stops into each of the side pieces (see p. 117). The housing's sides are long enough to span the table's side rails; the housing bottoms are shorter to fit between the kicker bottoms. The housings fit snugly into the gaps left in the kickers.

Tight clearance provides smooth action with no play The slides have about ¹⁄₆₄ in. clearance for a snug fit inside the housings. The maximum length of the slide is determined by the distance between the side rails, plus the thickness of one side rail, plus ⅜ in. for a finger pull that extends beyond the outside of the rail.

With the supports cut to size, I laid them in position in the housings, with one end extending over the table's side rails, and scribed the intersection on top of the rails with a sharp knife. Then I sawed and chiseled out the slots to allow the supports to extend through the rails. Next I glued stops in the appropriate locations on the sides of each support, and I drilled for and inserted thin, nylon stem bumpers on both ends of the top of the supports. The bumpers make the supports slide much easier.

Finally, I disassembled and finished all the parts and drilled screw holes though the kickers for attaching the tabletop. Then I glued the kickers and support housings into place (see photo above), positioned the sliders, and attached the tabletops with leaves that were already in place.

CHRIS BECKSVOORT builds custom furniture in New Gloucester, Maine, and is a contributing editor to *Fine Woodworking*. He is also the author of *The Shaker Legacy* (The Taunton Press, 1999). Visit him online at www.chbecksvoort.com.

Designing on the Go: A Coffee Table Takes Shape

BY PETER TURNER

My sister Wendy offered me a deal I couldn't refuse. She'd give me one of her watercolor paintings if I made a worktable for her studio. She sent me a rough sketch showing a long, low table with a shelf beneath the top.

Then I started thinking. Why not turn Wendy's worktable into a prototype for something I could sell as a stock item in my booth at craft shows? Something everyone

needs—a coffee table. This barter proved to be the start of a design-and-build process that produced four versions of this Shaker-style coffee table and culminated in the table you see in the front photo. It gracefully serves its purpose and is not difficult to build.

Small Changes Produce Big Results

Along the way, I tried three different leg designs, three approaches to the shelf and top construction, and several different dimensions on the top. Wendy's worktable, at

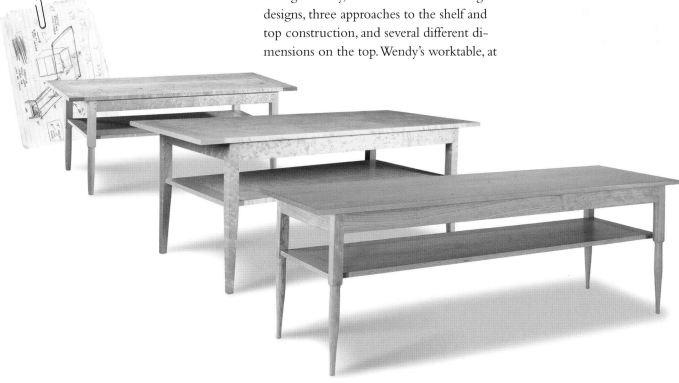

SHAKER SIMPLICITY IN A COFFEE TABLE

An ample overhang on the top, turned legs, and restrained design gives this coffee table a decidedly Shaker look. All joinery is mortise and tenon.

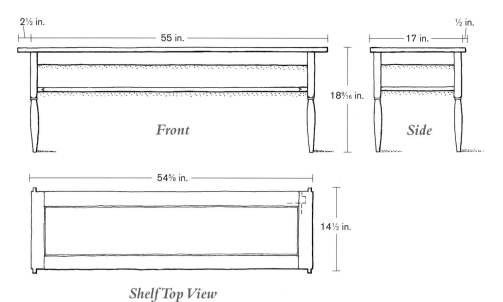

2½ in.

55 in.

½ in.

17 in.

18⁹⁄₁₆ in.

Front

Side

54⅝ in.

14½ in.

Shelf Top View

KEEP TRYING. Peter Turner's work on this coffee table began with a request from his sister and a sketch (p. 119). After several tries, he settled on a graceful design that he could build quickly.

THE TOUGH PART IS THE TRANSITION. The point where the leg turns from square to round is easy to ruin. An initial cut with a skew (left) can prevent chipping. A parting tool (above) helps form the collar.

20 in. high, was a little too tall to correspond to most sofas. I lowered the second version to 18 in. and added a 48-in. by 23-in. top. The legs, turned from 1⅜-in. stock, were slightly tapered and ended at ¹⁵⁄₁₆ in. at the floor (see the back table on p. 119). Both the top and the shelf had breadboard ends. Although very useful, the table's narrow width reminded me of an aircraft carrier, and the legs ended up looking like cigars.

A shortened incarnation, 36 in. by 18 in., with square, tapered legs followed (see the center table on p. 119). I added a more intricate breadboard design with multiple tenons. That was as much to try a new technique as it was to provide more strength and stability.

But some of these design features made the table too expensive. So to make the table easier and faster to build (and as a result less expensive), I reduced its complexity while retaining its usefulness and grace. Breadboard ends were eliminated on the top and replaced on the shelf with a frame-and-panel design, which I think is easier to make. And along the way, I refined the turned leg from its initial cigar shape to

a more delicate form. The first of these simpler versions was 18 in. high with a 48-in. by 18-in. top. I finally settled on a slightly longer version, with a 60-in. by 18-in. top that is ⁹⁄₁₆ in. thick. The shelf is ⅝ in. thick.

Simple Construction Complements the Design

There aren't many pieces to this table, and it doesn't require much material—in all, about 25 bd. ft. of 4/4 lumber and 4 bd. ft. of 8/4 wood for the legs. I use mortises and tenons to join both the apron pieces and the frame-and-panel shelf to the legs.

I start by turning the legs from 1¼-in.-sq. stock. I'm by no means a master turner, so I use only a few turning tools on the legs: a roughing-out gouge, a skew, a scraper, and a parting tool. The gouge does most of the work, and the only tricky part is turning the pommel at the transition where the leg goes from square to round. The danger is chipping out corners of the leg where it remains square. So I use the tip of the skew to make a shallow cut at the transition point (see the left photo above),

THINNER IS MORE GRACEFUL

An early version of this turned leg was ¹⁵⁄₁₆ in. dia. at the floor, but to the author it looked too much like a cigar. He then developed this pattern, with a ½-in.-dia. foot.

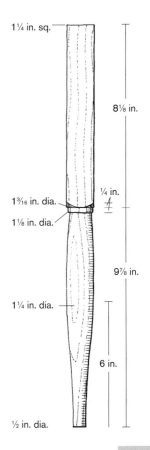

1¼ in. sq.

8⅛ in.

1³⁄₁₆ in. dia.

¼ in.

1⅛ in. dia.

9⅞ in.

1¼ in. dia.

6 in.

½ in. dia.

JOINERY IS SIMPLE AND EFFECTIVE

All joinery is mortise and tenon. Apron tenons, ⅜ in. thick and ⅞ in. long, are mitered at the corners.

Biscuit slot for buttons

2⅜ in.

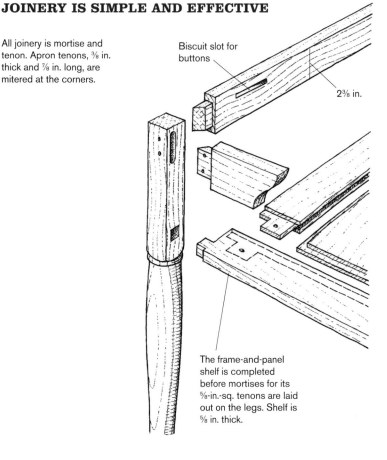

The frame-and-panel shelf is completed before mortises for its ⅝-in.-sq. tenons are laid out on the legs. Shelf is ⅝ in. thick.

then a scraper to round over the corners very gently. The detail I especially like is the ¼-in.-wide collar at the transition from round to square (see the right-hand photo on p. 121).

Once the legs are turned, I cut apron mortises in the legs and cut stile mortises in the shelf frame rails using a Multi-Router®, which is a router-based joinery tool. But it doesn't matter how you cut the mortises. They could be done with a router, a mortiser, a drill press and chisel, or entirely by hand. I make grooves for the shelf in the frame parts on a tablesaw to match the mortises.

When I cut apron and shelf frame tenons, I make sure the length between shoulders on both apron ends and shelf rails is identical so the legs stay square. This means I make the long aprons first and then the shelf, which has a ⅝-in. by ⅝-in. tenon at each corner. I clamp a long apron between two legs and mark shelf mortises

DON'T SKIP THE DRY-FIT. Gluing up all the table parts shouldn't be a nightmare. A dry run pinpoints problems while they can still be corrected.

Making It Shaker When the Shakers Didn't Make It

Can't imagine a living room without a coffee table? The Shakers could. They didn't build coffee tables. To give my design a feeling that is reminiscent of Shaker work, I turned to my reference library (the four books I find most useful are listed here).

If you want to know more about the religious and social basis of Shaker craft, you can start with something called "Orders and Rules of the Church at Mount Lebanon: Millennial Laws of Gospel Statutes & Ordinances." This summary of Shaker habits—described in some of the books I used—was published for church elders in several versions between 1821 and 1887. Laws covered general approaches to furniture, and they could be very specific: The 1845 laws required beds to be painted green and limited bedroom mirrors to 18 in. by 12 in.

For the design of this table, I looked at photos of Shaker work. The greater the variety and number of photographic examples I absorbed, the stronger my vocabulary became in the elements of form, scale, proportion, and balance. This accumulated understanding allowed me to use specific design characteristics in this coffee table. Thin tops, ½ in. or ⅝ in., and ample overhangs, 2 in. to 3 in., on table ends are common on Shaker tables, so I adopted those elements here. The leg transition from square to collar to round came from a Shaker side table made in Enfield, New Hampshire. Along with sound joinery and little decorative elaboration, the prudent selection of design elements evokes a harmony and balance present in the majority of Shaker work.

My list of most useful books includes the following:

The Complete Book of Shaker Furniture by Timothy Rieman and Jean Burks (Harry N. Abrams, 1993)

Shop Drawings of Shaker Furniture and Woodenware, vols. 1, 2, and 3 (Berkshire Traveller Press, 1973–1977)

The Book of Shaker Furniture by John Kassay (University of Massachusetts Press, 1980).

Illustrated Guide to Shaker Furniture by Robert Meader (Dover Publications, 1972)

---

in the legs directly from the shelf tenons. Once the shoulder-to-shoulder distance on the shelf is established, I cut the short apron pieces to match.

When fitting the shelf panel, I take the shrinking characteristics of the wood and the time of year into account. Various books provide formulas for figuring out how much each species of wood moves with changes in seasonal humidity.

I fitted the panel in this table in early October, when the weather was still warm, so I guessed the wood was close to its maximum width. The reveals around the edge of the panel are sized accordingly. The panel is flush on both sides of the shelf.

A tenon on each corner of the shelf fits into a corresponding mortise in the leg. I rough out these mortises on the drill press and clean them up with a chisel.

After Assembly, Finish Up with Citrus Oil

Final assembly begins with a dry-fit (see the photo on the facing page). Then I glue together the long aprons and legs. The short end aprons and the fully sanded shelf are then glued into place and pinned (I use ⅛-in.-dia. dowel for pins), two pins for each apron joint and one for each shelf joint. To attach the top, I use wooden buttons with tongues that fit biscuit slots cut on the inside edges of the aprons.

After bringing everything along to 320-grit sandpaper, I finish it with three coats of Livos® oil, which has a pleasant smell and produces a nice satin sheen.

PETER TURNER is a woodworker who lives and works in South Portland, Maine. You may visit him on the web at www.petersturner.com.

Designing Table Legs

BY GRAHAM
BLACKBURN

More often than not, legs are the defining features of a table. Once you decide on the shape and color of a tabletop, making it is largely a question of providing the required surface area with the chosen stock. But the support for the tabletop is a different matter. Table legs—whether in the form of monolithic blocks, single pedestals, trestles, or in groups of three, four, or more—may be provided in a bewildering array of forms. The variety of legs is virtually endless, both from stylistic and construction standpoints.

Providing reliable support may be the most fundamental requirement demanded of any leg, but deciding on an appropriate form and shape requires a reasoned understanding of the table's function and style. Whether you are designing with a certain period look in mind or venturing out into original designs, there is something to be learned by studying the furniture of the past. Frequently, period styles are characterized by features that produce distinguishing effects. If the purpose of these effects is understood, they can be duplicated in original designs that don't represent any particular period.

When planning a leg design, consider a few basic concepts that guide the process. Is the wood choice appropriate for the table design? Do you want the table to appear solidly grounded or delicate and refined? Should the table appear formal or relaxed? This chapter presents an overview of leg types, as well as their functions and construction methods, to make choosing a style and design easier for every table builder.

Function and Form

Very often a table's use will determine much of its leg design. The legs on a dining table, for example, must make sitting at it convenient: No matter how handsome any given leg may be, if it prevents a comfortable seating arrangement, it will be a functional failure. Similarly, if it is to be a heavy-load-bearing library table, it should not have delicate, spindly legs. A table that must be movable, adjustable, or expandable should not rest on massive, stretcher-bound legs.

After a table's function has been taken into account, the question of style remains. Sometimes this merely means designing legs that are coherent with the table's essential character—stout, sturdy legs for a chunky, heavy-duty piece or delicate legs for a refined piece—but more often than not the table will contain references to a particular period or style. Adding inappropriately designed legs can result in an awkward combination that will spoil an otherwise soundly constructed piece.

APPROPRIATE MATERIAL. Some styles just beg for a particular wood species. For example, simple, square oak legs look great on a Mission-style table.

LIGHTNESS. For a Shaker side table with a large overhang on the top and a narrow skirt, plain pine legs, tapered on two sides, lend a delicate look.

SOLID GROUNDING. A weight-bearing library table built in dark walnut needs hefty legs, a solid skirt and bottom stretchers to support heavy loads of books.

SOBRIETY. A Federal writing table built with deep walnut and mahogany tones calls for a restrained, classical leg design with stringing and a shaded holly inlay.

FLIGHTS OF FANCY. Poly- chrome geometric solids add visual interest and a sense of humor to this large dining table of post-Memphis design.

Stylistic Appropriateness

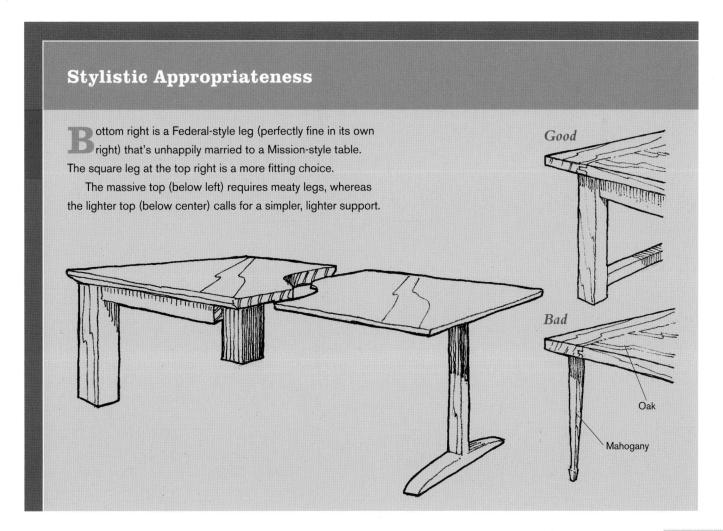

Bottom right is a Federal-style leg (perfectly fine in its own right) that's unhappily married to a Mission-style table. The square leg at the top right is a more fitting choice.

The massive top (below left) requires meaty legs, whereas the lighter top (below center) calls for a simpler, lighter support.

Good

Bad

Oak

Mahogany

Designing Tapers

A shallow taper on one side (left) affords an elegant line without sacrificing the look of strength. Adjacent sides can be tapered to produce a light appearance (center). Or opposite sides can be tapered (right) and the legs inlaid to achieve a period look.

End views

Feet Must Fit the Style

Adding a foot to a table leg can help ground a piece. The pad foot (center) and bun foot (left) are inappropriate for this Federal-style leg from the late 18th century. This design calls for a simpler foot (right), lightening the piece and making the table appear to float.

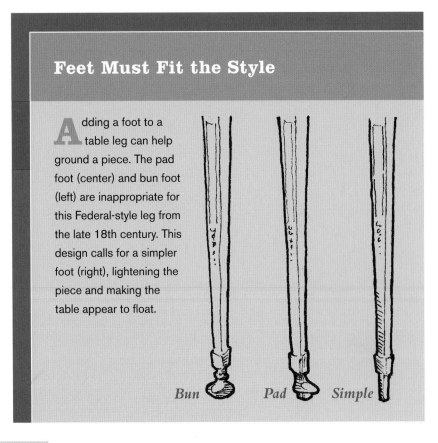

Bun *Pad* *Simple*

Words like "inappropriately" and "awkward" may sound dangerously subjective, but in fact, style can be analyzed and understood quite objectively.

Design guidelines When attempting to reproduce a particular period or style, wood choice is one of the main concerns. Mission pieces, for example, were traditionally made of solid oak—a material that accounts for much of the character of this style. To reproduce the Mission style, oak is the obvious choice but not necessarily the only option. If you choose to build in another wood, it should be for a sound reason. Woods close to oak in color and grain pattern, such as ash or elm, may complement the design. Or you may want to soften the heavy look of this style by altering the scale or by building in a lighter wood like cherry, but you should realize that you're no longer building a period piece.

A table may have the appearance of being solidly grounded, or it may take on a more delicate look. A leg that rests on a solid base and is joined to other legs by low rails or stretchers gives the appearance of sturdiness. Using a substantial foot at the end of a leg also makes a table appear balanced and solid. A tapered leg, whether plain, square, or turned, will give the look of delicacy, even of floating. This idea can be developed further by altering the form of the taper: for example, tapering a square leg on one, two, three, or four sides.

A classically designed leg in the Federal style might be more appropriate for tables requiring a dignified appearance. Conference tables, library tables, or formal dining tables often need this sense of sobriety. But there is also room to be playful. Flights of fancy embodied in curvilinear pieces, both regular and free-form, can transform an ordinary table into a contemporary expression of individuality.

Whatever style you choose, make sure that it is environmentally compatible. This simply means that you must take the surroundings into account—either locally, in terms of the pieces directly around it, or globally, in terms of the larger surroundings in which the piece will live. Sometimes, of course, none of this is known to the maker, and you can do no more than aim to be as true as possible to the piece's own character—square legs on square tables, for example.

Designing legs that are appropriate to a particular era requires that you recognize the design parameters underlying the style. Knowing how particular styles developed, the features and techniques that were used, and the characteristics the builder was after will help you design legs that are comfortable and right on any given table. It will also steer you away from infelicitous mistakes like trying to graft Jacobean legs onto a Chippendale piece.

From Gothic to Contemporary: A Brief History of Legs

What follows is a chronological look at some of the major periods of Western furniture. It should provide not only a broad outline of the more important styles but also tell you what to look for when you're trying to decide whether a particular leg detail will be appropriate for the situation at hand.

Gothic/Medieval Apart from various esoteric pieces from antiquity, such as Egyptian chairs found in pyramid tombs and Greek and Roman furniture known primarily from artistic representations, furniture from the 14th and 15th centuries constitutes the first period from which actual examples are readily found. These were vigorous, if not violent, times, and the furniture that remains is, appropriately enough, decidedly sturdy, relying largely on heavy hardwoods such as oak and chestnut.

Early tables often were placed upon trestles for mobility. These "proto-legs" were often ecclesiastical in character. They were

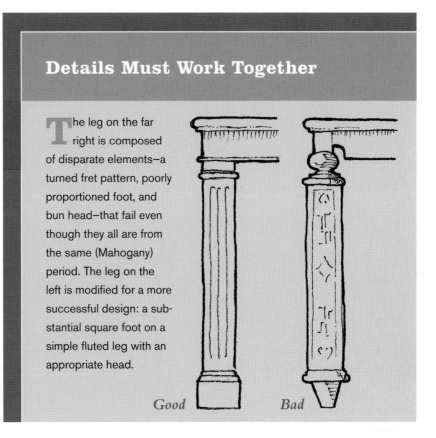

Details Must Work Together

The leg on the far right is composed of disparate elements—a turned fret pattern, poorly proportioned foot, and bun head—that fail even though they all are from the same (Mahogany) period. The leg on the left is modified for a more successful design: a substantial square foot on a simple fluted leg with an appropriate head.

Good   *Bad*

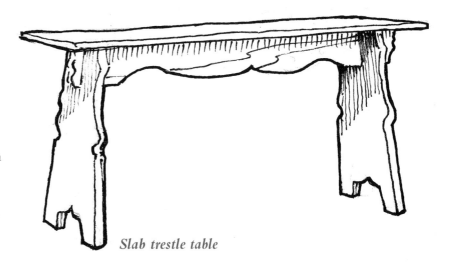

Slab trestle table

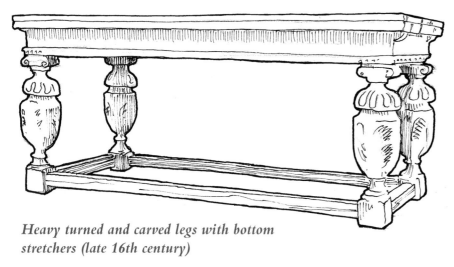

Heavy turned and carved legs with bottom stretchers (late 16th century)

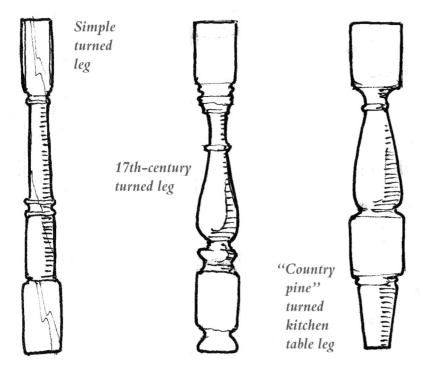

Simple turned leg

17th-century turned leg

"Country pine" turned kitchen table leg

sometimes carved with graceful Gothic tracery, using intersecting circles to form pointed arches and other geometrically inspired shapes. More commonly, they consisted of pairs of simple slabs, occasionally made single and supported by one broad foot.

The age of oak As more permanence was achieved, "joined" tables became common in the 16th century. Dining tables were invariably massive, with large legs typically joined near their bottoms by sturdy stretchers that served not only to strengthen the legs but also to provide a place to rest one's foot—off a drafty and perhaps dirty stone floor. Early types employed a central stretcher connected to pairs of legs. This stretcher system has the advantage of providing plenty of space for the sitter's legs.

Square legs were frequently chamfered and cusped, with square stretchers mortised into them and secured with pegs. Turned legs range from basic cylinders with simple rings and square ends to those with exaggerated shapes sumptuously carved and displaying a variety of motifs—from acanthus leaves to satyr heads.

Contemporary uses for legs made in this style might include a single turned and carved leg for a round dining table or simpler versions of the turned variety with square ends used in a kitchen or on a work table—as seen in much so-called English country pine.

Seventeenth-century walnut By the 17th century, tables—from large dining tables to smaller altar or writing tables— became more delicate and fanciful. Their legs were no longer merely straight but often curved and exhibiting pronounced turned elements—spirals, double twists, cups, and a variety of inlay. Stretchers connecting the legs also became more varied, with lighter, curved pieces replacing the heavy, structural members found on earlier tables. There is a distinct Renaissance influence in much of the carving of this period.

Although it is possible to divide the period into numerous categories that vary widely from one to another—such as Jacobean in Europe and Pilgrim Century furniture in America—legs from this period were generally more sophisticated and refined than those from the Gothic/Medieval and Oak periods. At the same time, the legs were more inventive and decorated than those of the succeeding periods. The 17th century probably presents the contemporary designer with more choices than any other period,

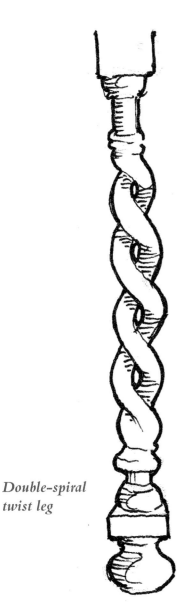

Double-spiral twist leg

17th-century spiral twist leg with curved stretcher

especially if he or she is not constrained by matching or harmonizing the piece with any other furniture or a particular surrounding. Although the construction tends to be traditional, the shape, ornamentation, and material are susceptible to infinite invention, as a visit to any museum with tables from this period will demonstrate.

Queen Anne walnut At the beginning of the 18th century, a stylistic reaction to earlier exuberance set in. The so-called Queen Anne style—which lasted much longer than Queen Anne's actual reign—was typified by restraint and a lessening of ornament. More attention was paid to purity of line and elegance of design, and this was particularly typified by the Queen Anne cabriole leg with pad foot and later the ball-and-claw foot, both with minimal carving.

This was the beginning of the classic 18th-century style of furniture, which came to be known in Britain as the Georgian period. In America this period was represented by such luminaries as Thomas Affleck and other Philadelphia cabinetmakers. Many other sought-after makers, such as the Goddards and Townsends of Newport, Rhode Island, were recasting

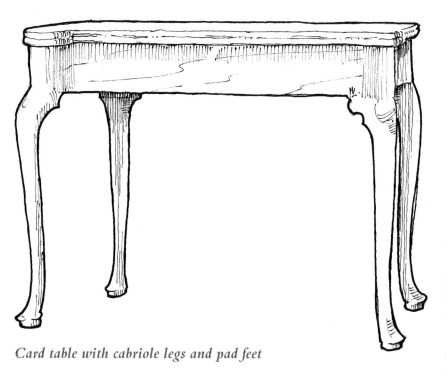

Card table with cabriole legs and pad feet

design. These men based their designs on classical paradigms and proportions derived from Greek and Roman architecture.

If you wish to design in this style, it is important to learn something about the underlying proportional system that dictates fundamentals—height-to-width ratios, for instance. Start by paying close attention to the wealth of published material that is available on this period.

Mahogany furniture As the 18th century wore on, there was a return to ornamentation, and by the time of Chippendale, table legs were once again heavily carved with lions' feet, fretwork, flutes, and all manner of brackets.

Although successful designs in this style require at least a passing awareness of basic underlying design principles, there are a

Correct Details Are No Substitute for Overall Balance

The cabriole leg at far right is composed of congruous details but designed with no attention to the overall form. Not understanding or being sensitive to the underlying proportional rationale, the builder creates a leg that is misshapen and unhappy. The leg does little to give the table a feeling of comfortable support (it looks like it might easily break) or appropriate elegance. Poorly understood period pieces look silly, but overall form is even more important with contemporary pieces, where the design vocabulary is much more relaxed.

Correct bracket

Graceful, subtle curve

Well-proportioned web foot

Good

Leg is set back too far.

Unbalanced and badly exaggerated curve

Webbed foot is correct in detail but too small.

Bad

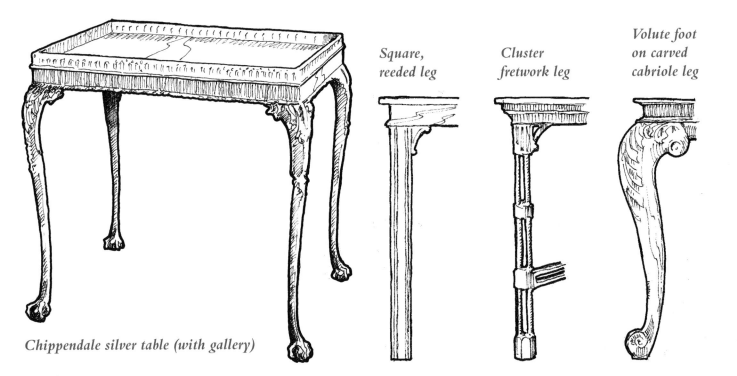

*Square,
reeded leg*

*Cluster
fretwork leg*

*Volute foot
on carved
cabriole leg*

Chippendale silver table (with gallery)

host of details that identify separate varieties. Often, randomly mixing and matching in an attempt to reproduce the general flavor of this period fails and simply looks silly. But if you choose the details carefully—a particular foot, a certain stretcher type, an overall shape or proportion—and keep an eye on overall balance, both in terms of weight (as implied by the actual size and dimensions of various parts) and form (as constituted by color, wood species, and ornamentation, such as carving or inlay), you can produce something new and exciting from ideas that have stood the test of time.

The important thing is to avoid replicating a particular style exactly—such as a New York side table from 1790—and, from a lack of familiarity, giving it something incongruous, such as a Boston foot. Details should always be subservient to the whole. However much a particular detail may appeal to you, do not hesitate to alter or adjust it appropriately for the sake of the design as a whole.

Hepplewhite/Sheraton-style table with stretcherless legs that are tapered and inlaid

Shaker table: Absolute simplicity

Late 18th century By the end of the 18th century, designers such as Robert and James Adam, Thomas Sheraton, and George Hepplewhite had introduced even more classical elements: stretcherless tapered legs; architectural details such as classically inspired spandrels, pilasters, and fluting; and a great deal of inlay in the form of shells, urns, stringing, and banding. This was possible, of course, because cabinetmaking techniques—based mainly on veneered construction—had largely overtaken the older forms of solid-wood joinery.

Realizing this, you can avoid using these techniques on legs destined for a table designed in an earlier style. Put another way, it is invariably better to restrict your design ideas to those elements that go hand-in-hand with the type of construction being employed.

Overall Form Is More Important Than Correctness of Detail

This table is composed of elements—such as the fretwork skirt, heavily carved knees, and biche (deer) feet—that are all from different periods, making the table stylistically incorrect. But the design works because the overall form is graceful, and the various components make structural sense.

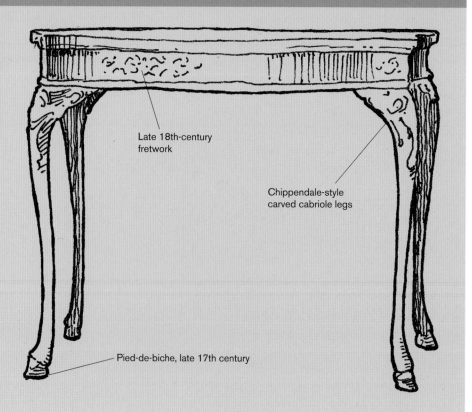

Late 18th-century fretwork

Chippendale-style carved cabriole legs

Pied-de-biche, late 17th century

Nineteenth century In the 19th century, the general introduction of powered machinery and the large-scale production of furniture began to affect the one-man, several-apprentice shops that had previously been the norm. It was also a period given to stylistic revivals. Consequently, there are as many distinct forms, fads, styles, and schools originating from this period as from practically all preceding centuries.

A close look at some of these styles can be instructive. To start with, the very popular Shaker style is well known as a model of simplicity and unadorned sobriety. Construction is honest and straightforward. Very little is added that does not have an essential structural purpose. This demand for functional furniture results in simple turned or plainly tapered legs sufficient for the job of supporting the table. Legs were usually made from the most practical material at hand, eschewing the use of rare and exotic species that might require additional work. Try using these principles by designing a leg that represents the minimum possible construction for sufficient support.

In sharp contrast to Shaker simplicity was mass-produced Victorian furniture, which sought to embody whatever fantastic element was the fashion of the day. This included applied veneer pieces, pressed patterns, gilded incised designs, spindled galleries, machine fluting, and coarse carving (often on two-dimensionally shaped members). One well-known example of revivalist fashion is furniture inspired by the designer Charles Eastlake, who was responsible for introducing the principles of the English design reform movement to America. Originally conceived as a reaction against the melodramatic red plush and extravagant furniture of mid-century, this resulted in a series of more simplified styles drawing upon earlier models, such as Modern Gothic and Queen Anne Revival.

Today, much of this furniture can seem excessively busy, but it serves the contemporary designer as a model of how earlier elements can be reinterpreted. Although some of the results may be seen as a travesty of the pieces that inspired them, it is instructive to observe how they present a coherent identity when reinterpreted and incorporated into new work. This is another important idea to bear in mind: A well-designed leg—of whatever style—will stand on its own merits as long as you have fulfilled the structural requirements and have conceived the leg and the table as a whole.

Twentieth-century contemporary With the arrival of the 20th century, several factors converged to create a landscape that was, at least superficially, even more puzzling for the designer. On one hand, the 19th century's infatuation with rediscovering old styles—from Gothic to Turkish—had produced an almost limitless number of confusing design ideas. On the other hand, there was a severe reaction to everything overly ornamented and complicated. The Arts and Crafts movement's return to simple craftsmanship—starting with designers such as William Morris and continuing across the Atlantic to people such as Gustav Stickley in upstate New York—had produced, by comparison, a spartan and foursquare approach that foreshadowed

Victorian table leg is an eclectic mix of Gothic, Tudor, and Romanesque.

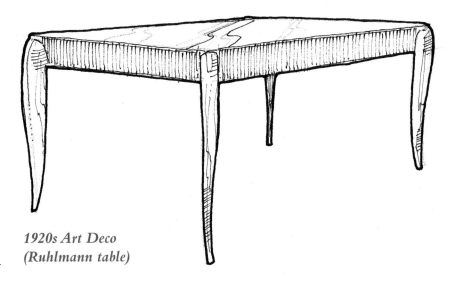

1920s Art Deco (Ruhlmann table)

*Krenov-style
silver table*

the Art Deco movement. This resulted
in the exciting use of new and different
materials, including sharkskin, aluminum,
and laminates. Designers such as Jacques-
Emile Ruhlmann and Wendell Castle
have expanded our ideas of what can be
achieved if the constraints of traditionalism
are laid aside.

More recently there has been a flower-
ing of talented new designers produced by a
renewed interest in high-quality woodworking. There are now schools in Britain and
America where the making of well-con-
structed and well-designed furniture—both
contemporary and traditional—is taught.

The result has been a century with more
choices than ever for the designer. It would
seem that anything goes. But for all of the
apparent variety, the fundamentals of good
design remain: Overall harmony, structural
sufficiency, and balance cannot be ignored.

James Krenov's furniture may be well-
known for its sensitive and delicate attention to overall harmony of color and grain,
George Nakashima can be appreciated for
his use of natural forms, and the Memphis
style may stand out by virtue of its uncom-
promising and radical approach to color
and geometrics, but all three of these superficially different approaches succeed because
their fundamental concern is with the given
piece as a balanced whole. The successful
and varied elements of earlier periods are
still important and endlessly instructional.

No matter what construction methods
you use, no matter what style you prefer,
strive always to design a leg that bears the
lessons of the past in mind. Remember,
above all, to design legs that are an integral
part of the whole piece.

GRAHAM BLACKBURN is a furniture maker, illustrator, author, and the publisher of Blackburn Books
(www.blackburnbooks.com) in Bearsville, New York.

the later Bauhaus movement of the mid-
century. Added to these diverse approaches,
the increase of machinery, new methods of
production, and changing market condi-
tions (due especially to World Wars I and II)
all provided an extremely fertile ground for
a variety of new styles.

Some lines of development continued
the simple approach. Out of the Arts and
Crafts movement came designers concerned with honesty, simplicity, and good
workmanship. People such as Edward
Barnsley, Allan Peters, and even James
Krenov have continued to embody this
approach. At the other end of the design
spectrum, a purely artistic spirit produced
the fluid and nature-inspired shapes of the
Art Nouveau movement, which merged
with the increasingly modern ideas of

Joining Legs to Aprons

BY GARRETT HACK

The life of a table is often not easy. Legs get kicked; the table gets pushed and pulled across uneven floors, leaned against, and sometimes even sat upon. To make matters worse, the very nature of wood adds to the stress. As the tabletop shrinks and swells with seasonal changes, the movement works against the integrity of the table's structure. Where is all this stress felt? It's the leg-to-apron joint that holds a table together and gives it rigidity. When that joint fails, the table falls apart.

Leg-to-apron joints must withstand three different kinds of stress. One is shear: a vertical load directly above a joint, such as when someone sits on the corner of a table. Leaning heavily on the top of a table midpoint above the apron causes the joints to undergo a bending stress trying to lever them apart. Shoving the table sideways or bumping against a leg gives the joints a mixture of twisting forces. Also, as a tabletop that is fastened too tightly to the apron expands or shrinks, it can try to twist the joints. The best defense against these stresses is a well-designed, tight-fitting mortise-and-tenon joint that locks apron to leg. The mortise and tenon is not only a good joint for tables; the same principles apply to designing joints for cabinet doors and chairs.

A STURDY LEG-TO-APRON JOINT

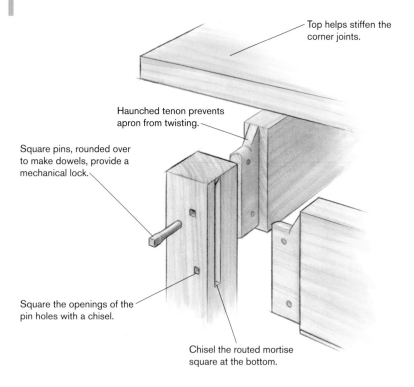

Top helps stiffen the corner joints.

Haunched tenon prevents apron from twisting.

Square pins, rounded over to make dowels, provide a mechanical lock.

Square the openings of the pin holes with a chisel.

Chisel the routed mortise square at the bottom.

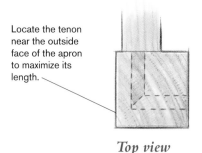

Locate the tenon near the outside face of the apron to maximize its length.

Top view

If tenons are mitered, cut them slightly short to leave a small gap between them.

Tenon should be a little more than one-third the thickness of the apron.

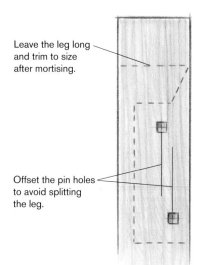

Leave the leg long and trim to size after mortising.

Offset the pin holes to avoid splitting the leg.

Side view

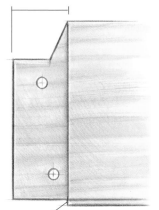

Length of the tenon should be three to four times its thickness.

Small shoulder at the bottom ensures a clean line at the joint.

Size the Tenon

When deciding on the sizes of joinery components, the key is to attain a workable balance. Too large a mortise and you risk weakening the leg; too skimpy a tenon and you lose glue and mechanical strength. The ideal joint would have a large tenon with lots of glue surface, it would be the full height of the apron to best resist twisting, and the mortise would be cut from the center of the width of the leg for maximum strength. But it's not just the sizes of the mortise and tenon that you have to balance: The shoulders on both sides of the tenon must be substantial enough to do their work. They butt against the leg and resist bending and twisting forces trying to lever apart the joint. A good rule of thumb is to size the tenon thickness a little more than one-third the thickness of the apron.

Although the one-third rule is a good general guide to follow, sometimes it's better to make exceptions. If I'm building a table out of butternut or a similar softwood, with aprons only ¾ in. thick, I make the tenons at least 5⁄16 in., maybe even 3⁄8 in. thick. Any smaller and a sharp bump to the leg might snap the tenon right off. Because you rarely see the thickness of an apron, one good design strategy is to make it thicker—7⁄8 in. or 1 in. will provide larger, stronger shoulders.

Maximize tenon length Two other aspects of the tenon affect the joint strength. One is the amount of long-grain glue surface on the cheeks of the tenon; the other is the length of the tenon, which is affected by where the mortise is cut on the leg. Naturally, a longer tenon has more glue surface and provides more mechanical strength to the joint. As a general rule, the longer the tenon, the better, assuming the leg can accommodate it. A tenon length that's three to four times its thickness is quite adequate. When laying out the size and placement of tenons, a full-scale, top-view drawing will help you understand the orientation and relationship of all of the parts.

One engineering principle states that the stress on any part is least along the centerline or neutral axis. A centered mortise or tenon is stronger because it has all of that wood on both sides bolstering it. For this reason, I prefer to have a shoulder on both sides of a tenon (rather than one side only) to better resist bending stresses from either direction. Even a small shoulder will cover any bruised edges on the mortise that result from cutting the joint.

A centered mortise might be ideal, but the farther to the outside of the leg you position a mortise, the longer the respective tenon will be. Too far out and the cheek of the mortise is more vulnerable to splitting under stress. Deciding on the exact placement is a judgment call that varies with each project. I have butted tenons together inside the leg, but doing so makes one tenon shorter than the other. Butting tenons together works when joining aprons of unequal width, where the wider tenon can be the shorter one because it has extra glue surface. I've also cut half of each tenon long and the other half short and locked one tenon into another with a bird's-mouth cut, as Chinese furniture makers sometimes do. But I prefer to miter the tenons within the joint without actually joining them. This is easy to do, and it can add 15 percent to 20 percent more glue surface and length to the tenons. If I must incorporate drawers into an apron, the size of the rail usually calls for a completely different tenon design (see "Unique Solutions for Different Design Problems" on p. 141).

Shorten the Tenon Height with a Haunch

A tenon the full height of the apron affords lots of glue surface and strength against bending and twisting forces. But there's a trade-off: A full-height mortise weakens the leg, especially if there are two mortises

WHERE TENONS MEET

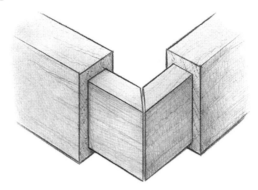

Miter them, but skip the glue on the very ends. Hack does not bother to glue the end grain of the miters, reasoning that the bond is unreliable.

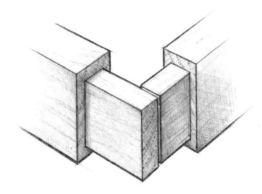

Butt them together if you have tenons of unequal width.

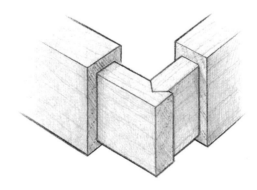

Bird's-mouth joints often are found in Asian furniture. This design offers additional strength because the tenons interlock.

Begin by Routing the Mortise

ROUTERS ARE QUICK AND ACCURATE. Although his mortises often require additional handwork, Hack cuts most of them with a machine he made from scrap parts. It has a router mounted horizontally to a sliding table that can be adjusted in three dimensions.

CUT THE BOTTOM SQUARE. Use chisels to clean out the bottom corners of each mortise as an index to seat the tenons later on.

SCRIBE LINES FOR THE HAUNCH. A marking gauge extends the lines of the existing mortise that indicate where to cut the angled haunch.

CHISEL THE HAUNCH BY HAND. There is no other practical way to cut the slope for this shape. Hack leaves the table legs long to keep them from splitting along the top edge while he chisels the haunch.

CHECK THE RESULTS USING A SMALL SHOPMADE TEMPLATE. The template makes it easy to check your progress as you cut the angled mortise.

at the corner of the leg. With the top of the mortise open, any serious stress on the apron can more easily split the top of the leg. So the strength of such a joint relies almost entirely on the glue bond because the mechanical strength is compromised.

A simple solution, and one I prefer, is to shorten the tenon considerably for the top ¾ in. to 1 in. or so and cut an angled haunch. With this design detail, what little glue surface you lose is balanced against having a much stronger mortise.

I cut the haunch on the tenon by hand with a dovetail saw and then clean it up with a chisel. For speed and accuracy, I lay a wooden template on the tenon to mark out the haunch and use another one made as the mirror image of that pattern to size the mortise at the haunch end. To cut the mortise for the haunch, I first mark out the sides aligned with the mortise with a mortise gauge, chop the waste, and refine it using the template and a chisel. Because I cut many of my mortises with a router

Fit the Tenon to the Mortise

TENONS ON THE TABLESAW. With the workpiece firmly clamped against this tenoning jig, the tablesaw can cut tenons cleanly and accurately.

TRIM TENONS TO SIZE AND SHAPE. A matching template made to the negative shape of the one used to check mortises shows where to cut the angled haunch on the tenons. The first cut is made with a stop block on the miter gauge.

THIS HANDWORK IS FAST AND ACCURATE ENOUGH. A dovetail saw makes quick work of trimming the angled haunch and mitering the ends of the tenons.

Glue and Pin the Joint

YOU DON'T NEED A LOT OF GLUE.
With snugly fitting mortise-and-tenon joints, a thin layer of yellow glue spread evenly is all you need for a good bond.

bit, I keep the top of the mortise below the haunch round for a small measure of added strength. Also, a small ⅛-in. shoulder at the bottom of the apron tenon will hide any small inaccuracies in cutting the mortise, and it allows for vertical alignment when the table is assembled.

Adjust the Fit and Use Glue Sparingly

The best design and the strongest glue won't overcome a joint with carelessly fit shoulders or a sloppy fit between tenon and mortise. Even when I cut these joints with accurate machine setups, I still often find it necessary to improve the fit with a few passes of a shoulder plane or a chisel. I want the shoulders to fit tightly over their entire surface and the tenon to slide into place with a minimum of force for a good glue bond.

Part of the long-term strength of the joint is the snugness of the fit, or what I call its mechanical strength. Glue adds strength, but how long does a glue bond last? By its very nature a mortise-and-tenon joint has wood fibers running cross-grain to one another, which weakens the bond. Flexible modern glues can accommodate some of this movement.

Before gluing, I always dry-fit and clamp the parts together to discover any problems that may arise while there's still time to solve them. To ease assembly, I chamfer the ends of each tenon. Glue-ups can be stressful, but it is worth taking care to place the glue so as to avoid drips and oozing joints that would be a headache to clean up later. With a thin stick about half the width of an ice-cream stick, I apply a light amount of glue into the mortise and on both tenon cheeks. The flat edge of the stick is perfect to squeeze out the glue in a thin, even layer. Another trick that works well is to cut a light chamfer around the mortise to contain any squeeze-out. Ideally, the joint should slip together under light clamping pressure.

For large tables and for peace of mind, I often pin the leg-to-apron joints. I use a hard, straight-grained wood such as rosewood, ebony, or maple for the pins. A contrasting wood can add a pleasing visual detail, and two small pins are stronger than one large one. Most often, I drill holes for the pins after gluing and drive them in either from the outside or inside of the leg, depending on whether or not I want them to show.

GARRETT HACK is a contributing editor to *Fine Woodworking* magazine.

PINS ARE AN INSURANCE POLICY. Small hardwood pins will hold the joint tightly, even if the glue fails. Hack leaves the outside end of the pin square and holds it with a wrench as he hammers it home.

Unique Solutions for Different Design Problems

Not all aprons call for a single haunched tenon mortised into the leg. The problems presented by some leg-to-apron joints require uncommon solutions. One example is an apron that incorporates drawers into the design, such as those you'd find on a desk or some kitchen tables.

Aprons with drawers often have a narrow rail under the drawers that joins into the leg, and such rails have tenons that can't be any higher than the height of the rail, nor probably any longer than the other tenons joining into the leg. Still, these tenons are doing quite a bit of structural work. The solution is to make double tenons parallel to one another, which doubles the glue surface and provides good resistance to twisting and bending forces.

Extrawide aprons offer another example of design problems that require different solutions. Wood movement over such a wide apron is, of course, a consideration. But more than that, a long mortise can weaken the leg. The long sides of the mortise can flex easily, and the apron-to-leg joint loses vital mechanical strength. The solution is simply two mortises with a groove for a stub tenon between them and an angled haunch at the top. The two mortises still have plenty of glue surface and lock the apron along its full height. If wood movement is a concern,

glue only the top part of the tenon, then pin the lower part with elongated holes, as you would on a breadboard end, so that the apron can move slightly. Also, cut the bottom mortise a little long to accommodate the anticipated movement.

TWO TENONS ARE BETTER THAN ONE. Narrow rails under drawers need beefier tenons. Doubling them up maximizes the strength you can get from such a small piece of wood.

WIDE APRONS NEED A BREAK. A mortise longer than 4 in. or so can threaten the structural integrity of a leg. A break in the middle for a haunched tenon alleviates that problem but still keeps the apron from twisting.

Top rail is dovetailed into the leg.

A double tenon is used on the bottom rail.

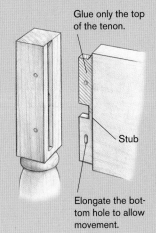

Glue only the top of the tenon.

Stub

Elongate the bottom hole to allow movement.

Attaching Tabletops

BY MARIO RODRIGUEZ

Attaching a top to its base is a critical aspect of table design and construction. Regardless of the method you choose, it should meet the following criteria: The top must be firmly attached to the base, the top must remain flat, a solid-wood top must be allowed to move seasonally, and the attachment method shouldn't compromise the design of the table or complicate its construction. I'll describe six ways of attaching a tabletop that meet these requirements, along with the reasoning behind each method.

The most important factor to consider when deciding how to attach a tabletop is wood movement. We all know that solid wood moves seasonally across the grain. It's a fact; you can't do anything to stop it. In the summer, a board will expand across its width because of an increase in humidity. During cold months, the same board will shrink and become narrower. If no allowance is made to control or direct this seasonal movement, a tabletop might buckle, or worse, crack and split.

When calculating how much a board will move, I usually allow from ⅛ in. to ³⁄₁₆ in. for every 12 in. of width. Therefore, I would anticipate that a 42-in.-wide tabletop might move about ½ in. overall. This is only a general guide, and certain factors must be

Controlling Wood Movement

Although you cannot prevent a solid-wood tabletop from moving seasonally, you can direct this movement so that it doesn't disrupt the looks or the use of the table. The following are examples of how to secure the tabletop to the frame to control expansion and contraction.

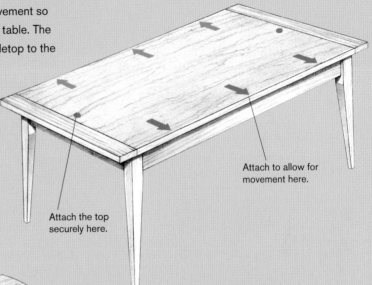

Attach to allow for movement here.

Attach the top securely here.

SECURED AT THE CENTER

On a table with an overhang that will be seen from and used on all sides, pin the tabletop at the center of both end rails. Secure the top to the long rails in a way that allows for seasonal movement.

SECURED AT THE BACK

Because a demilune table often is placed against a wall or locked to a larger section of a table, the top should be secured at the rear so the wood expands toward the front.

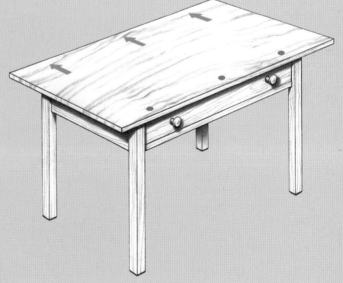

SECURED AT THE FRONT

If one side of a table is going to be used more than the others, secure that edge to the rail and confine seasonal movement to the opposite edge.

Pocket Holes

This method is probably the oldest way of attaching a tabletop. It involves drilling into the rail a ½-in. flat-bottomed pocket hole at a 10-degree angle. Then a smaller pilot hole (to accommodate the shank of a #8 wood screw) is drilled into the center of the pocket hole.

Common on antique furniture, pocket holes make no allowance for wood movement, which may explain the number of cracked and split tabletops. On small solid-wood tops (up to 9 in.) or veneered plywood tops, pocket holes can be the only attachment method. On larger pieces, they should be limited to areas needing movement restricted.

POCKET-HOLE JIG. Construct a small jig to hold the rail at approximately 10 degrees while drilling pocket holes with a Forstner bit.

A HOLE IN THE POCKET. Drill a smaller-diameter pilot hole for the screw that will be driven into the tabletop.

taken into account. For instance, in parts of the country with low humidity, wood movement might be minimal.

Another factor is the type of wood you're using: Cherry moves less than white oak but more than mahogany, and flatsawn wood moves more than quartersawn. For more on this subject, read *Understanding Wood* by R. Bruce Hoadley (The Taunton Press, 2000).

Once you accept that the tabletop will move, you can control or direct this movement so that it doesn't disrupt how the table works or looks (see the drawings on p. 143). For a freestanding table with a uniform overhang, I anchor the top to the base at the center of the end rails. That way, any cross-grain movement will occur evenly along each long-grain side. On a demilune (half-round) table, I pin the back edge of the top, which typically is placed against a wall. Conversely, on a writing table I might fix the top along the front of the table so that movement occurs toward the rear.

Fastening a Tabletop

For this chapter, I have illustrated six methods of securing a tabletop. The methods are listed by ease of installation, starting with the simplest. The hardware for two of the methods can be purchased relatively cheaply from hardware catalogs, whereas the rest can be made from shop scrap. This is a low-budget process.

MARIO RODRIGUEZ, a former contributing editor to *Fine Woodworking*, builds commissions and teaches classes at the Philadelphia Furniture Workshop (www. philadelphiafurnitureworkshop.com).

Metal Table Clips

These clips, also known as S-shaped clips or simply as tabletop fasteners, are probably the easiest and quickest method for attaching tabletops. They fit into a groove or slot cut on the inside face of a rail.

The easiest method is to cut the grooves in the rails on the tablesaw. The grooves must be cut before the base is assembled.

The clips are installed after the base has been assembled. Place one end of the clip into the groove and screw the other end into the underside of the tabletop. Because the groove runs the length of the rail, any number of clips can be used. This method nicely accommodates any cross-grain wood movement whether the clips are parallel or perpendicular to the tabletop's grain: The clips on the end rails move along the groove as the wood moves, whereas the clips on the front and back rails move in and out of the groove.

An alternate way to install the clips is to cut slots in the rails using a biscuit joiner. This method removes less wood from the rails, and it has the added advantage of being doable after the base of the table has been glued up.

SECURE BUT FREE TO MOVE. Driving the screws too tight will prevent the wood from moving and defeat the purpose of using the clips.

GROOVES OR SLOTS. The clips are installed in grooves cut on the tablesaw or in slots cut with a biscuit joiner.

Flat Twin-Circle Clips

Also known as a desktop or figure-eight clip, this unobtrusive fastener requires only a shallow flat-bottomed recess in the top edge of the rail. The diameter of the recess should accommodate that of the clip, but the recess should be drilled to place the center of the clip past the edge of the rail. This location will let the clip pivot slightly, allowing for cross-grain wood movement.

For large tabletops, you can increase the clip's ability to move side to side by chiseling away a little of the rail on both sides of the clip. However, because the clips do not handle wood movement perpendicular to the rail very well, they are best confined to end rails. Like the metal table clips (p. 145), these fasteners should be relegated to casual, day-to-day furniture pieces.

PRECISION DRILLING. The recess for twin-circle, or figure-eight, clips, should be close to the inside edge of the rail to allow for movement.

ATTACHED TO THE RAIL. The twin-circle clips can be screwed to the rail either before or after the base has been assembled. Check that the clips are free to move.

ATTACHED TO THE TABLETOP. These fasteners are best fitted to either small tables or to the ends of large tables. They do not allow for much wood movement when fitted perpendicular to the grain of the tabletop.

Simple Wooden Blocks

These wooden blocks are either glued or screwed to the inside of the rail and screwed to the tabletop. This type of fastener offers the advantage of using shop scrap that matches the piece. The blocks need to be tailored to each location around the rails: Blocks at the center of each end rail can have just a single screw hole because there is no wood movement here, and they can keep the top centered on the rail. Blocks at the extremity of each end rail will require a slot that runs parallel to the rail, whereas those attached to the front and rear rails will have slots perpendicular to these rails. In all cases, ensure that the blocks are designed so that the long grain—not the end grain—is glued to the rails.

Two methods work well when gluing the blocks to the rails: With the table base the right way up, glue and clamp the blocks using a straightedge to ensure that the block tops are level. The other method is to lay the base upside down on a flat surface covered with wax paper and then rub the glued blocks onto the apron until they stick tight. When the glue has dried, tear off any paper that has stuck to the wood.

ATTACHING THE BLOCK. With the rail sitting on a flat surface covered with wax paper, rub the glued block on the rail until it adheres. When the glue has dried, remove any paper that has stuck to the wood.

ROOM AT THE CORNER. Near the corner of the end rail, the block needs to have a slotted hole parallel to the rail. Make sure that the long grain, not the end grain, of the block is glued to the rail.

SCREW SLOTS ALLOW FOR MOVEMENT

The position of the block relative to the rail dictates whether the block has a round screw hole to prevent wood movement or a slot to allow the top to move seasonally.

Block is secured to prevent wood movement.

Block is slotted to allow wood movement.

Tabletop

Direction of the top's expansion

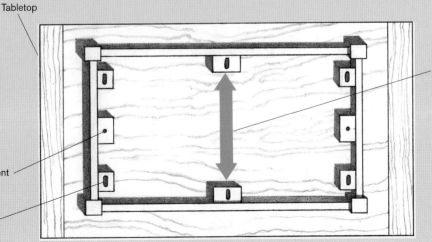

Tongue-and-Groove Blocks

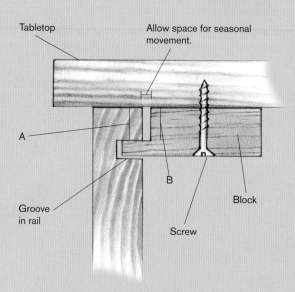

This type of fastener is made from project leftovers. These blocks are attached to the tabletop with screws and have projecting tongues that engage corresponding grooves cut into the rails. The rail grooves are slightly larger than the width of the blocks, allowing for movement and preventing the tabletop from splitting.

By carefully laying out the placement of the blocks and milling properly sized grooves, a more tailored and carefully crafted appearance is achieved. The best way to cut the grooves is with a router guided by a fence bearing on the rail. Properly spaced, tongue-and-groove blocks work very well for all sizes of tabletops.

Tabletop

Allow space for seasonal movement.

A

Groove in rail

B

Screw

Block

Make sure that the distance (A) is fractionally greater than (B) to ensure that the tabletop is tightly attached to the frame but still free to move.

TWO BLOCKS IN THREE CUTS. Make a cut about ⅜ in. deep in each end of a piece of wood. Next, cut perpendicular to the first cut to remove a small block of waste. The push block prevents the waste block from being thrown back when it is cut from the workpiece. Last, cut the piece of wood in half to produce two tongue-and-groove blocks.

CUT THE GROOVE. Select a straight bit slightly wider than the tongue of the block and, using a guide fence, rout a series of grooves in the rails.

ATTACH THE BLOCKS. The tongues of the blocks engage with the grooves in the rails. Then the blocks are screwed to the tabletop.

Beveled Cleats

This attachment method provides a clean appearance. First, rip a 3-in.-wide hardwood strip with the tablesaw blade tilted to a 15-degree angle. Then cut tenons on both ends of one piece and rout matching grooves in the side rails.

When the table base has been assembled, the tenoned cleat is inserted but not glued into both rails. Make sure that the wider side of the angled cut is placed against the tabletop. With the base positioned on the upside-down tabletop, take the other section of wood that was ripped, crosscut it slightly shorter than the distance between the rails, and place it next to the other cleat. Screw it to the tabletop using a single hole in the middle and slots near the ends of the cleat to allow for wood movement. On small tables, the top is attached at each end, but for tables more than 48 in. long, a third center support is necessary.

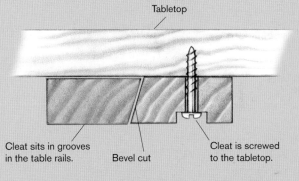

Tabletop

Cleat sits in grooves in the table rails.　　Bevel cut　　Cleat is screwed to the tabletop.

The tenoned half is attached to the rails, and the second half is screwed to the top. The bevel creates resistance to the top being lifted.

ONE CUT MAKES TWO CLEATS. Select a piece of wood 3 in. wide and a little longer than the end rails of the table. With the blade at a 15-degree angle, rip the board in half.

TENONS SLIDE INTO THE GROOVES. One cleat sits in grooves in the side rails. The wide side of the board should be against the tabletop.

MEETING ON THE BEVEL. Slide the second cleat against the first one and screw it to the tabletop. The center screw can be fixed, but screws closer to the edges should be in slotted holes to allow for wood movement.

WATCH IT ON THE WEB

For a video on making beveled cleats, go to www.finewoodworking.com.

Engineering a Table with Drawers

BY WILL NEPTUNE

I like to tell my woodworking students that there's a Shaker nightstand hidden in every table with drawers. I may be overstating my case, but only by a bit. At the North Bennet Street School, we taught strategy. Our largely traditional approach to building tables with drawers isn't the only approach, but it's almost endlessly adaptable; once you understand it, you can apply it to Chippendale writing desks, Pembroke tables, contemporary tables, whatever you like. An approach is liberating: It leaves room for good design and good workmanship while eliminating the need for mock-ups, prototypes, and reinventing the wheel.

There's nothing new about this attitude. Thomas Chippendale's *Chippendale Director* contains page after page of chairs and chair backs. No joints. No dimensions. Nothing about how to build a Chippendale chair. Chippendale assumes his readers already know how to build a chair and that chairs are all built the same way.

When students build a table with drawers, they learn a system. I recall one student who started a veneered Pembroke table after having done a simpler table with a drawer. "Remember when you built the Shaker nightstand?" I said to him. "Now here's what you're gonna do different." His eyes lit up

MANY TABLES, ONE APPROACH. The author's students at North Bennet Street School have used his system (mock-up at top) successfully in many styles of tables (above).

The Essential Table with Drawer

The author built this mock-up demonstration table to show the basic components that go into a simple table with a drawer.

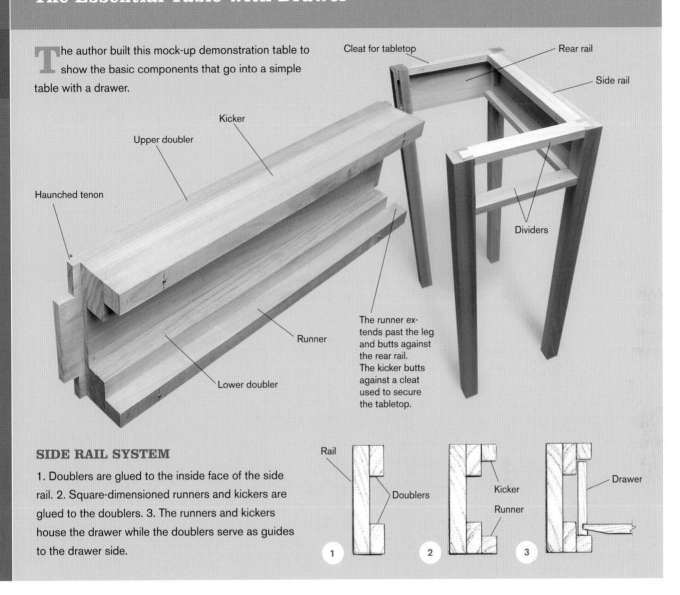

Cleat for tabletop

Rear rail

Side rail

Kicker

Upper doubler

Haunched tenon

Dividers

Runner

Lower doubler

The runner extends past the leg and butts against the rear rail. The kicker butts against a cleat used to secure the tabletop.

SIDE RAIL SYSTEM

1. Doublers are glued to the inside face of the side rail. 2. Square-dimensioned runners and kickers are glued to the doublers. 3. The runners and kickers house the drawer while the doublers serve as guides to the drawer side.

Rail

Doublers

Kicker

Runner

Drawer

1　**2**　**3**

Divider Joints

Cut a shallow rabbet on the bottom face of the dovetailed upper divider. For a perfect fit, place the 1/16-in. or 3/32-in. rabbeted shoulder on top of the legs, clamp up the table, and scribe the dovetail onto the leg. The shoulder on the twin-tenoned lower divider is optional.

DOVETAILED UPPER DIVIDER.

TWIN-TENONED LOWER DIVIDER.

Revealed: A Table with Multiple Drawers

In this demonstration table, the author reveals the components of a long table with multiple drawers. For illustrative purposes, he built two types of partitions.

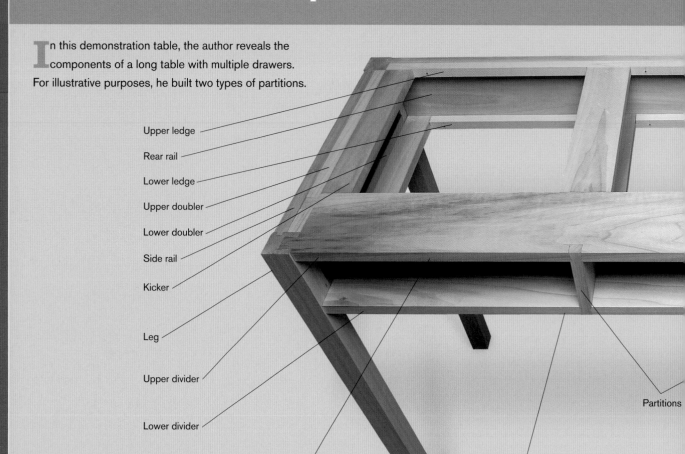

Upper ledge
Rear rail
Lower ledge
Upper doubler
Lower doubler
Side rail
Kicker
Leg
Upper divider
Lower divider

Partitions

DOVETAILED WIDE UPPER DIVIDER

A wide upper divider is dove-tailed to the doubler as well as to the leg. If the dovetail is too close to the leg, the short-grained end of the doubler can easily crack off.

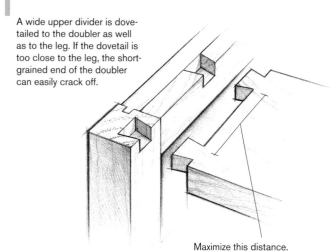

Maximize this distance.

TENONED WIDE LOWER DIVIDER

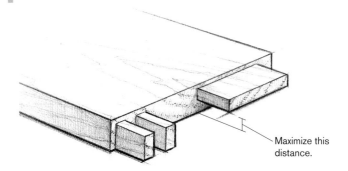

Maximize this distance.

A wide lower divider is twin tenoned to the leg and also tenoned to the doubler. The single tenon must be thick for strength. But it must be oriented horizontally and placed at the top of the divider so there is enough wood in the doubler below the mortise.

Tenoned at the Front

At the front, where strength is needed, the kicker and runner are tenoned to the dividers.

Half-Lapped at the Back

At the back, the kicker and the runner are half-lapped to a ledger strip. The runner should be half-lapped on top, so it rests on the ledger supporting the drawer. The kicker should be half-lapped on the bottom, because the drawer, if tipped, will push against the kicker from below.

Snapped into Place

Kickers and runners can be installed after the table frame has been glued up.

First insert the tenon of the kicker or runner.

Then slide in the ledger.

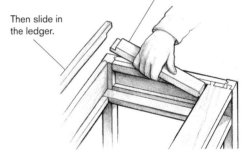

and he said, "Ah, and you just make this longer, and curve that and, oh, yeah, yeah, yeah." He already knew how to build a Pembroke table—he just didn't realize it.

The single-drawer demonstration table I built (see the top photo on p. 151) reveals the basic components of a simple table-with-drawer system: dividers, which replace the front rail to make room for the drawer; doublers, which fill out the side rails and serve as drawer guides; runners, which support the weight of the drawer; and kickers, which keep the drawer from tipping upward when pulled out. Some tables require ledgers to support the runners and kickers, and there are others that do without doublers. Nevertheless, if you took apart a Pembroke table, you'd find the basic components in one fashion or another. And you'd know the secret to building tables with drawers: Inside, they're all about the same. Knowing this is like having a deck full of jokers. You can just keep playing the cards.

A Strategy for Construction as Well as Design

It's worth taking a close look at the components that make up the table-with-drawer system, not only in terms of how each

functions as part of an overall design but also in terms of how each is constructed in concert with the other components. Although there's no reason why you couldn't apply my strategy to building a table by hand, I'm going to assume you will use a tablesaw and a thickness planer. For me, efficiency demands the use of machines, even for the construction of traditional furniture forms.

The key to efficient construction lies in designing joints that share like dimensions and like locations relative to the leg. The tablesaw cuts related parts to equal length; the planer establishes consistent thicknesses and widths. Together, the tablesaw and thickness planer allow groups of parts to have compatible machine-cut joints. When you plane the dividers to thickness, you can also plane a number of square-dimensioned sticks for runners, kickers, and ledgers. If you make the haunched tenons on the rails and the twin tenons on the lower divider the same length and location from the face of the leg, then you can cut all the mortises on a hollow-chisel mortiser with a single fence setting. And you can cut the main shoulders of these joints, as well as the dovetails on the upper divider, without changing the dado height or the fence setting.

Once you've milled the pieces, you're ready to put together the essential table: four legs, three rails, and two dividers. The upper divider is dovetailed into the leg; the lower divider can't be dovetailed, so it's twin tenoned (see the drawings on p. 152). With the table glued up, you can take your time installing the inner pieces—doublers, kickers, runners, and (if need be) ledgers.

The first pieces to go inside I call doublers because, roughly speaking, they double the thickness of rails. More important, the doublers bring the rail assembly flush to the inside face of the leg, so you don't have to notch the runners and kickers. Some people would call the doublers side guides, and that's what they are as far as the drawer is concerned: blocks that keep the drawer

from shifting from side to side as it's pulled out. Cut four doublers to length, and glue them to the top and bottom of the side rails. That's that.

Onto the surface of each doubler, glue one of the little square sticks you thickness planed at the same time as the dividers, one stick at the top of each upper doubler to serve as a kicker, one stick at the bottom of each lower doubler to serve as a runner. Taken together, a doubler and runner or a doubler and kicker form an L-shaped piece of wood, which you could make by rabbeting one piece. But they're much easier to make and install inside the table as two pieces. The wide face of the doublers remains stable when glued flush against the rail. The kickers and runners are such small squares that they won't curl or twist.

What to Do When the Span Gets Long

On a small table like my single-drawer demonstration table, gluing the runners and kickers to the doublers, letting them butt against the dividers and the rear rail (or a cleat for securing the tabletop), provides enough strength to support the drawer. On a larger or heftier table or on a table with multiple drawers (see the photo on pp. 152–153), you may need to join the runners and kickers at the front and back of the table. At the front, you can tenon the runners to the lower divider and the kickers to the upper divider. You may not want to tenon the runners and kickers at the back of the table, however, because you'd have to glue up all the pieces at once. Imagine doing that on a five-drawer lowboy with offset drawers!

To avoid having to glue up all those sticks at once, dado two small sticks (which you have milled and ready) across their width to accept a half-lap joint from each runner and kicker, and then brad the sticks temporarily to the rear rail as ledger strips (see the middle drawing p. 153). To allow

Two Partition Options That Support the Span

DOVETAILED PARTITION

A dovetailed partition is easier to install than a tenoned partition because it can be slipped into place after the dividers have been assembled.

TENONED PARTITION

The strongest way to tie together the dividers between the drawers is a vertical partition with through twin tenons or triple tenons. (The plan view drawing below is shown at the lower divider.)

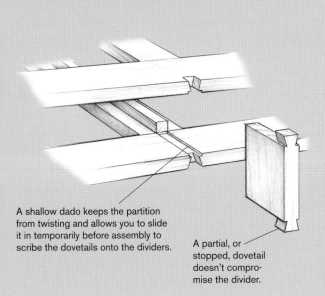

A shallow dado keeps the partition from twisting and allows you to slide it in temporarily before assembly to scribe the dovetails onto the dividers.

A partial, or stopped, dovetail doesn't compromise the divider.

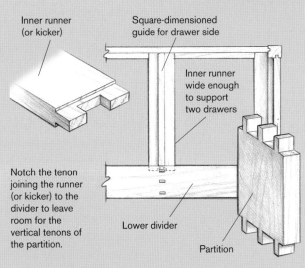

Inner runner (or kicker)

Square-dimensioned guide for drawer side

Inner runner wide enough to support two drawers

Notch the tenon joining the runner (or kicker) to the divider to leave room for the vertical tenons of the partition.

Lower divider

Partition

you to install the kickers and runners after the table frame is glued up, cut them a touch short. Cut the tenons relatively short as well. Even a ⅜-in. tenon will take the weight of a drawer. Just slide in the tenons and snap the pieces into place. Then slide in the ledgers, using the brads to locate them for gluing.

If the span of the table is long and you need the dividers to be stronger, there are only two things you can do: Make the dividers wider, or make them thicker. Making them thicker is, by far, the easiest route to take because a little thickness adds a lot of strength. But many designs simply won't allow for a thick divider.

If you settle on making wide dividers, however, you'd better make them really wide. An extra ½ in. of width isn't going to increase the stiffness of the divider to speak of, and an undersized divider will deflect downward. I'd make the divider 4-in. wide at least; a 4-in. divider is no more work than a narrower one. The trouble is, a wide divider stands a good chance of cupping or twisting. To resist racking, you have to join a wide divider not only to the legs but also to either the doublers or the side rails.

When you join a divider to a side rail or doubler, however, you run the risk that the movement of the rail as it expands and contracts will work the divider like a lever. To prevent movement in the rails from cracking the dividers, keep the rails relatively narrow (ideally less than 4 in. wide), and make the dividers really wide so that movement at the inner dovetail is spread out over a greater distance before it reaches the front dovetail.

Joining the dividers directly to the side rails is historically accurate, but it's tricky because you have to mill dividers longer than the rear rail and then notch the dividers around the leg. The other way to join wide dividers—attaching them to the doublers—is awfully tempting. A big advantage to attaching wide dividers to the doublers rather than to the rails is that you can make

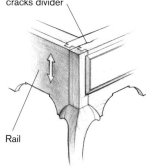

WIDE RAILS + NARROW DIVIDERS = CRACKING

Wide rail movement cracks divider

Rail

both dividers the same length as the rear rail. The dovetails are easy to cut because they share a shoulder, and all these shoulders can be cut with the same dado setup used for the rail tenons. The forward dovetail is joined to the leg exactly as it would be on a narrow divider. The inner dovetail can be either a full dovetail, as it is in my demonstration table, or a half-dovetail. In either case, leave as much space as possible between the inner dovetail and the end of the doubler. If the housing for the dovetail is close to the end of the doubler, the little short-grained piece that remains can easily crack off.

Joining the lower divider to the lower doubler is a little trickier. The lower divider, you remember, is twin tenoned into the leg, so you don't want to dovetail it to the lower doubler because then assembly would be difficult. Instead, join the lower divider to the lower doubler with a horizontal tenon, cut to the same length as the twin tenons. This inner tenon must be as thick as possible for strength, with little or no shoulder on top, so there is enough wood in the doubler below the mortise to provide adequate strength; the doubler will still have plenty of wood above the mortise (see the bottom right drawing on p. 152).

Whether you make the dividers wider or thicker, sizing them is a judgment call. Err on the side of overbuilt. If the table bounces, what are you going to do about it? If it's a bit sturdier than it needs to be, you'll never know, and you'll be none the worse for it.

How to Handle More Than One Drawer

A table with multiple drawers requires a partition tying together the dividers between each drawer and a complement of internal runners, kickers, and drawer guides. It makes sense to mill the partitions at the same time as the dividers; just be sure to leave the divider blanks long, and whack the ends off. There are your partitions, already at the proper width.

If you feel comfortable with the span of the dividers and you simply want two drawers for looks or functionality, then you can stop dado a nonstructural partition into the dividers from behind. But if the dividers are really long—for example, 3 ft. or 4 ft.—the stopped-dadoed partition may pop out when the table deflects downward.

The easiest way to strengthen the joint between the partition and the divider is to use the same twin-tenon arrangement used to join the lower divider to the legs. On my multidrawer demonstration table, the dividers are so wide, I used triple tenons (see the photo and drawing at right on p. 155), but the idea is the same. I usually run the tenons through the dividers and sometimes even wedge them. If you join a pair of 3-ft. dividers together with two partitions and join the whole assembly to the legs, then you've created a girder. It's amazing how stiff this system is.

So now that you have partitions between the dividers, how do you support the drawers in the middle of the table? You mill runners and kickers wide enough to support drawers on both sides of the partitions, tenon them to the dividers, and half-lap them to the ledger on the rear rail.

Treat these inner runners and kickers as you would the runners and kickers next to the doublers, with one big exception. You have to notch the middle of the tenons so they don't interfere with the vertical twin tenons of the partition. To keep the drawers from swimming around, take another square stick and glue it onto the center of the runner, long grain to long grain, to serve as a drawer-side guide. Problem solved.

You could also dovetail the partition to the dividers. A dovetailed housing cut across the full width of the dividers would compromise the dividers, so use a stopped dovetail in the front to tie the dividers together, plus a shallow 1/8-in. dado across the width

of the dividers to keep the partition from twisting (see the left drawing on p. 155).

Dovetailed partitions are easier to install than tenoned partitions, because with dovetailed partitions you can attach both dividers to the legs and then simply slip the partitions into place. The shallow dado allows you to slip the partition into the dividers and then scribe the tail onto the dividers before cutting its housing. It's possible to cut the dado narrower than the dovetail to hide it from the front, but now I'm getting into variations on variations.

The beauty of this approach to engineering a table with drawers is that it doesn't rely on the proportions or the style of the table. You can cut big legs or little legs; you can set the rails flush to the legs or inset them; you can turn the legs or taper them; you can make the table long and low and turn it into a coffee table or tall and long and call it a writing desk.

What I hope I've constructed here is a conceptual framework onto which you can overlay your own design ideas.

WILL NEPTUNE is a furniture maker and former woodworking instructor at the North Bennet Street School in Boston, Massachusetts.

An Illustrated Guide to Table Design

BY GRAHAM BLACKBURN

Tables must above all function on a practical level. So far as function goes, ergonomic decisions, the choice of material, construction method, joinery details, and finish are of greatest importance. But—and this is a very big "but"—for a table to be completely successful, aesthetic considerations are also extremely important.

For dining tables, the design begins with seating capacity. Unless you are planning to use extension leaves, you have to decide how many people you want the table to accommodate and live with that. Although it may be tempting to build a large table to account for any eventuality, you should consider how the table functions on a daily basis for the immediate family. If you need flexibility, extension tables are the best option but will require more effort to engineer the leaf supports.

With worktables, height might be the most important consideration. For example, a writing table will be too high for use as a computer table unless accommodation is made for a keyboard tray. Occasional tables have their own requirements, but height and width decisions are less critical. Still, consider how they will relate to existing furniture in the home. Sofas and armchairs, for example, do not come with standard arm heights.

Regardless of your woodworking experience, the design of your particular table will benefit if you spend time identifying its precise function, giving careful consideration to the material and the construction, and following some form of aesthetic rationale throughout the piece.

Function: Tables Need to Work as Intended

The original and quintessential function of a table is to provide a flat surface for writing, playing games, eating, or working. The form of any given table may be as varied as these uses. So it is of the utmost importance to be clear at the outset about the requirements of the table you intend to design. These include not only structural requirements—so that the table can do its intended job—but also ergonomic requirements. The most exquisite dining table will be a complete failure if it proves too small to sit at.

Attention to function is absolutely the designer's first responsibility. Familiarize yourself with tables designed for similar functions, and note features designed for specific purposes, such as sturdy legs for heavy loads, drop or draw leaves for tables that must expand, lipped tables designed to prevent objects from falling off, and added drawers or shelves for storage. A reference

Dining Dimensions

Although it's important to make sure a table is sized to fit its intended surroundings, these dimensions will get you within striking distance.

COMFORT IS A CRITICAL FACTOR

Overall table height, legroom below the apron, overhang on the table ends, and the space allotted for each diner should all be considered when designing a dining table.

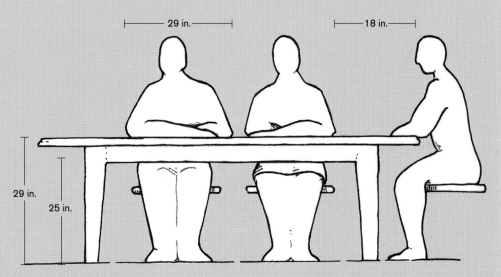

TABLE SIZE AND SEATING CAPACITY

Although 29 in. of elbow room per person is ideal, it's not an unbreakable rule. Less space can be allotted at the corners, and more space is rarely a problem.

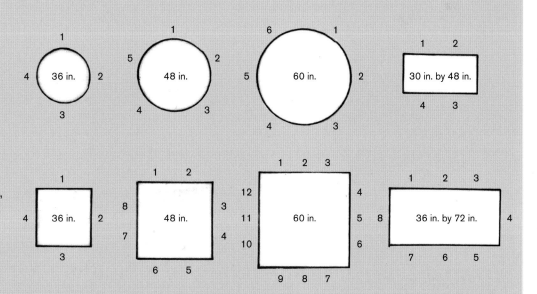

Table Height Guidelines

Although there are endless possibilities regarding style, shape, ornamentation, and proportion when designing furniture, start with proven dimensions suited to the function the piece will serve.

OCCASIONAL TABLES

A coffee table should afford views across a room, whereas an end table should be convenient to someone seated in an armchair or sofa.

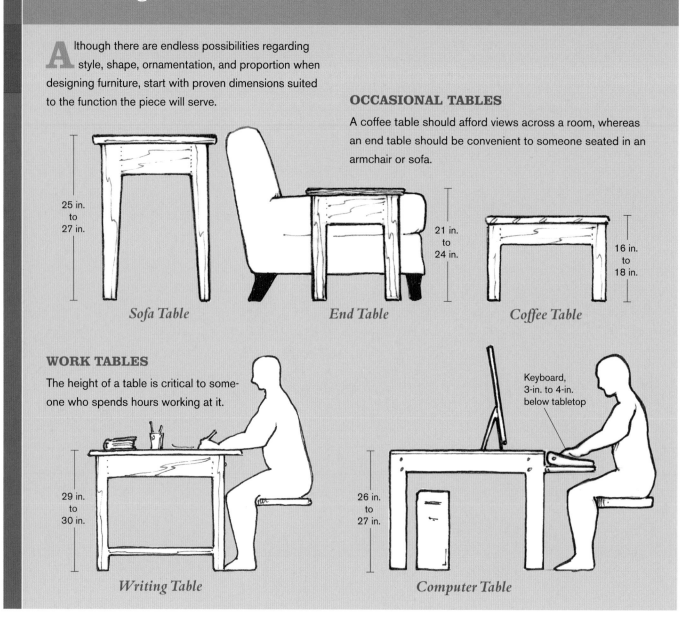

25 in. to 27 in.

Sofa Table

21 in. to 24 in.

End Table

16 in. to 18 in.

Coffee Table

WORK TABLES

The height of a table is critical to someone who spends hours working at it.

29 in. to 30 in.

Writing Table

Keyboard, 3-in. to 4-in. below tabletop

26 in. to 27 in.

Computer Table

such as *Architectural Graphic Standards* by Ramsey and Sleeper [Wiley, 2000] is a useful place to explore table types by function, and a basic reference for so-called standard or average dimensions.

Beware of "standard" dimensions. Few people are exactly "standard." Unless you are building many examples of a particular table, your client will be better served if the dimensions are uniquely suited to him. Nevertheless, certain aspects of many tables really

shouldn't be changed, such as the amount of leg room required beneath a skirt or the area a diner needs for greatest convenience.

There's More to a Table than Function and Style

A table may also be defined by various structural features. The construction should, of course, be consistent with the intended use: a knock-down trestle table for portability; a draw-leaf table for occasional enlargement.

Three Paths to Pleasing Proportions

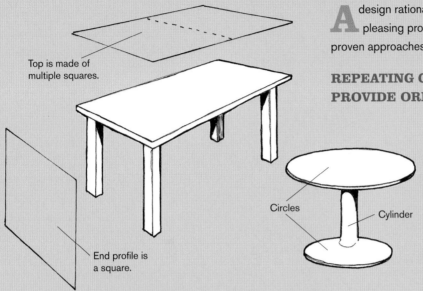

Top is made of multiple squares.

End profile is a square.

A design rationale is crucial to building tables with pleasing proportions. The three described here are proven approaches, but others are possible.

REPEATING GEOMETRIC SHAPES PROVIDE ORDER

Basic geometric shapes, such as squares, cubes, circles, ovals, or ellipses, can be used to define both the overall shape and the details of a table, thereby providing it with a repeated pattern that unifies the whole structure.

Circles

Cylinder

A NUMBER PROGRESSION IS A SUBTLE DESIGN DEVICE

Starting with a 1-in.-thick tabletop, for example, you might construct legs that measure 2-in. square and an apron that is 3-in. deep. Relating all dimensions to a common unit, either in multiples or regular increments, provides the table with an implied pattern that may not be immediately apparent but which lends it a fundamental unity.

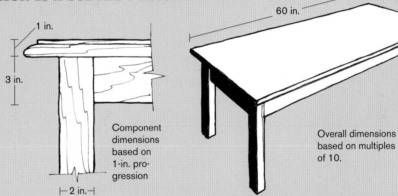

1 in.

3 in.

Component dimensions based on 1-in. progression

2 in.

60 in.

20 in.

30 in.

Overall dimensions based on multiples of 10.

CLASSICAL PROPORTION SYSTEM PLEASES THE EYE

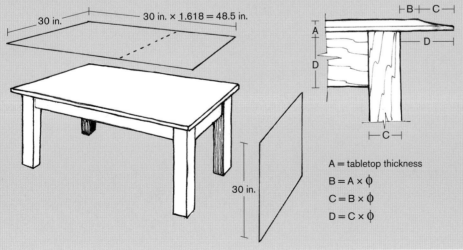

30 in.

30 in. × 1.618 = 48.5 in.

30 in.

B C

A

D

D

C

A = tabletop thickness

B = A × ϕ

C = B × ϕ

D = C × ϕ

The Golden Mean is the ratio of 1 to 1.618, represented by the Greek letter phi (ϕ). A tabletop might be designed so that its long side was 1.618 times longer than its short side. The ratio might also be used to determine the dimensions of the various parts of a table. The apron might be ϕ times the width of a leg, the leg ϕ times the thickness of the tabletop.

Table Base Options

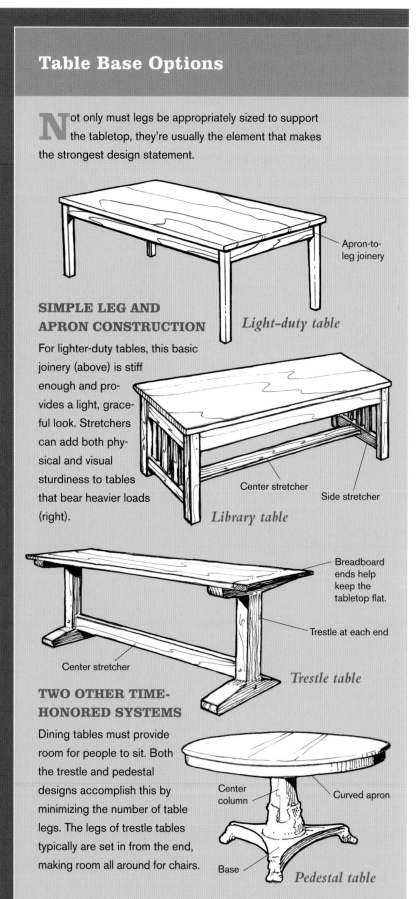

Not only must legs be appropriately sized to support the tabletop, they're usually the element that makes the strongest design statement.

Apron-to-leg joinery

Light-duty table

SIMPLE LEG AND APRON CONSTRUCTION

For lighter-duty tables, this basic joinery (above) is stiff enough and provides a light, graceful look. Stretchers can add both physical and visual sturdiness to tables that bear heavier loads (right).

Center stretcher

Side stretcher

Library table

Breadboard ends help keep the tabletop flat.

Trestle at each end

Center stretcher

Trestle table

TWO OTHER TIME-HONORED SYSTEMS

Dining tables must provide room for people to sit. Both the trestle and pedestal designs accomplish this by minimizing the number of table legs. The legs of trestle tables typically are set in from the end, making room all around for chairs.

Center column

Curved apron

Base

Pedestal table

Frequently, there are trade-offs to be considered. A gate-leg table, for example, has leaves that enlarge it when needed. The leaves are supported by hinged legs that swing out. When folded, the leaves can interfere with seating, and when opened, there sometimes seems an inordinate number of legs that get in the way of diners' legs. A group of four nesting tables that store in the space of one is great for occasional use. However, they are sequential in height and either the tallest or the shortest is apt to be at a less-than-optimal level.

Although your own experience and available tools will dictate to a large extent how any given table is constructed, resist the impulse to build only what you are comfortable with. It is worth the effort to research a new technique or a new joint for the sake of better function or more pleasing shape.

At the same time, do not get carried away by the urge for novelty. Successful construction entails the use of appropriate species, relevant construction methods, the right joint for the job—dovetail, mortise-and-tenon, dowels, biscuits, etc.—and a finish consistent with the intended use.

Legs Set the Style

To a great extent, all table tops are the same. They're flat, and intended to support something. Although the wood species, edge treatment, and apron certainly can make stylistic statements, it is the legs that most clearly establish a table's style and visual effect. As important as well-designed legs are, they will only be successful if they are considered as part of the overall design.

When viewing a table in a room that has enough light to make out forms but not details or wood species, it is still possible to discern the function of the table by looking at the legs. Four heavy legs joined by a horizontal stretcher tell us that this is a library table intended to support a load of books. Light and gracefully tapered legs that focus attention on the tabletop, as if it were floating, suggest that this may be a hall table for the display of some precious ornament.

Legs are frequently the key determinant of the table's style. For example, a Queen Anne table's top and apron are typified by restrained ornamentation. It is the cabriole legs that allow us to recognize the style. The same is true of the Shaker style, whose simple and efficient legs carry their load with no ornamentation or excess weight. And the Art Deco tables designed in the 1920s by Émile-Jacques Ruhlmann cast away traditionalism in favor of legs whose sensuous curves resembled nothing that had gone before.

Develop a Plan that Ties Together All the Elements

The final ingredient for successful table design requires that every detail be considered from the point of view of how the table will look.

Given that the functional requirements have been satisfied, and that the construction is sufficiently workmanlike, the most striking feature of any table is how well it fits in with its surroundings. This can mean designing in an established style such as Queen Anne or Arts and Crafts, or designing so that the general proportions, shapes, and colors are compatible with neighboring pieces. Compatibility can result from similarity or contrast. A severely modern design might fit very well with the relatively simple lines of a room full of Shaker furniture, but might look uncomfortably out of place in a room furnished in a ponderous Gothic or an ornate 18th-century style.

Designing in a particular period style can be difficult without understanding the underlying design sensibility of the period. It is not enough to employ superficial features of a period to achieve the right feeling. Slapping some misproportioned cabriole legs onto a table does not guarantee that it will look "Chippendale." Incorrect details can produce ludicrous and unhappy results,

similar to applying a distinctive Rolls-Royce hood to a Volkswagen Beetle.

Arts and Crafts furniture is not as uncompromisingly rectilinear as it may initially appear. And Shaker furniture, for all its apparent simplicity and lack of ornament, is often surprisingly sophisticated in its proportions. Before attempting to design a table in a period style, make sure that you understand the typical construction techniques, the common materials, and the forms that governed the proportions.

This last point—forms that govern proportions—is more important than almost anything else. The term simply means that, functional and structural requirements aside, some method has been employed to decide on all the dimensional details of your table. Making decisions about the exact width of a leg or the depth of a skirt or apron based on structural requirements alone may guarantee solid joinery, but unless you are the rare designer possessed of an inherently perfect "eye" it is unlikely that your table will look as balanced and graceful as it could if designed according to some plan.

There are, in fact, numerous design paradigms commonly used by designers, some exceedingly simple, others more sophisticated. You may, indeed, invent your own paradigm or plan—the point is that using virtually any plan is better than making decisions about exact dimensions based on nothing more than what material is conveniently to hand, or what size router bits are available.

GRAHAM BLACKBURN is a furniture maker, illustrator, author, and the publisher of Blackburn Books (www.blackburnbooks.com) in Bearsville, New York.

Expanding Tables

The ability to expand can greatly enhance a table's utility, but this versatility comes with challenges. Sturdiness and leaf storage are two prime considerations.

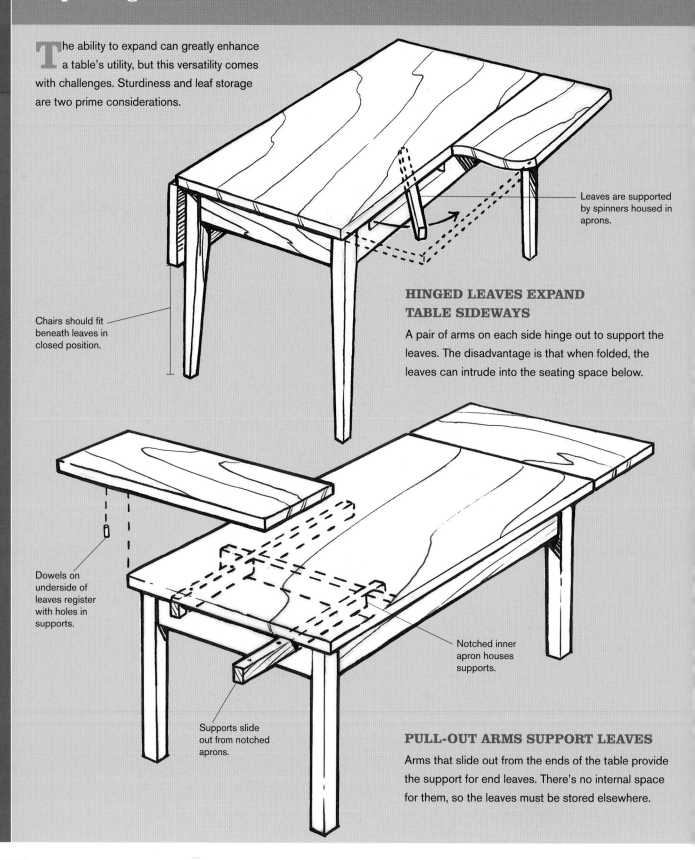

Leaves are supported by spinners housed in aprons.

Chairs should fit beneath leaves in closed position.

HINGED LEAVES EXPAND TABLE SIDEWAYS

A pair of arms on each side hinge out to support the leaves. The disadvantage is that when folded, the leaves can intrude into the seating space below.

Dowels on underside of leaves register with holes in supports.

Notched inner apron houses supports.

Supports slide out from notched aprons.

PULL-OUT ARMS SUPPORT LEAVES

Arms that slide out from the ends of the table provide the support for end leaves. There's no internal space for them, so the leaves must be stored elsewhere.

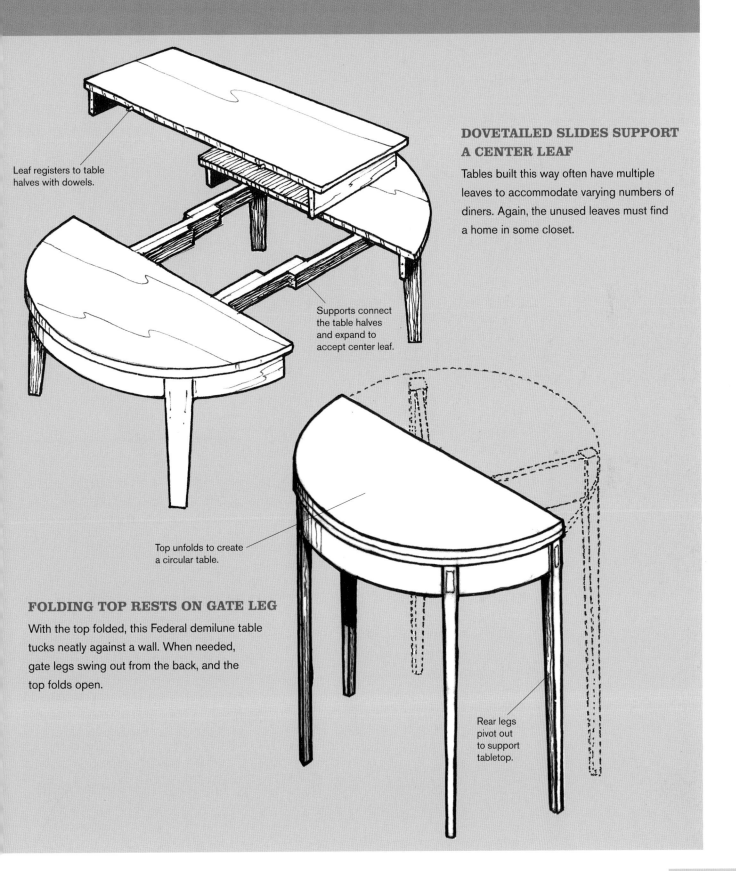

Leaf registers to table halves with dowels.

DOVETAILED SLIDES SUPPORT A CENTER LEAF

Tables built this way often have multiple leaves to accommodate varying numbers of diners. Again, the unused leaves must find a home in some closet.

Supports connect the table halves and expand to accept center leaf.

Top unfolds to create a circular table.

FOLDING TOP RESTS ON GATE LEG

With the top folded, this Federal demilune table tucks neatly against a wall. When needed, gate legs swing out from the back, and the top folds open.

Rear legs pivot out to support tabletop.

Building Bookshelves to Last

BY JEFF MILLER

Everyone can use a few more shelves. Indeed, in many homes an available shelf can be as difficult to find as the TV remote. So if you build a set of bookshelves, they'll probably be filled as soon as the finish dries.

Bookshelves can work in any room. You can make them freestanding or built-in. They can be big or small. And they can take any form, from simple screwed-together and painted plywood for use in a utility room to sophisticated formal library shelves made from beautiful hardwoods.

A Shelf Should Look Good

A successful bookshelf design must achieve a balance between appearance and function. A shelf with the perfect look might not be adequately strong. That often means making changes as you work out the design.

A good approach is to start by writing out a wish list that summarizes your ideal shelf design. The list should include the shelf depth, a factor determined by the width of the books going on the shelf. Next, choose a shelf length (bookcase width). Then, choose a shelf thickness—¾-in. stock is readily available, but let your eye make the final determination. After that, decide if you want the shelves to be fixed, adjustable, or some of each. Finally, choose a joint or mounting system that offers the look you want.

The design process is just beginning once you've worked out your bookshelf design "brief." Now you must determine if your initial choices will be strong enough. If not, you'll have to make some design changes. But before we get to that, it helps to understand how a shelf reacts to load.

Sag Is the Main Enemy

As the load on a shelf increases, the weight eventually reaches a point where the shelf bends, or sags. The same factors that affect appearance also affect shelf sag: the thickness, width, and length of the shelf; the wood species used; and the method used to mount the shelf.

As a general rule, our eyes won't notice sag if it's less than ⅟₃₂ in. (0.031 in.) per foot. With time, even if the contents don't change, a shelf's initial sag could increase by 50 percent or more as the wood fibers "tire." Wood engineers call this "creep." To be on the safe side, design shelves to limit any initial sag to no more than 0.02 in. per foot under a load of full-size books.

In extreme cases (loading a bookcase with your anvil collection, for example), shelves can deflect so much that the wood actually fails. This is not a common worry. More common, especially on long shelves, is that sag causes the effective length of the shelf to become shorter, causing it to slip off the shelf supports. Or too much weight on a long shelf can cause some adjustable shelf supports to crush the wood fibers in the case sides. As a result, the supports tilt downward.

Fixed or Adjustable

The method used to mount a shelf affects how much it will bend under a load. All else equal, a fixed shelf will bend less than an adjustable shelf. That's because on a well-secured fixed shelf the ends resist both tilting and being pulled inward by the sag (see pp. 168–171 for fixed- and adjustable-shelf options).

Be aware that fixed shelves aren't immune to failure. With enough weight (perhaps adding your spouse's anvil collection to your own on the same shelf) and its consequential sag, even fixed shelves can fail at the ends. When that happens, the shelf curves and effectively shortens, the ends pull free, and everything can head south in a hurry.

JEFF MILLER is a furniture maker, teacher, author, and frequent *Fine Woodworking* contributor.

Design Shelves for Maximum Load

Y ou don't need to guess at how much a shelf is going to sag. The chart on p. 172 provides a quick way to determine if your shelf will be sag-free. If the chart doesn't work for your shelf, you can use the Sagulator (www. finewoodworking.com/ sagulator), an online program that makes it easy to determine sag. Both the chart and the Sagulator assume unfixed shelf ends. Fixed ends sag less.

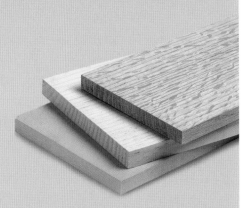

MATERIAL MAKES A DIFFERENCE. Some shelf materials resist sag better than others. Red oak is one of the better ones, eastern white pine less so. MDF makes a weaker shelf.

The chart is easy to use. It provides the maximum shelf-weight limits (in pounds per foot) and works for most designs. You need to know the thickness of the shelf (¾ in. or 1 in.) and its length (24 in., 30 in., 36 in., or 42 in.).

If the expected load exceeds the weight limit shown in the chart, you'll have to make compromises. To do that, use the Sagulator.

An answer of more than 0.02 in. per foot of shelf means you need to put less load on the shelf; use a stronger wood; make the shelf thicker, wider, or shorter; or add wide edging. With the Sagulator, you can adjust those values and calculate a new sag number.

The eye can detect shelf sag as slight as ⅟₃₂ in. per foot.

A severely sagging shelf may slip off supports.

APPROXIMATE SHELF LOADS

Hardcover books
(9 in. by 11 in.), 20 lb. per ft.

Magazines
(9 in. by 11 in.), 42 lb. per ft.

Fixed shelves attach to the sides of a case with either wood joinery, hardware, or a combination of both. Unlike adjustable shelves, fixed shelves help strengthen the entire case. And because they are attached to the case sides, fixed shelves sag less.

BISCUITS

Strength: Fair

Appearance: Excellent

It's easy to fix a shelf in place using a biscuit joiner. And because the biscuits are hidden when assembled, there is no joinery, support parts, or hardware to distract the eye. Use at least two biscuits on each end of the shelf. Add a third biscuit if there's room. The jig shown on p. 172 is a good one to use here. Invest a few minutes making it and you'll be rewarded many times over by the time saved.

DADO

Strength: Good

Appearance: Good (excellent if using a stopped dado or if covered by a face frame)

A dado joint effectively houses the ends of the shelf in a long notch, providing some mechanical strength. Because a dado joint produces mostly end-grain surfaces, adding glue increases the strength only nominally. The attachment strength of a shelf can be improved further by combining Confirmat screws (see "Confirmat Screws Add Strength," on p. 173) with either a dado joint or a rabbeted dado joint. The screws keep the ends of the shelves in the dado, and the dado adds extra shear strength.

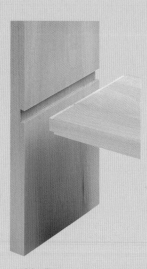

SLIDING DOVETAIL

Strength: Excellent

Appearance: Very good (excellent if stopped or covered by a face frame)

A sliding dovetail adds considerable mechanical strength, but sliding a 10-in.-long dovetail into a tight-fitting slot before the glue sets up is a challenge. Using a fairly slow-setting epoxy glue will help considerably. Epoxy is a slippery glue that helps get this type of joint together without excessive expansion and stress.

SCREWED CLEATS

Strength: Very good

Appearance: Fair

Screwed cleats let you add shelves without too much fuss, but they come up a little short in the appearance department. With the exception of the hole closest to the front, all of the holes in the shelf should be slotted to accommodate wood expansion. For the same reason, if you wish to glue this joint, bear in mind that you should glue only the front inch or so.

RABBETED DADO

Strength: Good

Appearance: Good (excellent if using a stopped dado or if covered by a face frame)

A minor variation on the dado joint is to rabbet the ends of the shelf to fit into a narrower dado. The main advantage is the ability to fit the joint more easily, especially if the shelf thicknesses are inconsistent.

This joint is useful when working with hardwood plywood, a material that typically measures less than ¾ in. thick. In this case, a dado cut by making a single pass with a ¾-in.-dia. straight router bit ends up too wide. However, with a rabbeted dado, you cut a narrow dado first, then the rabbet for a perfect fit.

MARK AND CUT THE RABBET. First, mark the rabbet location on the end of the shelf (above), then use a bearing-guided rabbeting bit to cut the rabbet (below).

A RABBETED DADO STARTS WITH A DADO. A T-square jig helps cut a dado across the side. The slot in the jig is just wide enough to accept the bearing of a top-mounted bearing-guided straight bit.

Adjustable Shelves Add Versatility

Adjustable shelves make it easy to change the spacing as needs change. But there is a structural cost: These shelves do nothing to hold the cabinet sides together. So, on taller bookcases it's a good idea to have one fixed shelf to help anchor the case sides.

SHELF PINS

Strength: Good (very good with sleeves)
Appearance: Good

Shelf pins come in a wide variety of shapes, sizes, materials, and finishes. My favorites are the machined solid brass ones from Lee Valley℠. I also like the very small round pins by Häfele® for smaller cases. Shelf pins also come with special clips for securing the shelves or for holding glass shelves. Sleeves are a great way to recover from poorly drilled holes. Stamped sleeves (short tubes with a flared and rounded-over end) tend to look like shoelace eyelets when installed in a cabinet. Solid brass machined sleeves look better, even though they accentuate the row of holes in the case sides somewhat. Some sleeves are threaded for specially threaded shelf pins.

SLEEVE ADDS REFINEMENT AND STRENGTH. You can improve both the appearance and strength of a shelf pin simply by slipping a brass sleeve into the pin hole.

SHELF-PIN HOLES IN A JIFFY. Thanks to this shopmade jig, the author quickly drills shelf-pin holes that are the same depth and perfectly spaced.

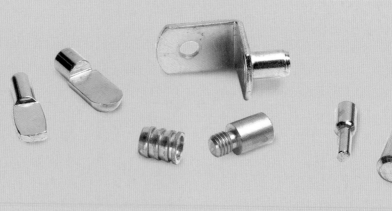

WOODEN STANDARDS

Strength: Very good
Appearance: Very good

Wooden shelf standards have been around in various styles for generations. They are easy to make and add an interesting look to almost any bookcase. The style shown in the top photo at left (I call it zig-zag) is one of the more common forms.

Another style (I call it half-moon) is shown in the bottom photo at left. To make a pair, you'll need a piece of stock that's at least double the width of each standard. Scribe a lengthwise centerline along the stock, then lay out the shelf spacing by making a series of evenly spaced marks along the centerline. Use a spade bit or a Forstner bit to drill a through-hole at each marked centerpoint. Finally, using a tablesaw, rip the stock down the middle. The net result is a pair of standards, each with a series of half-moon shapes.

Make the cleats just loose enough to slip in and out with ease.

HIDDEN WIRES

Strength: Good
Appearance: Very good

These bent-wire supports fit into holes drilled in the case sides. A stopped kerf cut in the ends of the shelf slips over the support, hiding the hardware. Structurally, this means the end of the shelf is thinner. This affects the shelf's shear strength, but will have little effect on sag.

METAL STANDARDS

Strength: Very good
Appearance: Fair

It's hard to beat metal shelf standards for ease of installation. Just run a pair of dadoes down each side of the case and nail, staple, or screw the shelf standards into place. Shelf supports usually just hook into place, although one new version has brass support pins that screw into threaded holes in the brass standards. In general, shelf standards seem out of place on finer furniture. But they are great for utilitarian pieces, and even in larger bookcases, where any support system will be pretty much invisible once the shelf is full of books.

SHELF WEIGHT LIMITS (POUNDS PER FOOT)*

TYPE		LENGTH			
Species	Thickness	24 in.	30 in.	36 in.	42 in.
RED OAK	¾ in.	49	21	9	5
	1 in.	116	47	23	12
	¾ in. with 2-in. edging	112	47	21	12
POPLAR	¾ in.	42	17	8	4
	1 in.	101	41	20	10
	¾ in. with 2-in. edging	97	39	20	10
EASTERN WHITE PINE	¾ in.	33	14	6	3
	1 in.	74	32	15	8
	¾ in. with 2-in. edging	76	32	14	8
FIR PLYWOOD	¾ in.	32	13	6	3
	¾ in. with 2-in. edging**	96	39	18	9
MDF	¾ in.	9	4	2	1
	¾ in. with 2-in. edging**	73	30	14	7

*Based on 11-in.-wide shelves
**Edging is red oak; other edgings are the same wood as the shelf.

Jig Speeds Biscuiting

A jig for cutting slots in the sides makes it easy to locate shelves accurately. The jig has just two parts: a cleat and a fence. The cleat keeps the end of the fence square to the side. Centerlines for the slots are marked on the end of the fence. With each new set of shelf slots, the fence is crosscut to a shorter length. Toss the jig when done.

CLAMP AND CUT. Clamp the jig to the case. Cut one set of slots, then use the jig to cut the same slots on the other side. Crosscut the fence to the next shelf position, and repeat until all slots are cut.

Confirmat Screws Add Strength

I'm not a fan of screwing shelves in place with the typical tapered woodscrew. They rarely hold up long-term. That said, I have found a specialized screw that works much better. Called a Confirmat® screw, it has a thick body with sharp, deep threads. It's mainly used with particleboard, melamine, and MDF, but it also holds well in solid wood. When used in a dado or a rabbeted dado, the joint strength is excellent. Confirmat screws require a pilot hole and a shank hole. A special bit is available that does the drilling in one step.

Zig-Zag Support in Three Steps

Start with stock wide enough to make four standards. Using the tablesaw, make a vertical cut at each shelf location (1). An auxiliary miter-gauge fence with a location pin in front (much like a finger-joint jig) makes it easy to position the stock for subsequent cuts. Follow with 45-degree cuts (2) after relocating the location pin. Remove the triangular waste piece, then clean the resulting flat with a chisel. Rip the stock to create four standards (3).

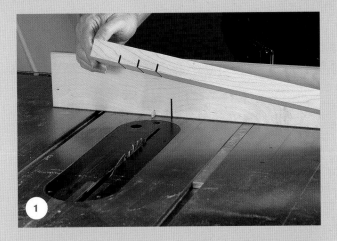

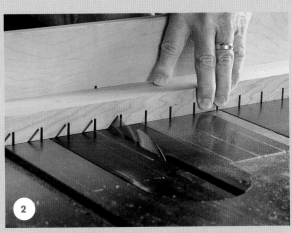

Anatomy of a Chest of Drawers

BY WILL NEPTUNE

Case furniture based on a dovetailed box is found in a wide range of styles and periods. Although the details vary, many pieces can be built using similar construction solutions. When I build a case, I work from a firm set of ideas—both traditional and modern—that I've found to be reliable and efficient.

The techniques required to make a chest of drawers are mostly common knowledge: dovetails, dadoes, miters, mortises, and tenons. The complex appearance is the result of a straightforward sequence of simple steps. At its most basic level, a chest of drawers is a stack of separate assemblies. However, based on moldings (or lack thereof), leg treatments, drawer styles, proportions, and materials, a wide variety of case pieces is possible. I will describe a basic, proven construction approach. The execution is up to you.

Start with a Dovetailed Case

When preparing your primary stock for the sides of the case, put aside strips to be used later to edge the top and bottom case panels as well as the drawer dividers. Using wood from the same board will give a uniform look to the case.

A chest of drawers begins with four panels: top, bottom, and two sides. The strips of primary wood that edge the top and bottom can be glued onto the secondary-wood panels after rough-milling. Match the grain direction of all parts during glue-up so they can be finish-milled as one piece.

The case is joined with half-blind dovetails, so lay them out for strength, not appearance. You may want extra tails near the edges, especially the front, to resist loads that could pop the front shoulder.

Another trick makes the joinery for the back a little easier. Run the rabbets for the back boards all the way up the sides without stopping. Then rip the top and bottom panels to be flush with this rabbet; the back boards will extend all the way up to the top and bottom of the case but be hidden by the true top, which goes on later. The back boards, lapped in some way to allow for wood movement, are screwed to the case.

Drawer Dividers: Three Options

Once the case dovetails have been cut, fitted, and dry-clamped, it's time to work on the system of drawer dividers and supports. For function and appearance, the divider frames must stay flat. Again, secondary wood can be used for all but the front edges. Choose the inner secondary wood for stability. Avoid secondary wood that was significantly bowed in the rough, and make

Dressing Up a Basic Box

A seemingly complex chest of drawers simply is a stack of components. By varying moldings, feet, drawers, and drawer dividers—not to mention proportions and materials—an endless array of case pieces is possible.

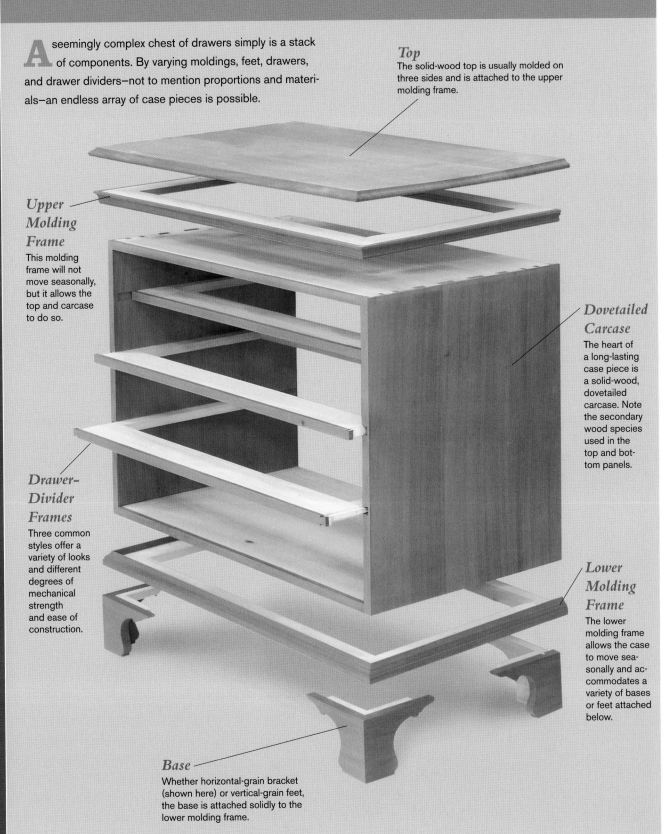

Top
The solid-wood top is usually molded on three sides and is attached to the upper molding frame.

Upper Molding Frame
This molding frame will not move seasonally, but it allows the top and carcase to do so.

Dovetailed Carcase
The heart of a long-lasting case piece is a solid-wood, dovetailed carcase. Note the secondary wood species used in the top and bottom panels.

Drawer-Divider Frames
Three common styles offer a variety of looks and different degrees of mechanical strength and ease of construction.

Lower Molding Frame
The lower molding frame allows the case to move seasonally and accommodates a variety of bases or feet attached below.

Base
Whether horizontal-grain bracket (shown here) or vertical-grain feet, the base is attached solidly to the lower molding frame.

CARCASE AND BACK CONSTRUCTION

This case is joined with half-blind dovetails, which are hidden from view.
Traditionally, the back consists of shiplapped boards.

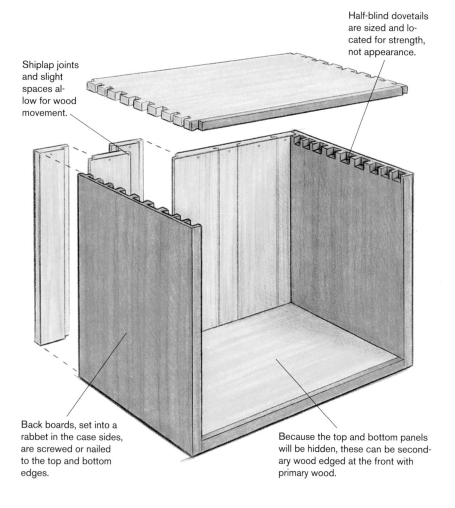

Shiplap joints and slight spaces allow for wood movement.

Half-blind dovetails are sized and located for strength, not appearance.

Back boards, set into a rabbet in the case sides, are screwed or nailed to the top and bottom edges.

Because the top and bottom panels will be hidden, these can be secondary wood edged at the front with primary wood.

Back-Panel Options

A more attractive frame and panel can be fit into the rabbet.

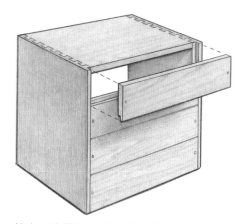

Horizontal shiplapped back boards help prevent tall sides from bowing outward.

---

the front divider wide for extra stiffness. I make the fronts 3½ in. to 4 in. wide, and the less-critical back dividers 2½ in. to 3 in. The runners can be narrower, about 2 in., because they are held in dadoes. Leave the parts a bit thick to allow for leveling the frame after gluing.

Although there are other divider systems, I typically use one of the three shown on the facing page. For all three types, I prefer to glue up the mortise-and-tenoned frame first and fit the unit to the case dadoes. But you also can fit and glue the pieces together in the case, using the dadoes to align the parts. One last note: The right time to glue up the case is after the dadoes have been cut but before building and fitting the divider frames.

Stopped dadoes This simple approach offers a streamlined look and straight-forward joinery. The main liability is the lack of sound glue surfaces between the frame and the case. Usually this isn't a problem, but for a tall case or one with unstable wood, you may want one of the other frame systems that use lap dovetails to tie the ends of the case together. The other types also offer the traditional look of exposed joinery.

Start by laying out and cutting the dadoes, which are about ¼ in. deep. I do the layout while the case is dry-clamped, using a story stick to avoid measuring errors. The goal is to get the pairs of dadoes at equal height and parallel to the inside faces of the top and bottom. Square up

Drawer Divider Frames

Only the front 3 in. or 4 in. are glued to the case, allowing the case sides to move. Choose a frame type based on the desired look and the need for strength.

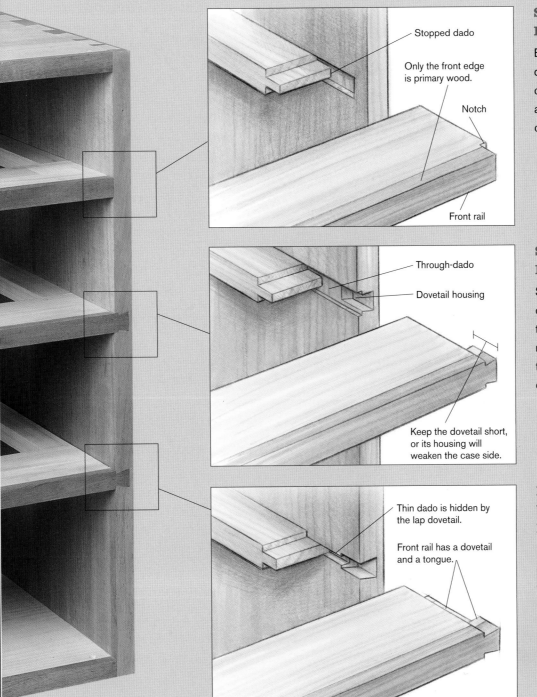

STOPPED DADOES

Basic stopped dadoes offer a clean, contemporary look and the easiest construction.

Stopped dado

Only the front edge is primary wood.

Notch

Front rail

STEPPED DOVETAILS

Stepped dovetails offer a more traditional look and a mechanical connection between the case sides.

Through-dado

Dovetail housing

Keep the dovetail short, or its housing will weaken the case side.

DOVETAILS WITH HIDDEN DADOES

Dovetails with hidden dadoes not only tie the case sides together but also offer a clean look.

Thin dado is hidden by the lap dovetail.

Front rail has a dovetail and a tongue.

the front ends of the stopped dadoes at an equal distance from the front edges of the case (about ½ in.). The front of the frame should be flush to the case edge, but the back should be inset about ⅜ in. from the rabbets to allow the sides to shrink. Gauge the length of the dividers from the bottom of the dadoes, and cut them about 1/32 in. undersize to make the frames easier to fit.

To join the divider frames, I use mortises with open ends; then the runners need only tenons. When clamping and gluing up the frames, take diagonal measurements to check for squareness, and be sure that the frames are flat. A good tip is to level the joints on the top of the frame first. Then, as you test the frame and slide it into the dadoes, you can do all of your fitting from the bottom. The front 3 in. to 4 in. of the frame should be snug, but the rest can be eased to make it slide in the dadoes with less drag.

You still need to cut a shoulder in the front of the frame so it can extend past the stopped dadoes to the front of the case.

Stepped dovetails Adding lap dovetails to the front of the frame gives it a strong mechanical connection to the case sides. The front rail will resist forces pushing the case sides outward, and it can be used to pull in bowed sides slightly. This traditional solution is called a stepped dovetail because both the dado and dovetail are visible at the front. I like this joint with lipped drawers, where the side lip matches the dado depth. Be prepared to spend extra time on these joints, though, because there are many surfaces that must fit at the front edge, and gaps will be obvious.

This joint uses a shallow (about 3/16 in. deep) through-dado, with a lap dovetail at the front extending into the case side.

Start by penciling in the lap location on the case sides. This gives the length of the front rail. Before gluing up the frame, notch the front rail to leave the stubs for the dove-

tails. Now build the rest of the frame and shape the dovetails on the front stubs. This joint will show any gaps, so work carefully and test the dovetail fit as you pare. When you install the frame, rub the rear part of the dado with paraffin wax so that any glue that drags back won't keep it from floating.

Lap dovetails with hidden dadoes The third frame type uses a narrower through-dado that is hidden at the front by the lap dovetail. This dovetailed frame gives the same mechanical strength as the stepped version but has a cleaner look. When used with flush drawers, it has a neat, logical appearance. This system has another advantage over the stepped dovetail: Because the dovetail fully covers the dado, there are fewer surfaces that must close up. Use a standard dado size that is 1/16 in. or so smaller than the base of the tail, and make the dadoes about ¼ in. deep.

Once the frame has been made, you need to form the tongues, stopping them at the front and leaving extra wood for the tails. Because the tongues and dadoes will be hidden, only the shoulders for the dovetails need to be tight, and the tongues don't need to bottom out in the dadoes; however, the tongues should be snug in thickness, especially at the front.

A Few Tips for the Drawers

Once the frames have been fitted and glued in, you may build and fit the drawers by any method you're comfortable with. Drawer fronts, of course, have a lot to do with the appearance of a chest, so look over the wood and plan the overall grain pattern before you begin.

I present to you two options: a flush drawer and a lipped drawer (see the photos on p. 180). Both types need stops (the fragile lip molding is there only to cover the clearance gaps). One reason why I locate the stop blocks on the rear dividers is that it's easy to clamp them in place while testing the drawer. Just remember to size your drawers to make room for the stops. But the great trick here is that putting the stops on a floating frame keeps the drawers flush at the front even as the case changes depth through the seasons.

Ease the Transitions with Moldings

Visually, top and bottom moldings have a powerful effect. They frame the case with their strong horizontal lines and play of light. Their projection at the bottom gives the base a sense of stability and strength. An upper molding provides a transition to the overhang of the top and also balances the bottom molding.

Many times you'll see old work with moldings attached to the case itself, but these tend to fail over time as the case shrinks. Using separate frames for the moldings will give the same appearance while allowing for case movement.

These top and bottom frames can be built using either of two methods (see p. 182). Both can use secondary wood for the inner part of the frame. The first is a simple mitered frame with a molded edge. A more complex, rabbeted frame system wraps over the sides and front edge of the case. With this system you can choose how much of the front case edge shows, giving a wider range of effects.

Both frame systems should overhang the back to allow for expansion of the case. Fasten the frames to the case with screws, tight along the front but with elongated holes along the sides and back to allow the case to move.

Flat frame is quicker to build The first step for the flat frame is to know the exact dimensions of the molding you want, its projection from the piece, and the width of the primary wood. The next step is to glue the primary wood strips onto the inner-frame stock and then mill the blanks to thickness.

Scribe for a Perfect Fit

NOTCHING THE DIVIDER

A DIVIDER IN A STOPPED DADO IS INSERTED FROM THE BACK. **The front rail must be notched to reach the front of the case.**

SLIDE THE DIVIDER TO THE FRONT OF THE DADO AND SCRIBE THE SHOULDER. **Then cut the notch in the rail.**

DOVETAILING THE CASE SIDE

DOVETAILED DIVIDERS GO IN FROM THE FRONT. **The dado is cut first; the dovetail housing is cut second.**

SLIDE IN THE DADOED SECTION AS FAR AS POSSIBLE. **Then transfer the layout of the dovetail onto the case side.**

Drawers

The two common drawer styles are flush and lipped. On the lipped style, the drawer front covers the gap for a more refined look.

MATCH THE DIVIDER TO THE DRAWER. The dovetail with hidden dado offers a clean look for flush drawers (top right), whereas lipped drawers look better with the stepped dovetail (bottom right).

Get the front miters fitting correctly before mortising in the flat, unmolded rear rail. Join the mitered corners with biscuits or stopped splines. Last, mold the desired profile on the outside edge.

Build the rabbeted frame in two parts

The second frame system is built in two stages. The inner, secondary wood frame is thinner than the molding, based on how much of the case edge you want covered. I build the frame first, slightly oversize, then trim it to fit the case exactly. Let the back edge overhang to hide seasonal case expansion.

Now form the rabbet with the three thicker molding blanks. Dry-fit the parts carefully, making sure the miters come together exactly at the corners of the case, keeping the end pieces long at first to allow room for adjustment. Then glue the blanks to the edges of the frame and mold the profile. The frame is held with screws as before, with slotted holes to allow for movement.

Attach the Top

The top of the case is often molded on three edges and usually has an overhanging back to hide shrinkage and to avoid a large gap between the case and the wall.

If a molding is used below the top, it's important to let the case, the molding frame, and the top move independently. All three parts are held tight with screws along the front edge to keep the miters and reveals constant. But along the sides and back, use elongated screw holes between the frame and top, as well as the case and frame. People commonly lift cases by the top edge, so all of these connections should be very strong.

Moldings and Case Top

The trick is to find a way to attach moldings across the grain of the case sides and the top. Molding frames are the key.

Elongated screw holes along the sides and back edge of the molding frame allow the top to move seasonally.

Elongated holes for the screws that attach the case to the molding frame allow the case to move.

Round holes along the front edge of the case and molding frame keep all three aligned where it counts most.

ELONGATED SCREW HOLES ARE THE ANSWER. These are elongated along the bottom side only, allowing the pieces to shift against each other without coming apart.

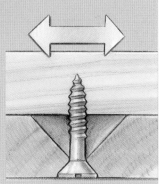

THE CORRECT SEQUENCE. First, attach the molding frame to the top (above) and then to the case using the elongated holes only. Last, screw all three parts along the front edge (right).

Flat versus Rabbeted Molding Frame

The type of molding frame will determine how much of the top or bottom edge of the carcase is visible.

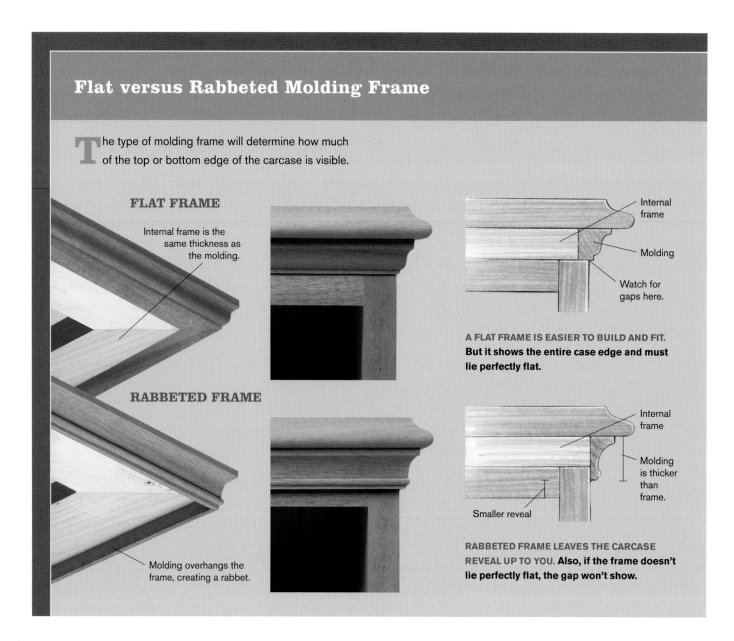

FLAT FRAME

Internal frame is the same thickness as the molding.

Internal frame

Molding

Watch for gaps here.

A FLAT FRAME IS EASIER TO BUILD AND FIT. But it shows the entire case edge and must lie perfectly flat.

RABBETED FRAME

Molding overhangs the frame, creating a rabbet.

Internal frame

Molding is thicker than frame.

Smaller reveal

RABBETED FRAME LEAVES THE CARCASE REVEAL UP TO YOU. Also, if the frame doesn't lie perfectly flat, the gap won't show.

BRACKET FEET

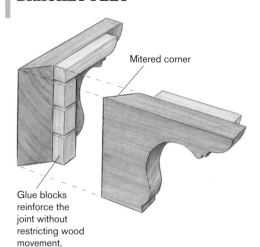

Mitered corner

Glue blocks reinforce the joint without restricting wood movement.

Molded or unmolded, with a wide variety of cutouts, bracket feet are used in many periods and styles. They are glued to the base molding frame (or attached to the case).

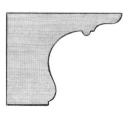

Flat Bracket Foot

Ogee Bracket Foot

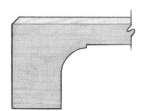

Flat Bracket Base

Choose a Base

The final bit of woodworking is to prepare a base. You will learn about the two most common systems, each adaptable to many leg styles. Bracket feet are cut from blanks with horizontal grain and are mitered at the front. The other leg style has vertical grain, which usually features narrower legs, often braced by flanking side pieces.

Bracket feet Start the flat bracket feet with one long board about ¾ in. thick. The six blanks should be taken out of a single board, if possible, so the grain pattern wraps around the base, matching at the miters. It's also nice to use the same board here as you did for the base molding to help hide the joint between the base frame and the feet.

The rear feet are braced with secondary wood. The joint at this back corner can be half-blind dovetails or, more simply, a tongue and dado. The miters for the front parts can be reinforced with a spline, but usually it's enough just to butt them.

Cut and dry-fit the joints before cutting the foot profile. The assembled feet are glued to the base frame. All of the foot and base joints should be reinforced with glue blocks. A single vertical block can cause the foot to crack, so I use three short blocks with ⅛ in. of space between them.

Vertical feet with support pieces The second construction system is seen in the saber leg with flanking transition pieces. Its main advantage over bracket feet is that the vertical grain direction allows a strong foot of a much smaller size.

Generally, a round or square tenon is cut in the top of the foot blanks to match a hole or mortise cut through the base frame. The mortise should be located away from the corner of the frame so that the miter joint isn't weakened. The transition pieces are tenoned into the foot. As before, these assemblies are glued to the base frame.

This sums up the approach I rely on for fine-quality casework, but many variations are possible. The great thing about this is that 10 people will use this information to build 10 very different chests, each one a record of that maker's taste and skills.

WILL NEPTUNE is a furniture maker and former woodworking instructor at the North Bennet Street School in Boston, Massachusetts.

Bases

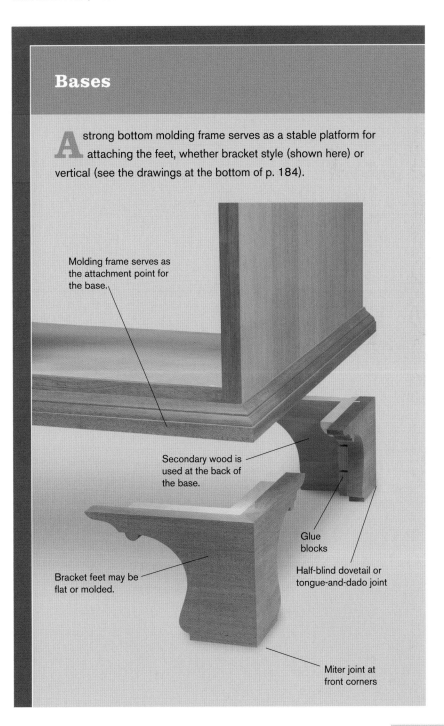

A strong bottom molding frame serves as a stable platform for attaching the feet, whether bracket style (shown here) or vertical (see the drawings at the bottom of p. 184).

Molding frame serves as the attachment point for the base.

Secondary wood is used at the back of the base.

Glue blocks

Half-blind dovetail or tongue-and-dado joint

Bracket feet may be flat or molded.

Miter joint at front corners

Details Define the Style

PERIOD OR CONTEMPORARY? The choice of moldings, drawers, feet, and hardware offers a wide range of design possibilities.

This construction system will produce a wide variety of case pieces, depending on the combination of the individual elements. An 18th-century piece (top) combines moldings, drawers, and feet common to that period. Lipped drawers soften the line of the front. A wide base molding and classic ball-and-claw feet give the piece a broad stance. The top is carefully dimensioned and molded to relate to the rest of the piece.

The bottom chest of drawers offers a more contemporary look, with harder lines and surfaces, including a flush front. The curved, tapered legs flare outward, broadening the stance of the piece without looking heavy. The base and top moldings are beveled to complement the style, and the top is chamfered to make it appear thinner and to match the other elements.

These two examples are the tip of the iceberg. You could make the case taller than it is wide, or use a different array of drawers. And consider the effect of other wood species or figured wood for the drawers.

VERTICAL-GRAIN FEET

Round tenon attaches to the molding frame.

Transition pieces are tenoned into the foot.

Vertical-grain foot

Vertical-grain feet come in a wide array of styles, from turned bun feet to 18th-century ball-and-claw feet to more contemporary saber feet. Most have flanking transition pieces.

Saber Foot

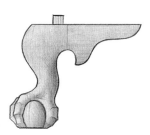
Ball-and-Claw Foot

Turned Foot

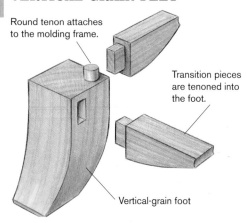

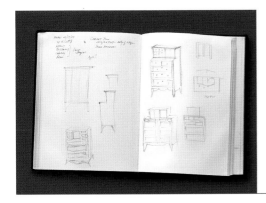

Designing a Chest of Drawers

BY GARRETT HACK

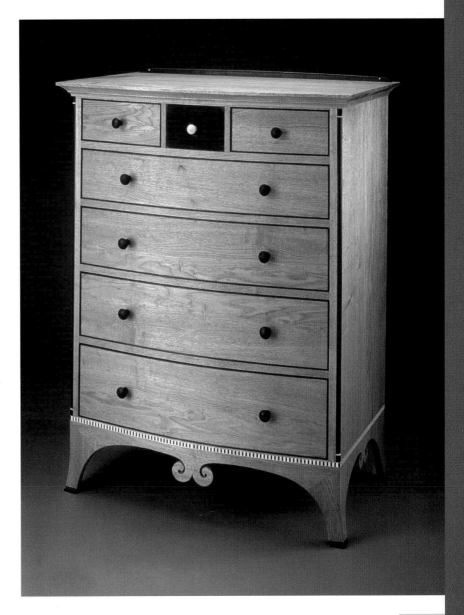

The chest form has been around at least 3,000 years, so it's hard to imagine designing something original today. I don't even pretend to. Instead, I freely borrow from this wealth of past ideas. Generations of craftsmen before me have played with chests in every way imaginable. They have refined everything from the sensuous sweep of certain curves to the basics of drawer joinery and case construction. Chests of drawers—from simple country chests to sophisticated highboys—are rich with ideas and lessons.

For me, originality comes not from trying to invent some new form or detail, but from some fresh and intriguing combination of ideas I've picked up along the way. I've been building and studying chests for years, and I've learned that knowledge builds on knowledge; you have to learn certain basics—about both design and construction—before you can understand more complex ideas. I can look at all sorts of furniture and absorb ideas, but only by actually building a piece that incorporates those ideas do they become part of my design vocabulary. And more important, I begin to understand new directions in which I can push those ideas next time. When thinking about a design problem, I often start by evaluating similar (and dissimilar) pieces I've built in the past.

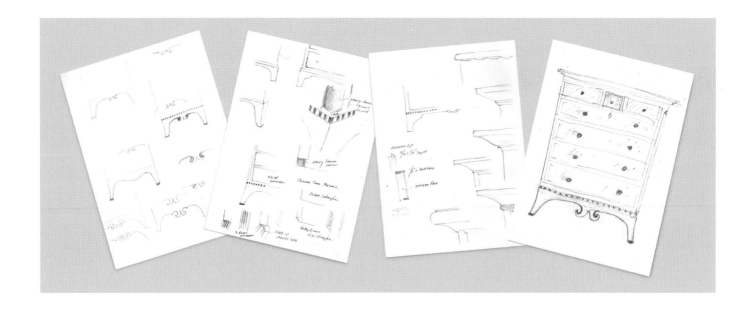

The most exciting designs are those with the fewest restrictions. For example, a man recently gave me a commission for a chest of drawers. He didn't have any fixed ideas of what he wanted. He favored cherry, but he was open to other light-colored native woods. He also liked the dimensions of another chest he owned, about 4 ft. high and a little less than 3 ft. wide.

Find a Starting Point

Designing a chest of drawers shouldn't be all that complicated, considering that it's basically a series of boxes that slide into a larger box. Thinking about wood choices is often a good place to begin the design process. Dark woods can make a large chest seem heavier, just as light woods have the opposite effect. Chests have a lot of surfaces—the sides, top, and drawers—that show off a wood differently than, say, the linear parts of a chair. Lots of heavy grain can dominate and distract from the quieter details. Fine-grained hardwoods take and hold small details that time would deface in a softer wood like white pine. With its quiet grain and rich color, cherry would have been a good choice for the client's chest of drawers, but I was a little tired of seeing it everywhere.

Butternut, another native species, soon came to mind. Commonly called white walnut, butternut has a warm amber color and subtle grain and works nicely with hand tools, although it's a little soft. I also had three exceptional wide boards stashed away—just enough to make single-board case sides and the top.

The widest case sides I could get out of the butternut boards were about 20 in., and the width of the top was limited to about 22 in. That size would allow drawers of a good usable depth. Defects in the boards limited the sides to 47 in. long. This would allow for a stack of five ample drawers. Four feet is also a nice height to stand at to see and use the top of the chest. Remembering that my client liked a chest of similar height, I used it as a starting point, drawing front and side views to proportion the drawers.

The smallest practical clothes drawer is about 4½ in. deep. Drawers deeper than 9 in. to 10 in. are prone to being overloaded and are not that efficient (imagine trying to find a particular shirt in a drawer with shirts stacked five high). I don't use any magic proportioning system for drawers; I just sketch out ideas. Sometimes it's as simple as increasing each successive drawer by an inch. Arranging larger drawers at the bottom and smaller drawers at the top is not only practical but also balances the composition. To give interest to the facade of this chest, I tried breaking up the top tier of drawers. First I tried two and then three smaller drawers. This seemed more flexible in terms of storage and created a small drawer perfect for small treasures. Should the facade of drawers be flush, lipped, flat, or shaped into a gentle bow front? As I developed other parts of the design, I would have a better idea about this.

The next problem was figuring out which base to use. I wanted a base that gave the massiveness of this chest a lift, maybe even to the point of exaggerating it a little. Too low a base would have given the chest a squat and heavy feel. Drawers close to the floor are also less comfortable to use. A high base cuts into the storage volume, but the visual lift it gives to the design more than makes up for this.

An idea that immediately appealed to me was four gently splayed feet known as French feet. Sometimes they splay to the side, and other times they splay forward as well. French feet create a sense of spring or tension, lifting the case. Flowing in an uninterrupted curve from the case, they would nicely complement the simplicity of the

Inspiration Is Everywhere

The richest source of inspiring forms and details is the furniture of the past in museums, books, antiques magazines, and high-end auction catalogs. But design ideas can come from architecture, old farm implements, nature, or even looking critically at your earlier work.

TRAIN YOUR EYE TO FIND THE RIGHT PROPORTIONS

The visual balance of the parts can sometimes be so subtle—they just feel right. Awkward proportions are often more obvious. There are a few guides to help you find pleasing proportions, but it is best to train your eye by looking critically at good design of all kinds.

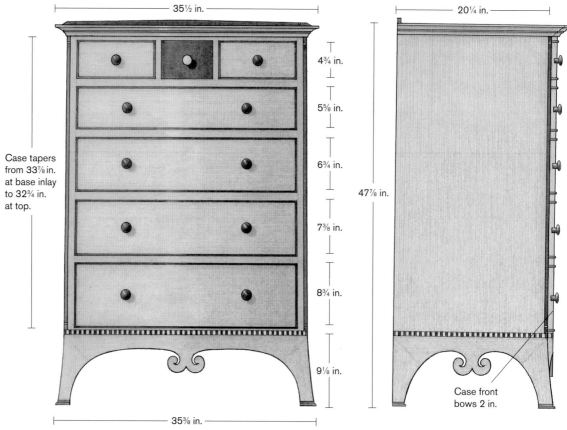

35½ in.

4¾ in.

5⅝ in.

6¾ in.

7⅞ in.

8¾ in.

9⅛ in.

Case tapers from 33⅞ in. at base inlay to 32¾ in. at top.

35⅝ in.

20¼ in.

47⅞ in.

Case front bows 2 in.

single-board sides. Quite foolishly (because I did not think about how much extra work this would be), I had the idea of emphasizing that upward curving energy by tapering the chest slightly, narrowing it at the top. In the drawings, I played with an inch or more taper, just on the edge of perception.

Why French feet rather than a more traditional design of a molded bottom edge of the case with bracket feet? Adding on the base in this way would have solved some of my problems with the defects at the ends of the case side boards and allowed me to build a higher chest. But such a base interrupts the smooth, upward sweep of the case, something my evolving design was emphasizing. I was also beginning to think about bowing out the drawers slightly, a curve echoing the out-swept feet.

Get Down to Specifics

At this point I had the beginnings of a design: a primary wood, rough dimensions of the case and drawers, curving French feet, and possibly bow-front drawers. I had a good idea of how I might build the chest using single-board parts. Nothing was cast in stone. I could only imagine how differently a Shaker brother or an 18th-century Boston cabinetmaker would have worked within similar parameters and the vastly different chests they might have created. Although there may be obvious differences, such as the shape of the case, drawers, and base, the most likely differences would be in the details.

Although the larger elements of form and proportion might catch your attention, the details keep you interested. Edge shapes, moldings, inlays, touches of color, and even the feel of surfaces can encourage your eyes

Apron Accents

Embellishing the apron with a whale's tail similar to ones used by the 18th-century Dunlap family of furniture makers connects this chest with its traditional roots. It adds interest to a part of the chest well below eye level, draws your eye up to the center, and balances the ebony center drawer. The inlaid black-and-white banding helps extend the curved lines of the whale's tail around the base.

and hands to play over a piece of furniture and come to know it more intimately. The details can often be a starting place for a design, or in this chest a way to draw the various elements together. The challenge is to provide plenty of details to explore while maintaining a harmony among those details. Similar to a musical fugue, they should be variations of a theme.

The base illustrates the movement details can create. The drawback to the French feet was that your eye could follow the curve of the side and foot right to the floor and dead end there. Little ebony pads on the bottom of each foot catch your attention before this happens. The vibrant black and the tiny bead cut along the bottom edge of the toes relate them to the cockbeads around each drawer and the ebony corner columns. Moving your gaze back up, the inlay band at the bottom of the case draws your eye horizontally around the two sides

Subtle Cove

To balance the splayed base, the top needs some overhang and mass, but not necessarily the mass of a thick top. The top is thick, but by covering its underside and adding another small cove molding, its profile is more elegant and interesting. The main cove is subtle and far enough below eye level that the author hopes it might be discovered as much by feel as it would by sight.

Details Unify the Design

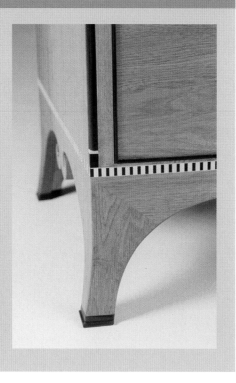

More exciting than chamfering or rounding the corners of the case, quarter-round ebony and holly columns boldly define these edges. They also help emphasize the verticality of the case and lead your eye to the upwardly sweeping French feet. Rounded columns echo the beads around the drawers and the ebony pads on the feet.

and facade. To draw more attention to the base and to relate this chest to earlier chests built in the area where my client lived, I carved the whale's tail details. They express some of the same curving energy as the feet and bow fronts, and perhaps propel your eye upward.

Practical Reasons Behind Details

The details that keep you exploring the forms can evolve for very practical reasons. Cockbeads, proud beads around drawer edges, originated as a way to protect the fragile veneered facade of the drawer. Using them meant flush, not lipped, drawers. Because I had only one other board from the same tree as the sides and top and I wanted good color and grain match, a solution was to laminate the drawer faces. I could then use any butternut for the backing laminates. Adding a cockbead allowed me to hide the lamination lines and nicely define the edges

of each drawer. The cockbead also helps hide the necessary gap around the drawer in its opening and some of the slight variation of how the bow-front drawer aligns with the facade. Laminating the drawer faces into a bow front was only slightly more work and makes for a more interesting design.

By the time I had envisioned a pattern of ebony contrasted with holly and butternut, the rest of the details followed. Ebony corner columns give those edges definition and the case more verticality. The small ebony center drawer with a holly knob attracts your eye to the center of the facade and to the curved top. The top's modest overhang draws a minimum of attention; under-beveling the edge presents a thin and elegant profile. The coved under-bevel repeats the similar curves of the legs and bow fronts. The small cove molding under the top smooths the transition from top to case. Ebony knobs are practical and add interesting dots of color.

I like to add details so subtle that they will be discovered only by a casual sweep of your hand someday. The ebony backsplash has such details—it balances the ebony feet and echoes the overall color pattern with the noticeable holly dots at the ends. Almost hidden between the dots is a very fine groove and bead cut along the top edge. Whoever finds the bead might find the small tapering chamfer defining the back edge of the backsplash as well.

Every furniture design is an experiment of sorts. You have to define the problem and pursue solutions that give you hints at a direction to keep going. Trusting your decisions is part of maturing as a designer. But what keeps it all interesting is the serendipity of furniture making. You can't foresee everything. I didn't plan the slight cant of the knobs down the front, but I like them.

GARRETT HACK is a contributing editor to *Fine Woodworking* magazine.

Dressing Up
a Basic Box

BY ROGER HOLMES

Most woodworkers that I know spend three-quarters of their time making boxes of one sort or another. Boxes for books, clothing, linen and blankets, dishes, cutlery, keepsakes, and odds and ends. We even spend a great deal of time making boxes for boxes; i.e., drawers for a chest or other case piece.

Designing with boxes is deceptively simple. First you figure out the right size and configuration of box or boxes to store or display the desired items. Then you try to make the boxes attractive. A recent request to build a pair of bedside cabinets for friends allowed me to explore methods of enhancing the basic box.

Wedged between the bed and a wall in many bedrooms, most bedside cabinets don't benefit from exposed joinery or lovely wood—you don't get much of a view of either. Trying to think outside the box, I started sketching various curvy alternatives, deciding on the simplest of them all—curving the front plane of the cabinet along a gentle arc. For centuries simple curves have been used to break the four-square rigidity of a box without sacrificing the advantages of rectilinear construction.

A good start, but it wasn't enough. I wanted to add some visual weight to the top and bottom, something a little more sub-

Details Make the Difference

MITERED CORNERS OF THIS CORNICE ARE NOT 45 DEGREES. Take angle measurements for the curved front pieces from working drawings.

DOVETAILS ON THE SKEW. Holmes cuts the dovetails on the skew rather than flattening the face where the joint comes together. Although tricky, it adds to the subtle details of superb craftsmanship of the piece.

PLINTH RAISES THE PIECE OFF THE GROUND. The plinth makes the box look less like a box and provides a structural base for the cabinet.

stantial than the ⅞-in.-thick edges of the box. The solutions—a 5-in.-tall plinth and 2-in.-high cornice—are also traditional, even classical. As far back as the Egyptians, architects have used the plinth to raise a box off the ground and, in a sense, put it on display. They added a cornice on top, like a crown, terminating the structure with a flourish. Furniture makers have used both elements extensively.

My plinth is slightly larger than the box it supports, and simple moldings make the transition between the two elements.

A bead molding announces the beginning of the cornice. The body of the cornice is the same size as the box, but the grain runs horizontally on the sides, setting it off subtly from the vertical grain of the box below. Set in slightly from the cornice body, the cove-molded top panel finishes the job.

Construction Notes

Adding a curve, plinth, or cornice is a time-consuming but rewarding way to make something special out of a simple box. I laminated the curved drawer front and rails for the plinth and cornice out of maple. I resawed the stock to about ³⁄₃₂ in. thick, then pressed the pieces between male and female forms made of medium-density fiberboard.

The plinth rails and legs were joined with mortises and tenons. Joining the curved front rail and leg required some careful layout but wasn't difficult to cut by hand or machine. The molding required slightly different cutter profiles for the curved and straight pieces to ensure an accurate fit at the corners. The molding was glued to the top of the rail-to-leg assembly. The plinth was screwed to the carcase through slots in the molding. The slots allow for seasonal movement.

The cornice was the trickiest element. I assembled the cornice frame, mitering the front corners. I attached the rabbeted cornice top to the frame, gluing the front edge and buttoning along the sides to allow for movement. Next, I attached the mitered bead molding to the carcase, gluing it down to the front edge and screwing it to the sides through slots, which allow the carcase to move. Finally, I glued the cornice assembly to the bead molding.

ROGER HOLMES designs and builds furniture in Lincoln, Nebraska.

AN ELEGANT CASE FROM TOP TO BOTTOM

Construction of this box is straightforward, except for the curved front. Holmes uses slotted holes for the screws where wood movement is likely to be an issue. The piece shown here is 18 in. deep by 19 in. wide by 28½ in. tall.

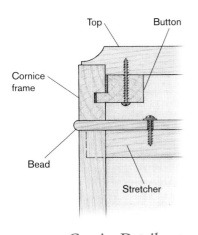

Top

Button

Cornice frame

Bead

Stretcher

Cornice Detail

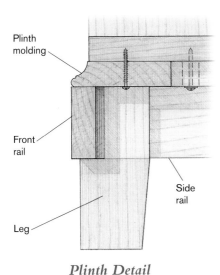

Plinth molding

Front rail

Leg

Side rail

Plinth Detail

Top, ¾ in. thick, is glued to the cornice frame along the front edge and attached with buttons along the sides and back.

Groove for buttons

Cornice frame is glued to the bead molding. Front rail is a bent lamination.

Bead molding is glued to the case along the front edge.

Bead molding is screwed to the cabinet sides. Slots allow for wood movement.

Stretchers are dovetailed into the cabinet sides.

Curved drawer front is a bent lamination.

Curved front rail is a bent lamination. Tenons follow the curve of the front of the rail.

Side rail

Plinth molding is glued to the rails and screwed to the cabinet sides. Slots allow for wood movement.

Graduated Drawers

BY CHRIS BECKSVOORT

The Shakers were among the primary proponents (and practitioners) of graduated drawers, although there are lots of cases—Chippendale, Federal, and Queen Anne—that have graduated drawers. Under the dictum "a place for everything and everything in its place," the Shakers built drawers to house specific items. There is no reason for a drawer that will hold cassette tapes to be as deep as one that holds CDs, or for your underwear drawer to be as high as your sweater drawer.

Also, I never build solid wood drawers much more than 9 in. high. Because of seasonal wood movement, anything higher will leave too wide a gap in midwinter (even with overlay drawers), and the drawer could bind in summer.

Another consideration is overall proportion. Small drawers in desks or in a collector's cabinet may graduate in only ¼-in. to ⅝-in. increments. In bureaus used for clothing, on the other hand, the drawers can be graduated in ¾-in. or 1-in. increments. If you are a stickler for detail, you may also want to consider graduating the size of the knobs or drawer pulls.

Find the Usable Drawer Height, Then Figure the Average Drawer Height

Once you know the height of the case and the number of drawers in the case, laying out graduated drawers is straightforward. To get the available drawer space, subtract from the total height the dimensions of the top, bottom, and all of the dividers. The number of dividers in a case will always be one less than the number of drawers: e.g., a five-drawer case will have four dividers. Dividing the available drawer space by the number of drawers will give you the average drawer height. Regardless of whether you're building a case with an odd or even number of drawers, the average drawer height is the most important dimension.

If you have an odd number of drawers, the middle drawer will be equal to the average drawer height. For the drawers above, simply subtract the amount by which you want the drawers to get smaller—the graduation interval—and add this amount to the drawers below the middle one.

When figuring drawer graduations for a case with an even number of drawers, you still need to find the amount of available drawer space and calculate the average drawer height. However, there will be no

A CASE WITH AN ODD NUMBER OF DRAWERS

A case with an odd number of drawers has a middle drawer with an equal number of drawers above and below it. The method of determining the average drawer height is the same as for a case with an even number of drawers. The formulas for the example here—a seven-drawer chest with 1-in. graduations—can be used for any chest with an odd number of drawers.

To get the usable drawer height, subtract the dimensions of the top (5¼ in.), base (6½ in.), and drawer dividers (6 × 3¾ in. = 4¼ in.) from the chest's total height (59⅛ in.):

$$59\tfrac{1}{8} - (5\tfrac{1}{4} + 6\tfrac{1}{2} + 4\tfrac{1}{2}) = 42\tfrac{7}{8}$$

To find the average drawer height, divide the usable drawer height (42⅞ in.) by the number of drawers (7):

$$42\tfrac{7}{8} \div 7 = 6\tfrac{1}{8}$$

For the drawers below the middle drawer, increase the drawer heights in 1-in. increments. For the drawers above the middle drawer, decrease the drawer heights in 1-in. increments.

5¼ in.

3⅛ in.

4⅛ in.

5⅛ in.

6⅛ in.

7⅛ in.

8⅛ in.

9⅛ in.

6½ in.

59⅛ in.

Six drawer dividers at ¾ in. = 4½ in.

A CASE WITH AN EVEN NUMBER OF DRAWERS

The formulas for the example here—a four-drawer chest with 1-in. graduations—can be used for any chest with an even number of drawers.

To get the usable drawer height, subtract the dimensions of the top (1½ in.), base (5¼ in.), and drawer dividers (3 × 3¾ in. = 2¼ in.) from the chest's total height (36 in.):

$36 - (1\frac{1}{2} + 5\frac{1}{4} + 2\frac{1}{4}) = 27.$

To find the average drawer height, divide the usable drawer height (27 in.) by the number of drawers (4):

$27 \div 4 = 6\frac{3}{4}$

To find the height of the drawer below the middle divider, add one-half the graduation increment—½ in.—to the average drawer height (6¾ in.):

$\frac{1}{2} + 6\frac{3}{4} = 7\frac{1}{4}$

Add 1 in. to the drawer height below and subtract 1 in. from the two above.

36 in.

1½ in.

5¼ in.

6¼ in.

7¼ in.

8¼ in.

5¼ in.

Three drawer dividers at ¾ in.: 2¼ in.

average-height drawer in the case when you are through; the average drawer height is just the starting point in your calculations. Determine an average drawer height, then add or subtract one-half the graduation increment to or from that average height to get started. Then proceed by full graduations.

Always remember that you have some flexibility. If needed, you can add a fraction of an inch to the top molding or remove a fraction of an inch from the base to make the numbers work in a simple way (making your life a lot easier) without compromising the chest. You probably can't change the dimensions of your dividers, though, which have to be a specific size if they are to fit into dovetails or dadoes cut with a standard router bit.

The illustrations shown in this article are examples of how to graduate the drawers

for a case with an odd number of drawers and for one with an even number of drawers. Here's an important thing to keep in mind: You can graduate drawers by any increment—1 in., 2 in., 3 in., even fractional inches—as long as you subtract the increment from the drawers above the average-height drawer and add the increment to the same number of drawers below the average-height drawer. The formulas can be used for any number of drawers, from the smallest case with 3 drawers to a floor-to-ceiling built-in with 16.

CHRIS BECKSVOORT builds custom furniture in New Gloucester, Maine, and is a contributing editor to *Fine Woodworking*. He is also the author of *The Shaker Legacy* (The Taunton Press, 1999). Visit him online at www.chbecksvoort.com.

Drawer-Design Strategies

BY GARY ROGOWSKI

It's always a wonder to me when I come across an old piece of furniture with drawers that slide as sweetly as they did the day they were made. How is it possible for old drawers to work so well? Odds are they have been weighted down, filled to overflowing, pushed, pulled, slammed home, tipped over, and otherwise abused by several generations of owners. Yet if a drawer is well-made, it will fit snugly in its opening and open and close effortlessly, regardless of the season. And it will continue to work that way for a long time.

With so many ways to put a drawer together, which way is best? There's no simple answer, but there are some basic considerations that can help you choose the right corner joint, materials, and method of supporting the bottom.

The object is to build a strong, stable, attractive drawer in a reasonable amount of time. How you do this will depend on your skills, your tastes, and the function of the piece that you are building. I built the drawers shown at left to showcase a number of the best possibilities for drawer construction in a fine case piece. These methods aren't the last word on drawer construction, but they should provide a good starting point.

Corner Construction

THROUGH DOVETAIL

Pros: Very strong, great mechanical strength, and large long-grain to long-grain glue area. The hand-cut through dovetail is aesthetically strong, too. End grain shows on the drawer face, providing a pleasing contrast in some furniture styles.

Cons: The end grain exposed on the face may be inappropriate on more traditionally styled pieces. Comparatively speaking, the dovetail is a time-consuming joint to cut, and it takes practice before you can cut it well. Router jigs used to make through dovetails are relatively expensive, and the resulting joint can look too uniform.

HALF-BLIND DOVETAIL

Pros: As with the through dovetail, half-blind dovetails are very strong and look great, too. And because the joint doesn't show on the drawer face, it's ideal for even the most formal and traditional drawers.

Cons: Even more time-consuming and finicky to cut by hand than through dovetails. Routed half-blind dovetails look routed because of the minimum width of the pins. Most jigs don't allow flexible spacing of pins and tails.

RABBETED HALF DOVETAIL

Pros: Simple to cut (one pass on the router table for each drawer component), simple to clamp, and quite handsome. When pinned with dowels, it's a mechanically strong joint.

Cons: Not as strong as through- or half-blind dovetails and without the traditional cachet. All glue-surface area is end grain to long grain, a weaker connection than long grain to long grain.

SLIDING DOVETAIL

Pros: Very strong, and easy to cut once set up. Can be made so the joint is visible at the top edge of the drawer or so the joint is hidden (stopped).

Cons: Difficult to fit and assemble. The fit should be a bit loose when the joint is dry because glue will start to bind the joint almost immediately. You'll need to work fast once you've applied the glue.

BLIND-DADO RABBET

Pros: Good production joint. It's quick to cut on the router table once it's set up. With a dedicated bit, setup is quick, too. Joint is hidden from front and looks nice if done well.

Cons: Time-consuming to set up unless you have a dedicated bit, which is expensive. Only fair mechanical strength and all glue-surface area is end grain to long grain. Side edges of drawer front are vulnerable to chipping if they're not beveled slightly.

Function: Make It Strong and Stable

When I'm working out the design for a piece of furniture that will include a drawer, I think first about function. A file cabinet or tool-box drawer obviously needs to be stronger than a drawer that will hold only socks or a few pencils. And, generally, the deeper a drawer is the stronger it needs to be.

Drawer joints, like all woodworking joints, derive their strength either from the amount of long-grain glue-surface area shared by the two joined parts or by the way the parts interlock mechanically.

Dovetails make the strongest joints In a chest of drawers, most any well-made joint will be strong enough because the weight the drawers will have to bear is minimal. But stuff a drawer with reams of paper, a dozen handplanes, or a blender, assorted bowls, and a food processor, and you've upped the ante.

In situations where I know a drawer is going to have to stand up to some heavy use, I like to use a dovetail joint. Through, half-blind, and sliding dovetails (see the photos on p. 198) will stand up to almost any use or abuse imaginable. Short of destroying a drawer, you're not likely to see a well-made dovetail joint fail. So choosing one of these three joints becomes a question of aesthetics and efficiency.

A simpler joint in the back Often a drawer is held together with two kinds of joints: something a little fancier in the front where it will show and something simpler in the back, where strength, not appearance, is the primary consideration. In the chest shown on p. 198, I joined the backs of the top four drawers to the sides with sliding dovetails because they're strong, and I can make them quickly with a router.

There's one situation in which you can't use a sliding dovetail at the back of a drawer: when you want to capture a plywood drawer bottom on all four sides, as I did on the bottom drawer in this chest. For that drawer, I used dado-rabbet joints at the back corners. The dadoes run from top to bottom on the drawer sides, just in from the ends. The back is rabbeted to engage the dado and is flush with the back end of the sides.

Quartersawn lumber is best Another functional consideration is stability: how much the drawer will move with seasonal changes in humidity. A drawer that's swollen shut is obviously useless, but one with a huge gap at the top isn't very attractive. So I try to use quartersawn lumber for the sides and backs of drawers whenever possible. It's much more dimensionally stable than flatsawn stock and less likely to warp or twist.

Regardless of whether I'm using quartersawn or flatsawn lumber, I make sure the drawer stock is thoroughly seasoned. I also try to let it acclimate in my shop for a few weeks before working it.

Choosing wood for sides, back, and runners For drawer sides and backs, I generally select a wood that's different from the fronts. Secondary wood saves a little money, and there's no need to waste really spectacular lumber on drawer sides or backs. I use a wood that moves about the same amount seasonally as the drawer fronts and is long-wearing. I also use this secondary wood for the drawer runners. This prevents the sides from wearing a groove in the runners or the runners from wearing down the sides.

Using a secondary wood for the sides of a drawer also can set up an interesting contrast when the drawer is opened, especially with a lighter-colored wood.

Aim for a thin drawer side Drawer-side thickness is a concern for both structural and aesthetic reasons. What you're trying to achieve is a drawer that's light, strong, and well-proportioned. For this chest, I used

Bottom Construction

Mix and match: You can support a drawer bottom in grooves cut in the drawer sides or in slips glued to the sides. Drawer bottoms can be made of plywood or solid wood. Either mate-rial is compatible with either method of support. Your choice will be based on time, cost, and the piece's function.

FULLY ENCLOSED PLYWOOD PANEL

SOLID RAISED PANEL IN A GROOVE

RABBETED SOLID PANEL IN A DRAWER SLIP

PLYWOOD PANEL IN A DRAWER SLIP

GROOVES

Grooved drawer sides provide plenty of support for most drawer bottoms, as long as the drawers aren't going to carry a lot of weight. Sides should be sized proportionally to the width of the drawer.

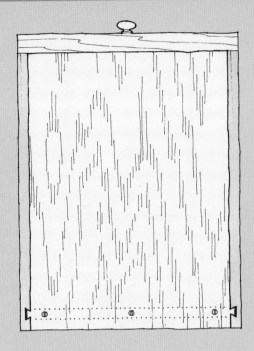

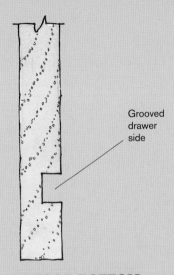

Grooved drawer side

PLYWOOD BOTTOM

A plywood bottom can be supported on three sides and screwed to the back of the drawer or totally enclosed and supported in grooves on all four sides.

SLIPS

Drawer slips add strength and rigidity and increase the drawer's bearing surface on the runners. Slips can be simple, grooved pieces of wood or they can be made more decorative, as shown at right.

Slip profiles

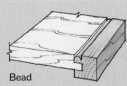
Groove

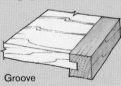
Bead

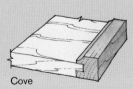
Cove

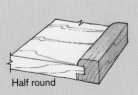
Half round

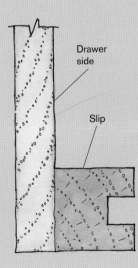

Drawer side

Slip

Solid–Bottom Profiles

Tongue

Rabbet

Raised panel

SOLID BOTTOM

A solid bottom can be cut to a tongue profile, rabbeted, or raised. Because solid wood expands and contracts seasonally, the panel should be oriented so that its grain runs across the drawer. The screw hole at the back of the drawer bottom should be elongated (right).

⅜-in.-thick drawer sides for the top pair of drawers. I added ¹⁄₁₆ in. thickness to the sides and back of each descending drawer. Graduated drawers distinguish this piece from production work; each drawer has sufficient strength and pleasing proportions.

Aesthetics: Make It Attractive and Appropriate

The next consideration is appearance. A nailed rabbet joint, for example, may work perfectly well but just wouldn't make it in a reproduction American highboy. All of the joints I used in this chest of drawers are attractive, but some are more refined than others. So the choice of joinery, especially at the front of the drawer, may hinge on the expectations or tastes of the client and the style of the piece.

To my eye, the through dovetail, the half-blind dovetail, and the rabbeted half dovetail work better aesthetically with this piece than do the sliding dovetail or blind-dado rabbet. But for drawers in a kitchen island or a child's bureau, I'd probably go with the sliding dovetail or the blind-dado rabbet because neither of these furniture pieces requires fancy joinery.

Efficiency: Can I Make It Quickly and Easily?

Ease and speed of construction are related concerns, especially if you make your living as a furniture maker. As a professional, I have to weigh the time it takes to cut and assemble a joint against what it adds to the piece. I also have to know whether the client is willing to pay for the extra labor. If you're an amateur woodworker, time probably is less of a concern, but there will still be projects you just want to finish.

The relative difficulty of making a particular joint also may be a consideration. If you've never cut dovetails by hand before, it's probably a good idea to practice before you start cutting into those figured-maple drawer fronts.

If you have no desire to cut dovetails by hand, a number of router jigs will cut dovetails that are just as strong or stronger than hand-cut ones. But with a few exceptions, they all give you dovetails that look rigidly uniform and machine-made. These may not be the right choice on a piece of furniture that traditionally would have had hand-cut dovetails. And even if routed dovetails work for you aesthetically, there's a learning curve for most of these jigs. So although there may be some gain in efficiency over time, you shouldn't plan to buy a jig on Saturday to speed you through your dovetails on Sunday.

A router can help you make other good-looking, simple joints that are plenty strong. The sliding dovetail and the blind-dado rabbet on the bottom two drawers of this chest fit the bill on all counts.

Supporting Drawer Bottoms

Corner joinery is only one facet of drawer construction. There's also the question of how to support the drawer bottom. What's wrong with a simple groove cut near the bottom of the drawer sides? Not a thing for most work (see the top drawing on p. 201), but if you check out a really first-rate antique, chances are good that the drawer will be riding on slips (see the bottom drawing on p. 201).

Drawer slips are strips of wood glued to the bottom inside faces of the drawer sides. They sit flush with the bottom of the side and are grooved to accept a drawer bottom. Designed to increase the running surface of the drawer, slips prevent the drawer side from wearing a groove in the runner. They also prevent a thin drawer side from being weakened by a groove. I used drawer slips on two of the drawers shown on p. 197: one with a plywood bottom and one with a rabbeted, solid-cedar bottom.

Slips are more than just functional additions to a drawer. They add a measure of finish and formality that catches your eye. I didn't add any decorative elements to the slips in this drawer, but you could bead the top inside edge of the slip, cove it, or round it over to add more visual interest, as shown in the bottom drawings on p. 201.

Plywood or Solid Wood?

The other big decision is whether to make the drawer bottoms from plywood or from solid wood.

Plywood is stronger but not traditional

Plywood has many advantages over solid wood, but for some purists it is simply unacceptable. Plywood is dimensionally stable, so you don't have to take wood movement into consideration. It is stronger for a given thickness than solid material, so you can use a thinner piece: 1/4-in. plywood is thick enough for a drawer bottom (I usually use a 1/2-in. panel if it's solid wood). This also makes plywood a good choice if you're concerned with weight.

One problem with using plywood is that the actual thickness of a 1/4-in. sheet is about 7/32 in. That means that if you rout a 1/4-in. groove in a slip or in your drawer sides, the plywood panel will flop around. Instead, I use a 3/16-in. bit and make two passes. I get a perfect fit, but it takes more time. Of course, there are dado sets available that will plow a 7/32-in. groove, but you can't always run the groove the length of the drawer piece. On some drawer fronts, for instance, you need a stopped groove.

Installing solid-wood bottoms For solid-wood drawer bottoms, the grain must run side to side in the drawer, rather than front to back, so wood expansion won't push the drawer apart and shrinkage won't create a gap at the sides. I usually either rabbet or raise a panel on a solid-wood drawer bottom so the edge is thinner than the rest of the field (see the solid-bottom profiles on p. 201). This lets me plow a smaller groove

in the drawer sides. The result is a strong, sturdy panel that will not weaken the drawer slips or sides excessively.

A rabbeted panel can be slid in with the raised portion facing either up or down. When I use drawer slips and a rabbeted panel, I put the panel in with the raised portion up, mark the panel, remove it, and then plane, scrape, and sand the panel so it's flush with the drawer slips. With the more traditional raised panel, I position the panel bevel-side down.

Keeping the drawer bottom in place

I don't glue drawer bottoms in place. It's easier to repair a drawer if the bottom just slides right out. To keep solid-wood drawer bottoms from sagging, I screw them to the drawer back with a single pan-head screw and elongate the hole so the bottom can move (see the lower right drawing detail on p. 201).

In spite of its strength, a 1/4-in. plywood panel is quite flexible, so I usually drive two or three screws into the drawer back. Otherwise, the bottom will sag (see the top drawing on p. 201).

Another possibility for plywood is to enclose it on all four sides (see the top left photo on p. 200). Because plywood is dimensionally stable, there's no need to leave the back open.

GARY ROGOWSKI, a contributing editor to *Fine Woodworking* magazine, runs the Northwest Woodworking Studio in Portland, Oregon. Visit his studio on the web at www.northwestwoodworking.com.

Where Furniture Meets the Floor

BY MARIO RODRIGUEZ

During the 1980s, when I operated a shop in Brooklyn, we received a steady stream of plain-Jane chests that had been picked up by interior decorators on their trips to the countryside or abroad. I was instructed to give these chests the "Cinderella treatment"—to revitalize them by changing the hardware, possibly adding stringing to the drawer fronts, or maybe making a new top.

By far the most dramatic change took place when I replaced a base. With a new base, a piece would assume a new personality. If I added just the right bracket feet, for example, a mundane Victorian behemoth could be transformed into an elegant Chippendale-style treasure. The careful selection of the base proved, time and again, to be critical to the success of the completed piece. And I've found just the same thing to be true in designing my own pieces or adapting period designs.

To demonstrate the impact that different attached bases can have on a basic chest and to show how approachable most are to make, I've built a single, unadorned chest of drawers and fitted it with four different bases: with bun feet, with saber feet, with sled feet, and with ogee bracket feet. All four of these bases are drawn from histori-cal examples, but as you'll see, they can easily be adapted to modern designs as well.

Why You Need a Base

A chest is essentially a box on a base. The box is where the action is—the drawers, the doors, the shelving. So the base, resting right on the floor, might seem likely to fall beneath our notice. But its impact is strong. First, it literally lifts the cabinet off the floor. The air it puts beneath the piece gives the cabinet definition and makes even an armoire appear lighter. Plunked right on the floor without a base, a large cabinet looks stunted and incomplete; it begins to seem immovable, like a part of the building. A Newport secretary minus its bracket feet would be about as impressive as the Statue of Liberty standing knee-deep in New York harbor.

The proper base should not only elevate the case but also enhance the other features of it. Instead of concentrating all of the detailing on the case and treating the base as an afterthought, I work out the details of the base along with the case.

My choice of a base is influenced by the size and weight of the piece. For instance, I wouldn't place a massive,

BUN FEET

SABER FEET

SLED FEET

OGEE BRACKET FEET

Bun Feet

A lathe-turned foot that has its origins in Europe, the bun foot is typically held to the bottom of a case by means of a wedged round tenon locked into a hole drilled into the case or into a molded frame below the case. A flattened section at the bottom of the spherical bun gives the foot a firm stance on the floor.

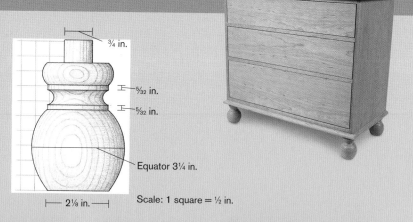

¾ in.

⁵⁄₃₂ in.

⁵⁄₃₂ in.

Equator 3¼ in.

2⅛ in.

Scale: 1 square = ½ in.

BUN FOOT STARTS WITH A GOUGE. Turn a rough cylinder, then use a pencil to mark out the major segments of the foot, including an equator for the foot's sphere.

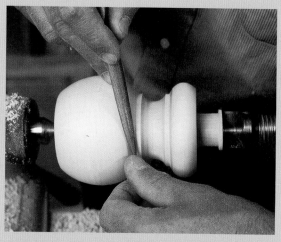

FINISH WITH A RASP. Use a rasp with a light touch to smooth the bumpy surface left by the gouge and to finish shaping the bun foot.

WRENCHING ACCURACY. To size the round tenon on top of the bun foot, hold an open-end wrench against the back of the foot while cutting the tenon to size with a parting tool. When the wrench slips over the tenon, it's the right size.

FOOTED FRAME. The round tenons of the bun feet are wedged into holes drilled in a molded frame. The frame is screwed to the bottom of the case.

multidrawer chest on dainty saber feet. Structurally, the feet might not support the great weight of the piece and its contents. And aesthetically, a large cabinet supported by diminutive feet might bring to mind a sumo wrestler wearing ballet slippers.

From a practical perspective, the lift a base provides also gives better access to the contents of a piece and protects them from moisture and dirt. In addition, an attached base can simplify construction of the carcase and can easily be replaced if it is damaged.

A Base with Bun Feet

The bun-footed base is a lively design that can animate even a very large piece of furniture. Yet with their low center of gravity and rounded form, bun feet are the sturdiest possible. The base is willing to carry great weight and will even endure being shoved and dragged across the floor. The ball-shaped feet introduce a nice counterpoint to the rectilinear lines of a chest. The balls can be full and round, almost forming perfect spheres, flattened like doughnuts, or elongated into cylindrical shapes.

Bun feet originated in Germany and Scandinavia and later were used on Kasten and blanket boxes in America. Bun feet were typically used on fairly massive pieces, but they found their way onto more refined case pieces such as desks and chests during the William and Mary period (1690–1730).

Bun feet are produced on the lathe. In the earliest examples, they were turned from a single block of wood; later, the block was laminated. Each foot has a stem or tenon at the top that is used for attachment to the case. Below that is a ringlike shoulder and then a narrow neck, called the reel, that swells into the ball. The most difficult aspect of turning a bun foot is executing a nice, round ball. If it looks like a potato, it won't work as a bun foot.

For a typical bun foot, start by turning a cylindrical blank. Mark out the major segments of the foot on the cylinder, including a line for the equator of the ball and a circle on the end of the cylinder to establish the flat portion where the ball will rest on the floor. Turn the reel and the shoulder first and then begin work on the ball.

Seasoned turners often use a large skew chisel to cut a sphere. By pivoting and rotating the tool, they obtain a smooth, arcing surface that requires little or no sanding. If you have less experience on the lathe, you might have better luck with a stout gouge. The surface you achieve may be a little bumpier, but the gouge is less likely to dig in and ruin the job because only a small portion of the tool's cutting edge contacts the workpiece. Even so, cut carefully, stopping frequently to check for symmetry.

You can use a rasp to perform the final shaping and smoothing. A rasp can be easily controlled and lightly applied to the rotating shape to correct the bun's outline. By varying the pressure, you can control the amount of wood you remove. And unlike a turning tool, the rasp won't dig into the work. Use sandpaper on the spinning piece to attain the final smooth surface.

There is a foolproof technique for turning the tenon on a bun foot to a precise diameter. From behind the rotating workpiece, press an open-end wrench against the tenon while removing material with a ⅛-in. parting tool. The narrow parting tool is used with a scraping action, so it doesn't require careful guidance and can be held in one hand. When the tenon is reduced to the precise final dimension, the wrench slips over the tenon.

The simplest way to attach bun feet to a case is to drill holes into the bottom of the carcase to receive the feet's tenons. But if the interior of the cabinet or chest will be visible, so will the ends of the tenons. In that case, attach the feet to a frame and then screw the frame to the underside of the chest. Make the frame of solid wood and cut a profile on its edge, which adds a molding to the bottom of the chest.

Saber Feet

The front feet on a Hepplewhite-style saber-footed base curve both to the front and the sides. The back feet curve only to the side, allowing the case to sit tight against a wall. Mortise-and-tenon joints hold together the rails and feet. Pine blocks strengthen corners. The base is screwed to the case through the blocks.

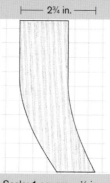

|— 2¾ in. —|

Scale: 1 square = ½ in.

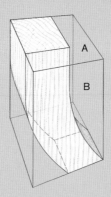

For the compound-curved front feet, trace the layout template on two adjacent faces (A and B) of a 2¾-in.-sq. leg blank. The tracings should meet at the foot's bottom tip. For the single-curved back feet, you need to trace the template only on one side.

FRONT FEET ARE CUT FOUR TIMES. The front feet on a saber-footed base curve to the front and to the outside, requiring four bandsaw cuts. The first two cuts are made with the blank resting on the same face.

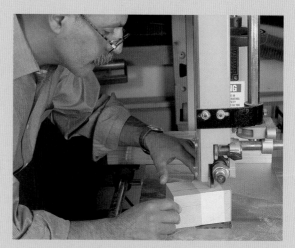

TAPE THE WASTE BACK ON. After making the first two cuts on the front feet, tape the waste pieces back on the feet. This will give you a flat surface on the bandsaw for the second two cuts.

A Base with Saber Feet

The sleek, graceful saber foot was most popular during the Hepplewhite period (1790–1805), when Baltimore cabinetmakers used it extensively. But with its hard edges and simple sweep, the saber foot transcends period classification and looks perfectly comfortable on modern pieces. Visually, the saber foot works best with pieces that are moderate to small in size, fairly rectilinear in form, and restrained in detailing. On the right case, a base with saber feet will confer a sense of poised nimbleness, like that of a dancer.

When designing saber feet, strive for a smooth, moderate curve. Start by making a cardboard template of the silhouette and use the template to trace the silhouette on a square blank. For the front feet of the base, which curve to the front and to the side, trace the template on adjacent sides of the blank; for the back feet, which curve only to the side, trace the template only on one side of the blank. As you design the curve of the feet, err on the side of moderation; a

block plane with a very small throat opening and a very sharp blade. I do any further cleaning up with a card scraper. On the concave sides, I begin with a curved soled spokeshave and follow that with rasps and sandpaper.

Saber feet are often linked with rails, creating a strong frame that can easily be screwed to the bottom of the case. Like table aprons, the rails are tenoned on the ends and fitted into mortises in the saber feet. It is simplest to cut the mortises in the feet while the blanks are still square.

A Base with Sled Feet

Solid and low slung, the sled-footed base suggests—and delivers—stability and strength. It can be used on both low storage chests and towering cupboards. I've seen sled feet on painted Scandinavian chests dating back to the 15th century, as well as on early 20th-century English Arts and Crafts pieces. To me, sled feet conjure up sturdy medieval coffers and cupboards reinforced with iron straps and hinges, or simple rustic furniture built and shaped with little fuss.

The sled-footed base is comprised of two parallel feet joined by a beam. The front ends of the feet typically extend beyond the front of the piece and are often chamfered, rounded over, or embellished with an ornamental scroll. A variation on this design that you sometimes see is one that raises the carcase off the feet with legs.

Because the shaped end of a sled foot is in front of the cabinet, its shape and finish must be crisp and attractive. Cut the shoulder of the scroll on the tablesaw and the curved outline on the bandsaw. Fair the curves and smooth them with fine rasps, files, card scrapers, and sandpaper. Start with a fine, 6-in. tapered rasp to create a flowing curve without any abrupt dips or blips. Work down from the bottom of the shoulder cut to the tip of the foot. Next, take care of the rough surface left by the rasp

curve that looks good on the template will often appear exaggerated when cut out of the blank, because each foot is a compound curve. Too radical a curve can make a foot look like it is straining under the weight of the cabinet. And, in fact, it may well be. The grain is short at the toe, and the farther the toe extends, the more vulnerable it is to breaking off.

The curves are cut on the bandsaw. After cutting one side of the front legs, temporarily reattach the cutoffs with masking tape. Then rotate the blank and cut the other curve. Clean up the convex curves using a

Sled Feet

This base of European origin is made of three main components: two sled feet and a perpendicular beam. The front of the feet typically protrude beyond the front of the case. A ⅞-in. tenon is turned on each end of the beam, and it is secured through holes in the feet with a wedge (see the bottom photo).

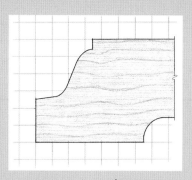

Scale: 1 square = ½ in.

CRISP CUTS START ON A TABLESAW. Cutting the shoulder on the front of the sled-footed base is best done on a tablesaw.

RELIEVING THE WASTE. Several bandsaw kerfs cut just to the layout lines of the front of the sled foot will make it easier to maneuver the wood around the blade for the tight corners of the finish cut.

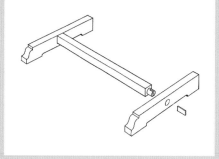

WEDGE TREATMENT. The back of each sled foot is cut square and flush with the back of the chest. Both feet are screwed to the bottom of the chest.

with a smooth round file and a card scraper. Finally, sand a bit for a silky surface. Make sure the curving edge is square to the sides, not lopsided. Refrain from breaking the edges, keeping everything crisp and clean.

Because the feet support the weight of the cabinet, the beam's purpose is mainly decorative. Not needing maximum strength, I joined the beam to the feet with round mortise-and-tenon joints. Turn the tenons on the lathe and size them with an open-end wrench to an exact ⅞ in. diameter. Then drill a corresponding hole in the feet to accept the through-tenon. For a decorative touch that also ensures a tight, clean joint, cut a thin kerf into the end of the tenon with a dovetail saw and later, when assembling the joint, tap a wedge into the kerf.

A Base with Ogee Bracket Feet

I always have fun with making ogee bracket feet and put great effort into their design. Ogee bracket feet give a rectilinear cabinet a fluid, sculptural touch, catching light and shadow in a pleasing way. This sculptural design was popular in the 18th century and typifies the Chippendale style (1760–1790). While displaying the sensuous nature of the wood, ogee bracket feet give a piece a sturdy, rocklike stance.

By definition, an ogee is a pair of complementary curves that form an "S" shape. The relationship of these curves can vary to suit your taste. The curves might be the same radius, or you might have a tight convex curve over a wide, shallow concave curve. The only requirement is that the convex curve be at the top and the concave curve below. A bracket foot with a convex curve at the bottom is called a reverse ogee.

A successful ogee profile will have a lively, curling contour, suggesting fabric unfurling. In addition to the undulating ogee, a bracket foot is defined by the profile at the end of each wing of the bracket. Some end quite simply; others end with a flourish of scrollwork. When designing a bracket foot, this end profile is read two ways—as a positive form (the foot) and as a negative form (the space beside the foot). You can explore this positive/negative relationship by cutting possible profiles in a light material and viewing them against a dark background.

To make ogee molding, cut the cove with an angled fence on the tablesaw and the convex shape with tablesaw cuts and hand tools. After milling long sections of ogee profile, cut them into 8-in. lengths. Next, designate adjacent pieces to be paired up as feet so that the grain will be continuous around the mitered outside corner of the bracket. The pieces must be marked left and right to produce a pair.

I often use splines to register and align the joint. To cut a groove into the face of the miter, set the tablesaw blade to 45 degrees. Clamp a scrap to the saw table to use as a stop to register the cut, and use the miter gauge to push the stock. Be careful to raise the angled blade no higher than the thinnest dimension of the ogee profile.

The grain orientation of the spline is critical to the strength of the joint: The grain should run across the width of the spline, not along the length. To produce a spline with the correct grain orientation, make a tablesaw kerf into the end grain of a scrap piece of molding. Then cut the spline free on the bandsaw. Most of the cutout work for the end profile of ogee bracket feet is done on the bandsaw. But to achieve a crisp result for designs that include tight inside curves, I begin at the drill press. I use whatever bit matches the radius I need—Forstner bits or circle cutters—to cut out the inside curves, then I cut the rest of the shape on the bandsaw.

MARIO RODRIGUEZ, a former contributing editor to *Fine Woodworking*, builds commissions and teaches classes at the Philadelphia Furniture Workshop (www. philadelphiafurnitureworkshop.com).

Ogee Bracket Feet

Popular in the Chippendale period, ogee bracket feet are made from sections of tablesaw-made ogee molding. The tight inside curve of each foot is cut on a drill press before the rest of the bracket is cut on a bandsaw. The rear feet are molded on the sides only. Flat pine blocks butt to the end of the rear feet and allow the case to sit tight to a wall (see the drawings on the facing page).

SPLINE TIME. An ogee bracket foot is made of mitered sections of moldings and held together with splines. After cutting the corner miter on a tablesaw, the author sets up the saw to cut a groove for the spline, taking care that the height of the spline cut is lower than the height of the thinnest part of the ogee profile.

LOW, INSIDE CURVE. Most of the cutout work on the ogee bracket foot is done on a bandsaw. An exception is any tight, constant-radius curve, such as the one near the bottom of the foot, which is more easily cut with an appropriately sized Forstner bit.

PROFILE OF REAR FOOT

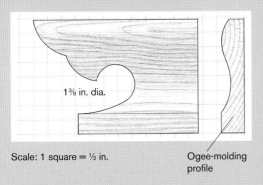

1⅜ in. dia.

Scale: 1 square = ½ in.

Ogee-molding profile

FRONT FOOT

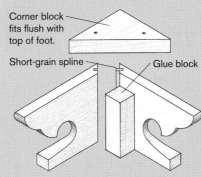

Corner block fits flush with top of foot.

Short-grain spline

Glue block

REAR FOOT

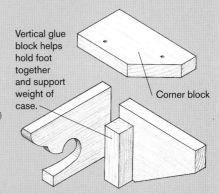

Vertical glue block helps hold foot together and support weight of case.

Corner block

TAPED AROUND A SQUARE BLOCK. To ensure a tight, 90-degree miter, set the splined-and-glued bracket foot around a squared block of wood. The miter is held tight with tape until the glue dries.

SCREW THROUGH TRIANGULAR CORNER BLOCK. The back feet on an ogee bracket base are not mitered like the front ones. Rather, the ogee bracket butts a flat pine block that will be invisible when the case is placed against a wall.

Sideboard Strategies

BY WILL NEPTUNE

It is all too easy to sketch something that looks good, only to discover that you have no reasonable way to build it. You either develop overly complex construction methods or sacrifice the design you really want because it's too difficult to build. The solution is to strike a balance between design complexity and construction simplicity.

Historically, sideboards were built using post-and-rail or frame-and-panel construction, but I prefer this method, which calls for a dovetailed box turned on its side. My alternative approach is less familiar, but when you start counting the joints necessary to build a frame-and-panel sideboard, you understand the logic of a dovetailed design. With this method, there are fewer joints to cut, and the ones you do cut aren't seen, so there's no need to be overly meticulous.

This construction system is based on a few rules concerning joinery: If a case part joins another at a corner, dovetail it; if one part meets along another's length, use multiple tenons. Dovetails and tenons are both strong joints that allow for wood movement and resist racking. Because all of the structural parts of the case have grain running in the same direction, the case expands and contracts together. Put simply, the case is still just a long, dovetailed box with legs attached.

Sideboards built using this approach may vary in size, line, and style, but they retain a family resemblance based on the construction system. The mocked-up sideboard shown on these pages is the most basic variation of this system, but it lays a foundation that can be used on more complex designs. Once you understand the construction system, you can focus on design and build in styles ranging from Federal to Arts and Crafts (see p. 222).

Basic Sideboard Design

A sideboard is typically a tall case piece that's often 40 in. high and taller, a convenient working height for a standing person. The height of a sideboard makes anything displayed on its top more visible because it isn't overpowered by the forest of chairs surrounding a dining-room table. A sideboard is also strongly horizontal because the tall legs hold the mass of the case off the floor and because the case length exceeds the height. The open space below the case keeps the sideboard from appearing too massive, an effect you get with many large case pieces. With lengths of 4 ft. and 5 ft. common, the facade can be divided using a combination of drawers and doors (see the drawings on p. 224).

In designing the mocked-up poplar sideboard seen on these pages, I wanted a

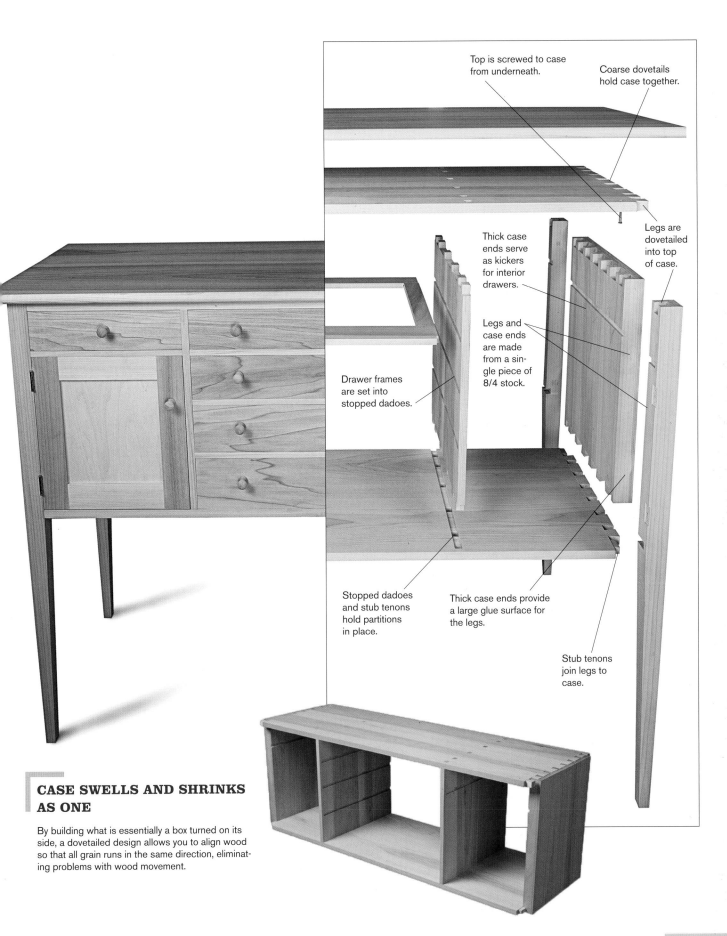

Top is screwed to case from underneath.

Coarse dovetails hold case together.

Legs are dovetailed into top of case.

Thick case ends serve as kickers for interior drawers.

Legs and case ends are made from a single piece of 8/4 stock.

Drawer frames are set into stopped dadoes.

Stopped dadoes and stub tenons hold partitions in place.

Thick case ends provide a large glue surface for the legs.

Stub tenons join legs to case.

CASE SWELLS AND SHRINKS AS ONE

By building what is essentially a box turned on its side, a dovetailed design allows you to align wood so that all grain runs in the same direction, eliminating problems with wood movement.

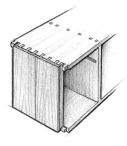

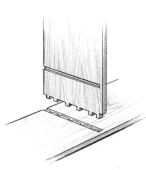

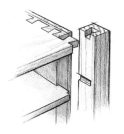

With this four-part construction system, you can design and build in any style.

simple piece with a country feel. In form, it refers to the Federal period but avoids the use of veneers, inlay, and hardware seen in period, high-style examples. To simplify construction, I decided on a small, four-legged version without the curved facade often seen in Federal examples. Country furniture makers made similar design choices in earlier times, using the grain and figure of local woods or even painted finishes to give a piece visual interest. These designs rely on proportion and line to create a sense of balance and harmony.

The Construction System

One key feature of this construction system is the use of built-up ends, which are thicknessed to the same dimension as the legs. The thicknesses of the ends provide large glue surfaces for the legs. In addition, the top and bottom join the legs and ends without having to be notched around the legs. This structural solution creates a lined interior for the cupboard areas.

The partitions that divide the facade are not only design variables, but also structural elements. The multiple stub tenons tying the long top and bottom together eliminate sagging almost completely. All of the drawers run on frames let into stopped dadoes.

In a real project, if saving primary wood is important, all of the case parts other than the legs can be made of a secondary species and faced or edged with your primary wood. Using a less dense secondary species also saves weight.

Using built-up ends Even though this entire mock-up is made of poplar, I laminated the ends the same way I might for a sideboard built in cherry or mahogany. By resawing a piece of 8/4 stock, you're able to show a book-matched pattern on the ends. The inner part of each end is glued up from the leftover pieces of the 8/4 stock. This is a nice way to keep the legs from appearing as though they were stuck on as

an afterthought. This effect is enhanced by good grain matches on the legs and ends, which make each assembly look like one solid piece (see the drawings on p. 219). This is particularly effective if you can choose an 8/4 board that is flatsawn and wide enough for the edges to have growth rings running at about 45 degrees (as seen on the end grain). This gives you straight grain on the legs, which helps disguise the glueline. As a bonus, the adjacent faces of the legs also match each other.

In the mock-up, I resawed the 8/4 stock thin, trying to avoid the green heartwood, but the thickness of the layers doesn't matter. The object is to calculate the width of each end so that little wood is lost between the ends and the legs, which would disturb the grain match. Also, you must start thick with both layers to allow for later milling. Once the inner and outer layers have been edge-glued, skim them with a handplane before gluing them together.

Alignment is much easier if you leave the parts long at this stage. The extra length allows you to nail the parts together in the waste areas when you clamp them up. The laminated parts should be given several days to move and reach equilibrium. After they are done moving, both the leg blanks and the ends can be flattened and thicknessed at the same time. When you trim the ends to finished length and width, remember to keep the book-match line centered and parallel to the edges.

Dovetailing the case The top and bottom of the case are milled and glued up like any large panels, then cut to final size. The dovetails that hold the case together are fairly easy to cut, either by hand or machine, but remember that the layout is different at each corner where a leg joins the case (see the top photos on p. 220). The top rear dovetails are cut narrow to make room for the back boards where the leg will be rabbeted. The case bottom has stub tenons that will be housed into the legs. These tenons are shouldered so that any later sanding won't change the fit of the joints. Once the piece is finished, none of the joinery will be visible, so the dovetails can be coarse (with wide pins and tails).

Filling out the facade The partition joints are somewhat fussy to cut, but they add considerable strength to the case (see the bottom photos on p. 220). Shallow stopped dadoes are used to locate the partitions. Tenons are positioned on the partition ends so that there is extra holding power at the edges, with enough tenons across the middle to help the top and bottom resist sagging. The partitions are held in line by the dadoes, which makes fitting the thickness of the partitions to the dadoes careful work. Partitions should be cut a bit longer than the ends to leave some extra tenon length for final flushing.

Because the partitions are fully housed in the dadoes, there are only small shoulders at the front. It is very important that when clamped the tenon shoulders bottom out in the dadoes, keeping both the top and bottom of the case parallel. Router planes can be fussy, but because the depth should be consistent, I took the time to run one through the dadoes of the mock-up.

To gauge the front shoulders, work in from both ends with a cutting gauge at the front until what's left between the lines equals the distance between the base of the pins cut on the case ends. Then add the depth of the dado and mark the space between the tenons. The trick is to get the small front shoulder to close at the same time that the end grain between the tenons bottoms out in the dado. This ensures that the top and bottom will remain parallel.

Once the tenons have been cut, locate the mortises in the dadoes. Line up the fronts of the partitions with the front of the case and mark around the tenons to establish your mortises. There is no need to run the tenons through, but it does add strength and keeps you from having to clean the bottoms of the mortises. When the partitions fit squarely into place, you've finished framing the basic case.

Attaching the legs to the case The legs are mortised to accept the stub tenons cut into the bottom board (see the photos p. 221). Because these tenons and the top dovetails share the same shoulder line, the legs should register flush to the case ends. Once the top dovetails are let into the legs, you can't trim any more wood off the legs and ends, so make sure this joint is accurate before you cut it. This method puts one serious requirement on the legs. They can be sawn to shape, turned, or carved, but the solid glue surfaces must meet the case ends.

To guarantee alignment, it's best to cut the dadoes for the drawer dividers using a router with the case ends and legs clamped up. Once the stopped dadoes have been cut, the case construction becomes fairly ordinary. Mortise-and-tenon frames that separate the drawers are glued in the front 3 in. or so but not at the back. Leaving space at the back ensures that when the case shrinks the frames don't push against the back of the case. Both the frame-and-panel doors and the dovetailed drawers are built using the usual methods, but I put small vertical stops behind the doors.

The rear legs and the bottom are rabbeted to accept the back. The back on the mock-up is a series of $\frac{1}{4}$-in. panels held by rabbeted cleats that are attached with screws. The top is ripped even with the bottom of the back rabbets so that the back boards run up to the exposed top. (This is not critical, but it does make it easier to fit the back.) A more elegant solution would be to resaw thin shiplap boards and run them vertically across the back. The top can be cut to allow some overhang, then molded and screwed down from below.

Sideboard Back

BACK RIDES IN RABBETED CLEATS

Rabbeted cleats are screwed to the rear top and bottom of the case. Three panels of ¼-in. plywood slide easily into place.

Panel

Cleat

Rabbet

Alternative Constructions

There are a number of places where construction can be altered to save wood or to produce a slightly different effect. People are often surprised by the use of a full-board top and bottom. Although it does use extra wood, it also adds strength to the case, resists cupping at the ends, and provides built-in kickers for the top drawers.

As a substitute, you could use two wide rails, with gussets or without. If your design has no cupboard space, you could use similar rails at the bottom. To allow for wood shrinkage, remember to fit any kickers with gaps at the shoulders and leave the rear tenons unglued.

The case ends could also be thinner than the legs, creating either a reveal where the ends join the legs or a recessed nook inside the case. Because of the added complexity of the case dovetails and drawer frames in the latter option, I would use it only if saving weight or wood is an issue.

It's easy to add decorative aprons between the legs (see the bottom right drawing on p. 224). At the lamination stage of making the case ends, glue on the outer layer long at the bottom. This creates a large lap for the dovetails, which, as before, are cut flush on the inner layer of the end. The outer layer hangs down and can be sawn to shape. To add an apron across the front, the bottom can be cut back and an apron piece glued onto the edge of the bottom. If the apron is wide at the center, it can be braced from behind. If it is wide at the leg, it should be tenoned into the leg to prevent racking and twisting.

The most common change to the case is to have the bottom step up in the middle. This introduces movement, breaks up the strongly horizontal case and allows different ways of arranging the doors and drawers. This type of case construction is more complex, but it uses the same joints as before (see the left drawing on p. 224). Just remember how this system works: If a case part joins another at a corner, dovetail it; if a part meets along another's length, use multiple tenons. When you add a step up in the center of the case, only the fitting sequence changes.

First cut and fit the multiple stub-tenon joints between the inner verticals and center bottom panel. All of the stub tenons can be cut at the same time, but put off dadoing

BUILT-UP ENDS

Using the Grain to Make Invisible Joints

By carefully planning the cuts, a single 8/4 board can be laid out to form leg-and-end assemblies that appear to be a single, solid board. The legs are cut from the straight-grained edge of the board, and the ends are book-matched and laminated from resawn stock. When the legs join the ends, you're left with virtually invisible gluelines.

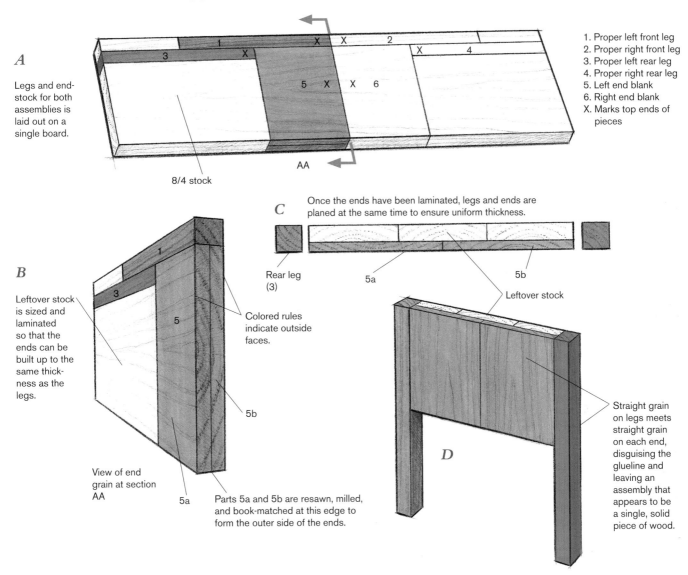

A Legs and end-stock for both assemblies is laid out on a single board.

8/4 stock

1. Proper left front leg
2. Proper right front leg
3. Proper left rear leg
4. Proper right rear leg
5. Left end blank
6. Right end blank
X. Marks top ends of pieces

C Once the ends have been laminated, legs and ends are planed at the same time to ensure uniform thickness.

Rear leg (3)

5a   5b   Leftover stock

B Leftover stock is sized and laminated so that the ends can be built up to the same thickness as the legs.

Colored rules indicate outside faces.

View of end grain at section AA

Parts 5a and 5b are resawn, milled, and book-matched at this edge to form the outer side of the ends.

D Straight grain on legs meets straight grain on each end, disguising the glueline and leaving an assembly that appears to be a single, solid piece of wood.

the top until the center panel is in place. The important thing here is to keep the inner verticals parallel. If the center panel clamps up shorter than planned, it's easier to move the dadoes in the top board (and make the center section smaller) than it is to live with verticals that aren't perpendicular to the case.

Now fit the dovetails of the ends to the top. While cutting the outer bottom panels, you can make any necessary adjustments. The most important thing is to keep the verticals parallel. Many things can creep in to change the exact locations of the verticals, but the top now tells you the actual distance between the inside faces of the verticals, a measurement that is more important than the overall length of the bottom pieces. So if the bottom location changed or you cut the bottom a bit short, adjust the gauge line

Dovetailed Box

THE BASIC CASE

A simple dovetailed box is modified to accommodate the legs. Dovetails can be cut coarse (with wide pins and tails) because the top will later cover them. Narrow tails at the front and back of the top and stub tenons at the case bottom are later fit to the legs.

Coarse dovetails are later covered by the top.

Narrow dovetail accepts top of leg.

Stub tenon holds leg in place.

Partitions

THROUGH-TENONS RESIST SAGGING

The partitions are set into stopped dadoes cut into the top and bottom of the case. Through-tenons on the partitions are housed in mortises cut into the case.

Through-tenon

Through-mortise

Dado stops just short of case front.

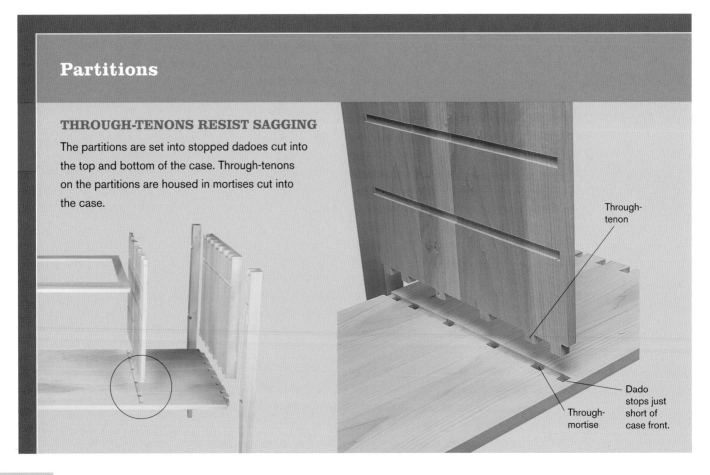

Dovetailed Legs

LEGS SLIDE INTO PLACE

By housing each leg in a narrow dovetail at the top of the case and a stub tenon at the bottom, the leg can be slipped into place from underneath after the basic case has been assembled. Stopped dadoes are cut to accept the drawer frames. Cutting the dadoes with ends and legs clamped up before assembly ensures perfect alignment. The exposed top is screwed to the top of the case from underneath.

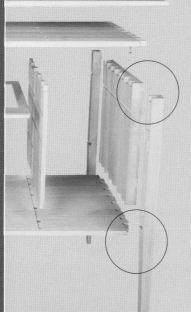

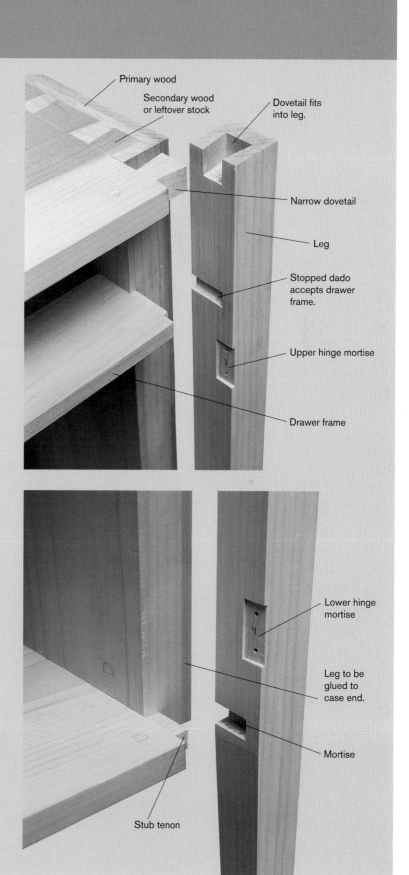

Primary wood

Secondary wood or leftover stock

Dovetail fits into leg.

Narrow dovetail

Leg

Stopped dado accepts drawer frame.

Upper hinge mortise

Drawer frame

Lower hinge mortise

Leg to be glued to case end.

Mortise

Stub tenon

FEDERAL By adding an inlaid apron and carefully choosing the leg style, a simple design turns into a Federal showpiece.

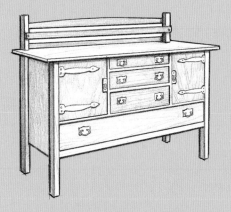

STICKLEY Typical of the Arts and Crafts movement, this design uses heft and hardware to create a solid sideboard with a medieval inspiration.

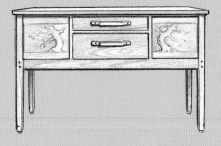

GREENE AND GREENE Ebony splines and details, rounded corners and carefully recessed legs can be used to build in a softer Arts and Crafts style.

With the construction system illustrated in this chapter, proportion and detail can be used to lend a sideboard a period feel. Working out a new design gives you a chance to try some of these possibilities and find a good fit for the design and style ideas of the piece you want to build. The size, shape, and proportions of a piece, along with the choice of materials, finish, hardware, and any embellishments, work together for an overall effect.

The mocked-up sideboard was designed only as a model for construction, but the size and proportions, along with the tapered legs, give it a country, Shaker feeling. This same design could be made of maple or cherry with a simple molding for the doors. I made the storage capacity as large as possible without losing the horizontal effect of the case. The central bay of drawers is wider than the side bays, partly to allow for some larger drawers but also because the narrow side bays keep the doors from looking too square. The resulting side bays have a vertical effect that frames and balances the strongly horizontal case.

Federal-period sideboards typically rely on large veneered surfaces for decoration. But a simpler, solid-wood construction inspired by the period could be built easily using this construction system (see the top drawing at left). Touches of inlay and the use of simple stringing (inlaid veneer strips) echo the effect of the more complex examples. I would use legs that are either tapered and inlaid or turned below the case bottom. Turned legs could be embellished by reeding the long tapers. The square top section of the legs could have a rectangular panel defined by holly stringing. To maintain the flat appearance of Federal veneered doors, two options come to mind: a solid-wood frame-and-panel door with the panel rabbeted to be flush to the frame, or a mitered solid-wood frame with a veneered panel for contrast. A small, curved apron below the bottom edge of the case would soften the shape of the case. The long, slender legs and small case section give the piece a delicate appearance.

Where the Federal piece exhibits delicacy and two-dimensional patterns, a Stickley-influenced, Arts and Crafts sideboard should be heavier looking to emphasize its medieval inspiration (see the middle drawing at left). To support this idea, I would use oak, fumed or stained to look old. Unlike the other examples, the legs could be thicker to stand proud of the case. The case ends as well as the front framing members would be set back $1/8$ in. to make the construction distinct. The divisions of the front space enhance the overall effect: The doors are square and severe, eliminating any sense of vertical lift. The large drawer at the bottom has a slablike appearance. The entire piece looks solid and heavy.

Also under the umbrella of the Arts and Crafts movement is the Greene-and-Greene sideboard in the bottom drawing on the facing page, which is based on a "Hall Cabinet" built for the Blacker House in 1907. The furniture and architecture of Greene and Greene are a bit more refined and softer than Stickley's, with more gentle curves. The piece pictured is strongly horizontal—even the doors are wider than they are tall. You can incorporate these and other details typical of Greene-and-Greene designs: carved door panels or stepped cloud-lift door rails, ebony splines and details, and bordering surfaces enhanced by setbacks and rounded corners. The overall effect should balance explicit construction with softness in detail.

The designs included here should show the endless variety of styles that can be built using this construction method. Feel free to incorporate ideas from any traditional form or to invent your own to achieve a design that better suits your tastes.

for the dovetails until the distance between them is the amount required. The slight change of length in the tails is absorbed in the lap of the pin piece. As before, the space below the raised center section can be filled with decorative apron pieces.

Proportions and Style

In designing a sideboard, it's important to consider the visual effect that the proportions and construction methods will have, then choose ones that help express the intent of the design. Before considering any decorative effects, sketch a few cases of different sizes and proportions (see p. 224). Then use tracing paper to try out a variety of partition locations and to vary the door and drawer sizes. This exercise gives you a sense of how changes in proportion alter the effect. You may find yourself discarding all of these sketches, preferring to develop a second set using your eye to judge correctness.

The methods used on the mocked-up sideboard should provide the basics of construction. Most of the alternatives discussed don't really change the construction methods much. They are additions to the basic case that either save wood or provide surfaces for design options. More complex cases are possible, but they are all offshoots of this basic method. You can choose details to design a sideboard with a refined period look, or opt for something more contemporary.

WILL NEPTUNE is a furniture maker and former woodworking instructor at the North Bennet Street School in Boston, Massachusetts.

Finding the Right Proportions

With a sideboard, as the case gets larger and the negative space between the legs grows smaller, the piece begins to look more massive. But take a look and compare cases 1 and 2. Case 1 is far more delicate in size, but the case divisions give a static effect because they are based on squares and 2:1 rectangles. Although case 2 is much bigger, both the vertical rectangles of the doors and the graduated drawer sizes help relieve any sense of heaviness. What if the drawers were the same size and the doors more square?

Putting the doors on the outer parts of case 3 leaves the drawer compartment overpowered, at least to my eye. Even though the initial placement of the partition gives equal divisions, once the central space is divided, it looks too small.

Case 4 uses proportions that I often rely on. Leaving 50 percent in the middle gives a strong impression but is not as obvious to the eye as halves or thirds. Dividing the total sideboard height in half is also satisfying but remarkably subtle because it takes a moment to see the relationship of the positive space to the negative. Overall, I like the interplay of vertical and horizontal rectangular spaces. But I would still be willing to adjust things by eye to get a more pleasant drawer spacing, for instance. For me, it's less important that the height be exactly divided in half than it is for the divisions of space to produce an impression of these proportions.

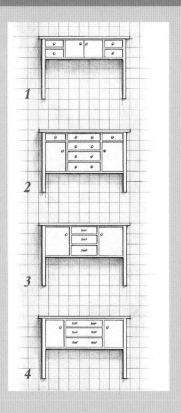

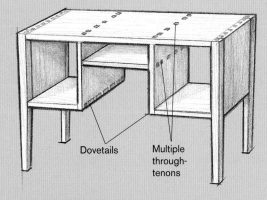

Dovetails

Multiple through-tenons

CONSTRUCTION BASICS REMAIN UNCHANGED

No matter how you change the design, the rules of construction are simple: Dovetail joinery is used at all corners and multiple through-tenons are used where a board joins another along its length.

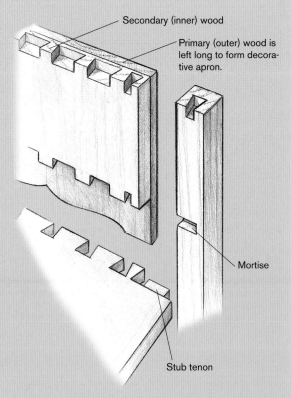

Secondary (inner) wood

Primary (outer) wood is left long to form decorative apron.

Mortise

Stub tenon

DECORATIVE APRON ADDS TO DESIGN

With the primary wood cut long and glued onto the secondary wood, an apron is formed and can be accented with scrollwork inlay. Cutting the secondary wood shorter allows you to employ the simple construction methods used on the basic case of the mock-up.

A Back for Every Cabinet

BY STEVE LATTA

Like many avid readers and collectors, I have a lot of bookcases. Over the years, I've jammed some of them so full that paperbacks are wedged into any usable opening. The shelves are so crowded, in fact, that it's almost impossible to see the back of the case. For strictly functional cabinets like these, a sturdy back can be as simple as a plain sheet of plywood.

But there are other types of cases that need a good-looking back, and some instances in which an attractive back also must be rock solid.

I have display cases, for example, that house ceramics, antique tools, and other prized possessions. For cases like these, the back needs to look good. The case that holds my collection of first-edition books needs a different kind of back. It has a pair of inset glass doors, so the back must look good and also be quite rigid. That helps hold the case square and keep the doors from racking and binding, regardless of the substantial weight of the books.

Fortunately, there are several ways to make an attractive back; some combine great looks with construction rigid enough for the most demanding applications.

Apart from that bare sheet of plywood, most cabinet backs fall into two basic

Two Stylish Options

A bookcase stuffed to the gills with paperbacks doesn't need a fancy-looking back. On the other hand, a case for displaying collectibles probably needs something dressier than a plain sheet of plywood. Slat backs (below left) made of solid wood are attractive enough to set off fine collectibles or rare books, and provide sufficient strength for an open-front cabinet. Frame-and-panel backs (below right) are even more handsome. With glued-in plywood panels, this back is also exceptionally rigid, making it the best choice for a cabinet with inset doors.

designs: slats or frame-and-panel. Slats offer a wide variety of looks—from rustic to refined—and their joinery allows for wood movement. They work well with open-front cases but aren't rigid enough for cabinets with inset doors. A frame-and-panel back, whether it's made with floating panels or glued-in plywood, is sturdier.

Slat-Back Options

The basic aesthetic goal for any slatted back is a pleasing, consistent pattern that doesn't involve very narrow or wide slats on the edges. I stagger the width of the slats, using pieces around 4 in. and 5 in. wide. Wider boards look better on larger backs.

For slatted backs, three basic forms of joinery come into play. In order of simplicity, these are shiplapping, splining, and tongue and groove.

Shiplapping Shiplapping involves rabbeting opposite sides of the same board so that the edges of adjoining slats overlap. Use a router table, a tablesaw with dado head, or a shaper; make the rabbets about ¼ in. wide and half as thick as the stock.

For small cases like the one shown here, (the back is 28½ in. wide and 42¾ in. tall),

CASE CONSTRUCTION

Regardless of solid-wood or plywood construction, the case should be built to accommodate sturdy attachment of the back. The key is to rabbet the sides and inset the subtop and case bottom flush with the rabbets.

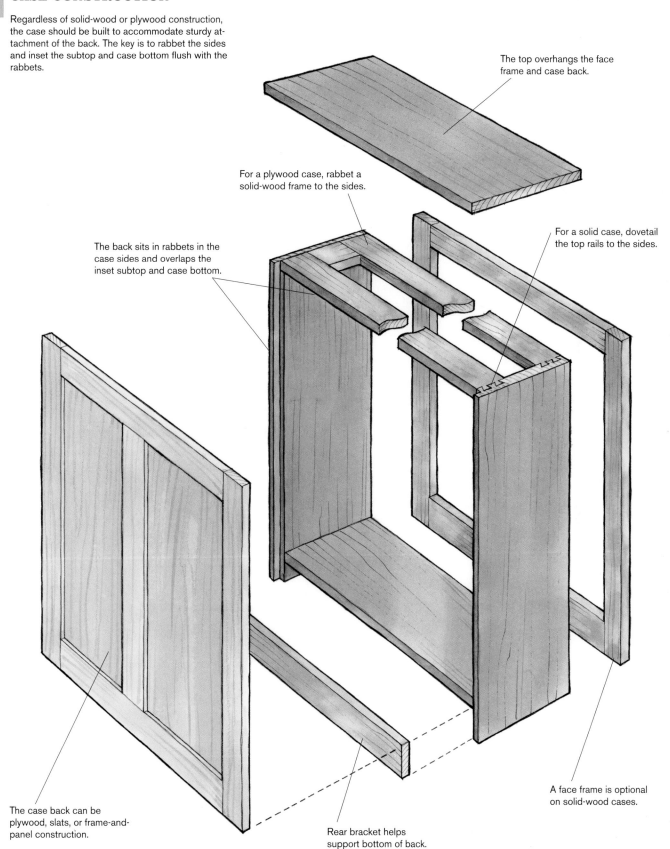

The top overhangs the face frame and case back.

For a plywood case, rabbet a solid-wood frame to the sides.

For a solid case, dovetail the top rails to the sides.

The back sits in rabbets in the case sides and overlaps the inset subtop and case bottom.

The case back can be plywood, slats, or frame-and-panel construction.

Rear bracket helps support bottom of back.

A face frame is optional on solid-wood cases.

A slat back is relatively simple solid-wood construction. Each of these joinery choices is designed to allow for its own wood movement, so don't glue the slats to each other. Each slat should expand and contract as an individual unit.

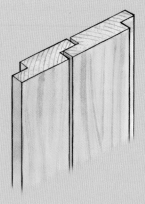

SHIPLAP

This is a practical choice for thinner slat stock because rabbetting divides the narrow edge of each slat into just two elements. In contrast, a groove plowed in the edge of a too-narrow slat will have skinny, fragile walls that could snap off.

MATCHED RABBETS FORM A JOINT. With the bit height set at half the thickness of the stock, all of the cuts can be made with one router-table setup.

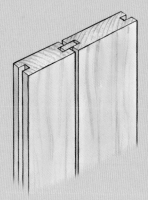

SPLINES

Cutting a simple groove along the edges of each slat allows the boards to be held together with splines. Stronger than shiplap, but not as strong as tongue and groove, a splined back is much quicker to make than the latter.

CUT A GROOVE. A tablesaw kerf is wide enough to house a spline. The spline should be slightly narrower than the combined depth of the grooves to allow for movement.

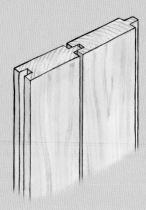

TONGUE AND GROOVE

Tongue-and-groove joinery makes a sturdier back. The joints interlock more securely than splined slats, reducing the likelihood of a piece cupping or twisting.

A SLOT CUTTER PLOWS A GROOVE. Tongue-and-groove joinery requires a wider groove. Make one pass in each direction to ensure that the groove is perfectly centered.

A STRAIGHT BIT CUTS THE TONGUE. Set the bit height to match the bottom of the groove.

slats as thin as $5/16$ in. would work. But because shiplapped joints are not truly interlocking, large cases require thicker slats to avoid having edges twist out and pull away from the case. Another strategy for this is to use a splined or tongue-and-groove back, both of which join the slats more securely.

Splining For boards of this size and length, cut a groove $1/8$ in. to $3/16$ in. wide. Keep the groove no deeper than $3/16$ in. to $1/4$ in. or you risk breaking off one of the sides. It's simplest to center the groove on the slat's edge unless you plan to add a bead or chamfer on the front of the board. In that case, cut the groove closer to the back of the board, but not so close that it compromises the strength of the groove's back lip.

On the tablesaw, use a featherboard and a tall auxiliary fence for safety and consistency of cut. A zero-clearance insert adds safety and prevents tearout.

You also can cut the grooves with a slot cutter mounted on a shaper or router table. Most slot-cutter sets are designed to cut a groove about $1/2$ in. deep, so I bury the cutter in the fence to get a shallower cut and to reduce tearout. A fence-mounted featherboard adds both safety and accuracy.

After cutting the grooves, I create splines by thickness-planing a board of slat stock to a little less than the combined depth of the two grooves and using the tablesaw to rip off strips that fit snugly in the grooves. When mounting the slats in the case, leave a slight gap, no more than $1/16$ in., between the pieces to allow for movement.

Tongue and Groove Positioning and cutting the grooves for tongue-and-groove slats is the same as for splining. Because these boards aren't very wide, there will be minimal movement, so the groove does not need to be very deep.

Amana® sells a two-wing, slot-cutting assembly marketed under the name of Quadraset™ that can be adjusted to cut both halves of the joint with a slot width as narrow as $1/8$ in. and expandable in $1/32$-in. increments. There is a distinct advantage in cutting both the top and bottom rabbets at the same time, because the tongue is guaranteed to be consistent and fit the groove. In my experience, cutting one side at a time, regardless of setup efforts, leads to variations in the tongue thickness that may require touch-up with a rabbet plane.

Embellishments Chamfers and beads are the two most common forms of edge detail on slat backs. For chamfers on splined or shiplapped slats, bury the bit into an auxiliary fence to ensure that the chamfer doesn't take up the entire edge. For tongue-and-groove slats, I make a special fence that allows me to chamfer both the tongued and the grooved slats with one router-table setup. I cut one of the lips off an extra piece of grooved stock, then bury the V-groove bit into the lower lip. (Don't use a chamfering bit here. The tongue on your slats will ride the bit's bearing and push the work away from the cutter.) The small flat that was left below the chamfer rides the edge of the rabbet.

I typically bead only tongue-and-groove slats, using a high fence and a beading bit in a table-mounted router. I cut the bead on the tongued section. When using thin stock, I don't bead the grooved edge because it will weaken the lip. This isn't an issue for larger cases with thicker back boards. If possible, set the top of the bead a little below the surface of the board so that it is not flattened during subsequent planing, scraping, and sanding stages.

Easy Frame-and-Panel

Frame-and-panel backs are much more rigid than slat backs and, as a result, are more effective at keeping a case from racking. Frame-and-panel backs are also quite attractive, and the use of contrasting panels adds a contemporary feel.

CHAMFERS

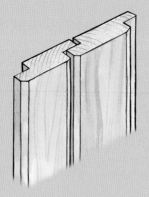

Chamfers work well on all three styles of slat backs, and they're easily cut using a block plane or a chamfering or V-groove bit chucked into a router table.

A SHIPLAP FENCE SIMPLIFIES THE WORK. Allowing the stock to overlap the fence means both edges can be chamfered with one router-table setup.

CUT A CHAMFER ON EACH EDGE. Make sure that the profile doesn't compromise the integrity of the rabbet at either edge.

BEADS

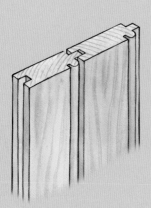

Beading works best on a shiplapped or tongue-and-groove back. On a splined slat, however, the bead can weaken one of the groove walls.

CUT THE DECORATIVE ELEMENT AFTER CUTTING THE JOINERY. Cutting the tongue first yields a cleaner cut because the beading bit isn't forced to hog away large amounts of waste material.

A very traditional back can be made with full tenons and a solid, raised panel, but I prefer another method, using plywood panels. This is just as attractive yet easier and more rigid. Plywood frame-and-panel backs can be made with a simple, quick method. For a case of this size, use ⅝-in. to ¾-in. frame stock with panels made from ⅜-in. or ½-in. plywood. Rotary-cut plywood is available in common species such as walnut, mahogany, cherry, and red or white oak. Because the panels aren't large, it is not difficult to cut a sheet for optimum appearance. Plain-sliced plywood has a more uniform look, but may not be as readily available in most species.

Size the back about ⅛ in. taller and wider than the rabbeted case opening. Design the back so that interior stiles and rails are proportional to each other. In my bookcase (see the photo at the bottom of p. 233), the back is divided into two panels for a balanced look. The center stile is about ½ in. narrower to compensate for the edges of the side, which rest in a rabbet in the case.

Making the frame I use stub-tenon joinery, which is a wonderful way to make frames quickly for a variety of applications such as cabinet backs and dust panels. By itself, this frame isn't as strong as one made with traditional mortise-and-tenon joinery. But with plywood panels glued in place, you wind up with a lightweight back that is more rigid than its traditional cousin.

The joinery is easy to cut. Start by plowing a full-length groove, ½ in. deep and ¼ in. wide, along the inner edges of the frame members. You can do this with a slot cutter or dado head. Lay out the tenons so they are centered on the stock. You can cut them quickly using any tenoning jig.

With all the joints cut, fit the frame together and size the panels. Measure the panel openings and add ⅞ in. to the length and width to account for the panel's rabbeted edges. Cut the rabbets about ½-in. to ⅜₆-in. wide. There is no need to make the reveal precisely even, as the rabbets are not visible from the front of the case.

Glue-up in stages It's best to approach the glue-up very systematically, starting with the top and bottom rails and the center stile. Next, apply a bead of glue along the back edges of the grooves only. In this way, any squeeze-out will be on the back of the plywood panel. Slide the panels in, mount the side stiles dry, and clamp the whole assembly, making sure everything is flat and square. After about half an hour, unclamp the assembly, glue on the side stiles, and reclamp.

Fit the panel to the case Taking special care to keep the panel square, size it for a snug fit in the case back. Racking is devastating if you plan to use inset doors. Rather than nails, use screws to hold paneled backs in place. This facilitates easy removal for finishing or any other reason that might arise.

STEVE LATTA, an instructor at Thaddeus Stevens College in Lancaster, Pennsylvania, is a contributing editor to *Fine Woodworking* magazine.

Installing Slats

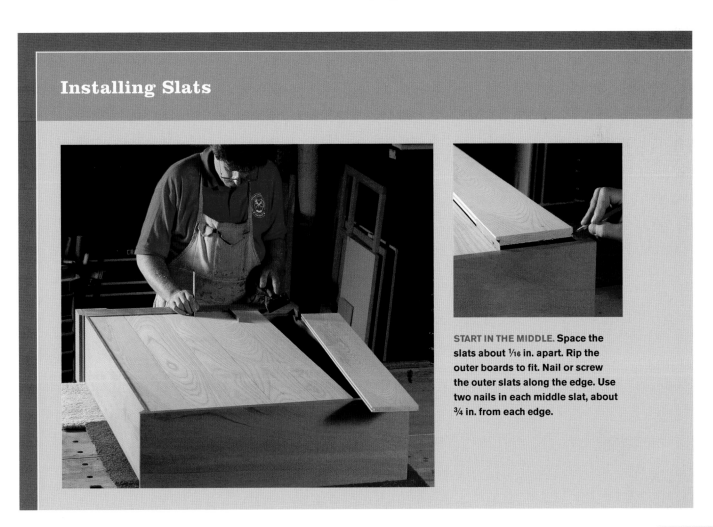

START IN THE MIDDLE. Space the slats about 1/16 in. apart. Rip the outer boards to fit. Nail or screw the outer slats along the edge. Use two nails in each middle slat, about 3/4 in. from each edge.

Frame-and-Panel Backs

Frame-and-panel backs are much more rigid than slat backs and as a result they're much more effective at keeping a case from racking. They are also quite attractive, and the use of contrasting panels adds a contemporary feel.

TRADITIONAL JOINERY WITH A SOLID PANEL

A traditional frame-and-panel back uses a solid-wood panel floating in a mortise-and-tenon frame.

Tenon is housed in a deep mortise.

Shallow groove for panel

Raised solid-wood panel floats in grooves.

STUB TENONS WITH A PLYWOOD PANEL

With plywood panels chosen for good-looking face veneer and glued in place, this approach is just as attractive as a traditional frame-and-panel back, but is both more rigid and easier to make.

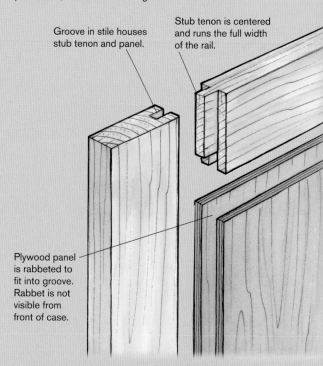

Groove in stile houses stub tenon and panel.

Stub tenon is centered and runs the full width of the rail.

Plywood panel is rabbeted to fit into groove. Rabbet is not visible from front of case.

CUT A CONTINUOUS GROOVE IN THE FRAME MEMBERS. On the stiles, the groove that houses the panel also serves as a mortise for the stub tenons on the rails. Because the cutter is buried into the fence, tearout is radically reduced. Make one pass in each direction to center the groove.

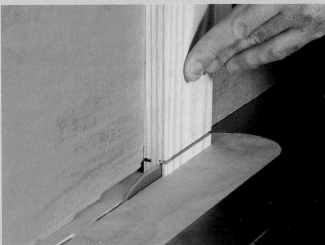

CUT THE STUB TENONS. Raise the tablesaw blade enough to barely nick the bottom corner of the groove (above left). This ensures a clean, snug-fitting corner at the base of the tenon. Raise the blade to trim the tenon cheeks (above right).

ASSEMBLE THE BACK. The ½-in.-thick plywood is rabbeted on the back side, ensuring a good fit in the grooves. Check carefully once the clamps are on to make sure the assembly is flat, tapping the components into place with a deadblow hammer, if needed, as you tighten the clamps.

What Makes a Chair Stand Up to Abuse?

BY JERE OSGOOD

When I was learning how to make furniture, my fellow students and I spent a lot of time designing chairs. Whenever we finished one, our instructor, Tage Frid, would sit in the chair. "Sit" isn't the right word. He would land on it hard, tip it onto its back legs, and wiggle around to see if it was going to fall apart. I never saw a chair break, but I witnessed a lot of sweating students.

Another Scandinavian furniture maker, the Swedish designer Carl Malmsten, once said that chairs are "the most difficult member of the furniture family to master." I think this is true. A chair, especially a dining chair, bears burdens unlike any other piece of furniture in a home. Its successful design depends as much on solid engineering as it does on aesthetic sensibility. To build a dining chair that is both beautiful and strong requires careful attention to the forces working against it.

What are those forces? First and foremost, a chair supports a person many times its own weight. This weight comes and goes, moves and shifts.

Different parts of a chair experience stress and strain at different times. As Tage Frid illustrated to us, the weight is deposited on a chair with force, not gently and gradually, so it must be able to withstand these moments

of impact. Chairs also get dragged around the house for all sorts of purposes, from eating and lounging to working and sometimes even changing a light bulb. Few pieces of furniture work this hard.

Every chair design accommodates these forces in different ways, making it difficult to establish ground rules that can be applied to all. Most wooden chairs, however, share a few critical connections holding the seat and legs together. The success of these joints will, in large part, determine whether a chair design will stand or fall after years of use.

Seat Rails Carry the Load

When Tage Frid dropped himself onto a chair, he would push his weight into the back, sometimes tilting onto the rear legs. You may be doing this right now as you read this chapter. If you are, notice how the back becomes a lever when you lean into it. This weight exerts tremendous force on the intersection between the back and the seat, pushing these pieces apart. Not surprisingly, this is one of the most important joints in a chair (see drawing on the facing page). If this joint is poorly designed—and I know this from experience—the seat rail will work loose from the back leg. It may not collapse, but the chair will soon wiggle.

In most wooden chairs (other than Windsor-style chairs) the seat rails have tenons that fit into mortises in the back legs. The tenon has to withstand the weight of the sitter as well as side-to-side racking forces. Therefore it must be thick—at least ⅜ in., but I prefer to make them closer to ½ in. I have seen tenons that were too small simply snap off. To get the most mechanical advantage, the depth of the tenon should be more than half the width of the back leg.

Another important consideration is the glue. Today more than ever we rely on adhesives to hold a chair together. This makes it possible to build strong chairs with less material, but it also means maximizing the strength of the bond. One way to compare different joinery options is to measure the total area of the long-grain gluing surface. I measure the long-grain faces of the tenon and the corresponding sides of the mortise and compare different joints to see which has the most gluing surface.

Chair joinery is a balancing act, though. A large tenon with lots of gluing surface will be stronger than a smaller one, but it also means that more material must be removed from the back leg to make the

IT LOOKS GOOD, BUT WILL IT HOLD UP? **Behind the lissome lines of this chair is a carefully engineered skeleton designed to withstand the substantial force of a 200-lb. dinner guest.**

THE FORCES WORKING AGAINST A CHAIR

People land hard in a chair, so the joints must be strong enough to withstand this stress. In this basic chair design, the strength of the joints between the seat rails and legs is critical. Improperly designed, the joints work loose and the chair wiggles.

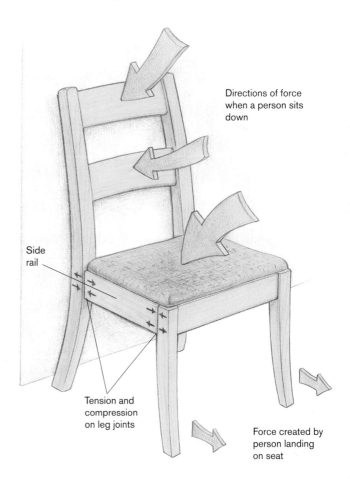

Directions of force when a person sits down

Side rail

Tension and compression on leg joints

Force created by person landing on seat

THE SEAT RAIL WORKS THE HARDEST

The joints between the side seat rails and the back legs bear the brunt of the weight. The top of the joint, under tension, is being pried apart by the force of someone leaning back. The bottom is in compression and will help resist this force.

To maximize the glue bond without weakening the leg, the author uses haunched or webbed tenons on the seat rails.

The width of the rail is more important than its thickness. The author recommends a minimum of 3½ in.

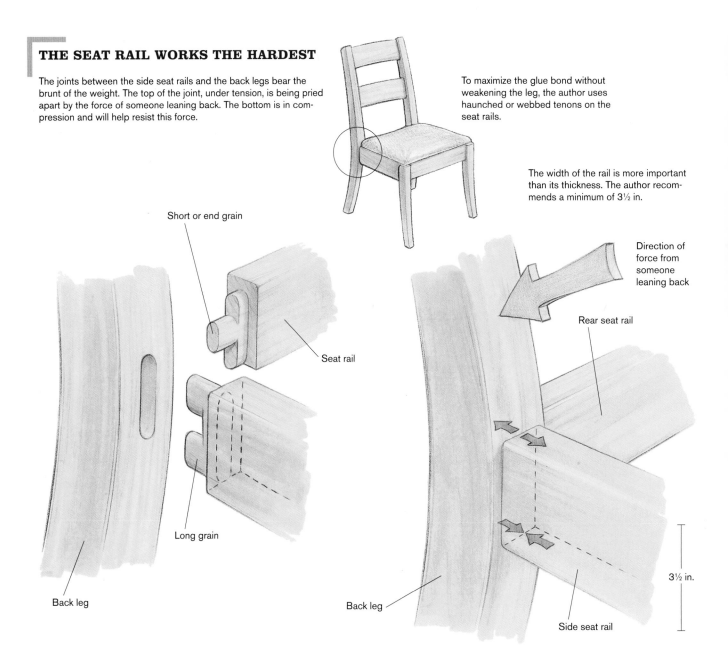

Short or end grain

Seat rail

Long grain

Back leg

Direction of force from someone leaning back

Rear seat rail

Back leg

Side seat rail

3½ in.

mortise. A gaping mortise in the back leg may fatally weaken its strength, defeating the purpose of the strong tenon. If the chair has a rear seat rail mortised into the back legs at the same spot, this will weaken the leg even further.

One solution is to make haunched or "webbed" tenons that are either T-shaped or U-shaped (see drawing above left). This reduces the size of the mortise without sacrificing the length of the tenon. Although there is less gluing area, it still makes a strong joint. Another way around this dilemma is to attach the rear seat rail to the

side seat rails just inside the back legs using stub tenons, but not so close as to interfere with the roots of the side rail tenon (see the bottom left drawing on p. 238). I can then run the back slats past the seat and either attach them into a lower stretcher or directly into the back legs.

The dimensions of the rails are as critical as the joints. No amount of joinery will help a chair survive years of use if the rails are too small. Width is more critical than thickness, because the rails must withstand tension and compression forces. A chair I made has rails that are plenty thick—nearly

BIGGER DOESN'T ALWAYS MEAN STRONGER. The author illustrates with this chair he made in the 1950s (above). The seat rails are plenty thick, but strength comes from width, not thickness. These rails were too narrow and wiggled loose over the years.

TRIM BACK THE TENONS. This will minimize the amount of material cut out of the leg for the mortises. Both the side and rear rails shown at right have ample long-grain gluing surface.

2 in.—but the width is far too narrow and the joint has failed (see the top left photo). I have found that the seat rail should be at least 3½ in. from top to bottom where it meets the back leg, especially if the chair has no stretchers.

Finally, the rear seat joints are stressed the most when someone tilts a chair onto its back legs. As an insurance policy, I try to position the bottom of the back legs further behind the seat than the top. The more the legs angle back, the harder it is to tip the chair onto the rear legs. There is a side benefit to doing this: The legs keep the

top of the chair from scraping against a wall. If the legs are angled too far back, though, they become a tripping hazard.

Front Legs Absorb Some of the Strain

The back leg-to-seat rail connection may bear the brunt of a 200-lb. dinner guest, but I have seen a lot of broken front legs, too. When someone sits down in a chair, the weight pushes the front leg out, making the joint between the front leg and the seat rail work hard to stay tight (see drawing on p. 235). A strong joint in front fights this

THERE IS MORE THAN ONE WAY TO CONNECT THE BACK LEGS

In many chairs, the back legs are connected by a seat rail, which is often mortised into the leg at the same spot as the side rails. Moving the rear seat rail so it spans between the two side rails means fewer mortises in the back leg. Corner blocks reinforce the joints and provide a secure place to anchor a slip seat.

THE ANATOMY OF A DINING CHAIR

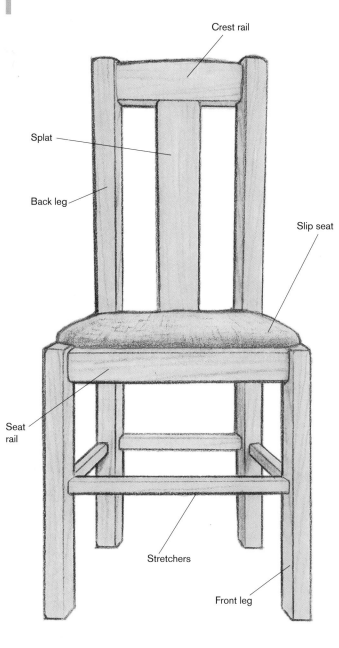

Crest rail

Splat

Back leg

Slip seat

Seat rail

Stretchers

Front leg

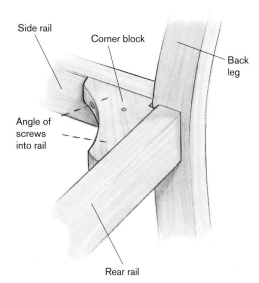

Side rail

Corner block

Back leg

Angle of screws into rail

Rear rail

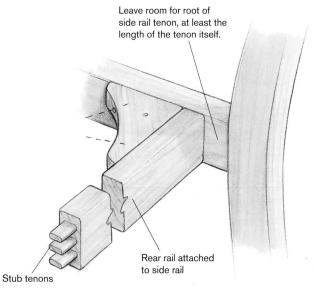

Leave room for root of side rail tenon, at least the length of the tenon itself.

Rear rail attached to side rail

Stub tenons

tendency. If this joint is weak, everything relies on the strength of that back joint.

For many years I have used a sliding dovetail to counterbalance the weight that pushes the front leg out (see drawings and photo at right). The dovetail is locked in place by the tenon on the front seat rail, creating a mechanical joint that has proven indestructible. With stronger glues, this may seem extreme, but I like insurance. It's not always possible to use a dovetail, but when you get the chance, take it. A locked dovetail is stronger than a mortise and tenon, and it will work even if the glue fails.

Corner blocks complete the seat frame. These small blocks, fastened to the inside of the seat rails, reinforce the joinery and provide a convenient spot to drive a screw into an upholstered seat frame. One word of advice: Don't rely on the seat itself to keep a chair rigid. A woven or upholstered seat may help tie things together at first, but seats invariably loosen with wear. If the chair is designed properly it should hold together with or without the seat.

Strength in Stretchers

The easiest way to strengthen a chair is by increasing the bulk of the parts, both the rails and the legs. Although this method can sometimes overcome engineering deficiencies, it usually results in a heavy, clunky chair that may not break, but isn't very inviting. One way to gain strength without sacrificing delicacy is by spreading the load among a greater number of parts.

A stretcher system below the seat, for instance, will help resist twisting and racking forces on the legs, reinforcing the seat joints (see drawings on p. 240). Shaker chairs often have several sets of turned stretchers encircling the legs. These chairs are quite strong, yet each individual turning is light and delicate. To achieve the same strength without stretchers would mean bulking up the seat frame, which would change the design.

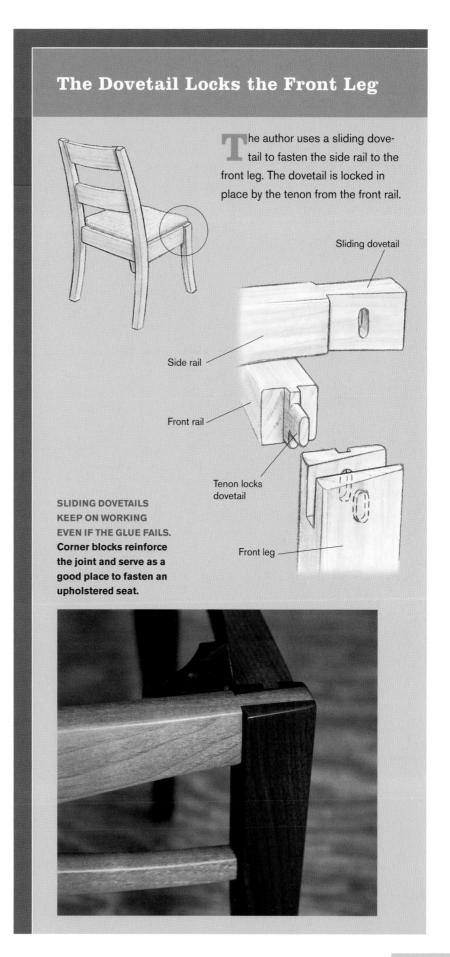

The Dovetail Locks the Front Leg

The author uses a sliding dovetail to fasten the side rail to the front leg. The dovetail is locked in place by the tenon from the front rail.

Sliding dovetail

Side rail

Front rail

Tenon locks dovetail

Front leg

SLIDING DOVETAILS KEEP ON WORKING EVEN IF THE GLUE FAILS. Corner blocks reinforce the joint and serve as a good place to fasten an upholstered seat.

STRETCHERS KEEP THE LEGS IN CHECK

Some chairs have no structure below the seat, but many have some sort of stretcher system which helps resist racking and twisting forces on the legs. Stretchers can be positioned any number of ways, as these examples show.

Box Stretcher

Shaker chairs often have delicate turnings, which means more parts are required to carry the load.

H Stretcher

The stretcher between the front legs is replaced by one connecting the two side stretchers, adding more room below.

Osgood's Split-Rail Stretcher

The rail splits to reinforce the front leg down low, where the extra support is needed.

Arms Act Like Upper Stretchers

Arms tie the legs together and reinforce the joint between the back and the seat.

Adding arms to a chair does the same thing as adding stretchers, although the strength is up higher where it can help stabilize the back as well as the legs. The crest rail also holds the chair together and helps keep the back legs in alignment.

Strength comes at a price, though, and you may not want to pay it. I like to tuck my feet underneath the seat, for example, so stretchers down to the floor would not suit me. Instead, I might make the stretchers a little bigger but use fewer of them, keeping the chair strong while leaving more legroom underneath.

A solution that I like to use is a split side rail and stretcher combination. The lower part of the rail becomes a stretcher and meets the front leg about 5-in. below the seat rail, counteracting some of the tension on the front leg. In this case the joinery at the back leg has proven to be quite strong, which is why I have the lower stretcher curve into the seat rail at the back of the chair. It also makes the design more fluid and less rectilinear.

There are countless ways to counteract the forces working against a chair. The classic Thonet cafe chair is completely different from a Shaker ladder-back. However you choose to address these structural problems, I strongly recommend full-size shop drawings and a full-size pine mockup. These are good places to analyze the joinery and engineering.

Structure and joinery are only two elements of any design. For me, making a chair is more about design than engineering. Comfort and style are far more important to most people. So durability has to be weighed against delicacy. Strength against comfort. Weight against beauty. Engineering is just one of the pieces to the puzzle.

JERE OSGOOD builds custom furniture out of his New Hampshire workshop. His work has been featured several times in *Fine Woodworking* magazine.

Anatomy
of a Bed

BY JEFF MILLER

Bed designs may vary widely, but sound construction is a critical part of any design's success. Fortunately, there aren't too many structural issues to deal with. First, you have to figure out the best way to support the mattress and box spring. Also, because most beds need to be transportable, they must come apart quickly and easily, and when put back together be rigid and silent. That means you must choose the best systems for joining the rails to the posts, and the posts to the headboard. I've built countless beds during my woodworking career. Using the techniques I've learned, you can make any style of bed.

Beds come in a variety of standard sizes, but these standards are not absolutes. If your mattress is larger than standard, you'll have to adjust the frame size; but if it is smaller, you should size the frame for a standard mattress so when the time comes to replace it, a new mattress will fit. In general, plan to leave ¼ in. to ½ in. of space on the sides to allow room for the bedding. I sometimes leave a little more room at the end, with a footboard that rises above the mattress, so there is some space to hang your toes off the end of the bed or to accommodate the cord of an electric blanket.

Construct the Headboard

The headboard (and footboard, if there is one) assembly usually is built as a unit, with mortise-and-tenon joints connecting the rail to the two posts. The mortise-and-tenon provides the maximum strength to this connection, but the details of the joint vary based on the bed's design. On a wide plank headboard, some allowance must be made for wood movement. With two separate tenons, glue only the upper one, or use a wide, short tenon floating in a long, shallow mortise, anchored in the center with a full-depth tenon that is glued.

On a four-poster bed, the headboard plank simply floats (without glue) in deep, slightly oversize mortises. The headboard then can be removed when the bed needs to be disassembled.

A headboard that has slats, spindles, or a frame-and-panel design will have a crest rail tenoned into the top of the posts. Be sure to offset the mortise-and-tenon joint toward the bottom of the crest rail so you leave as much wood as possible at the end of the post, above the joint.

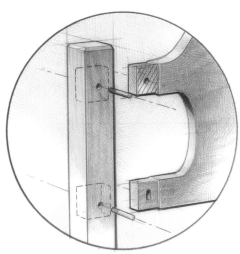

Headboard

Headboards vary in design and can be made from a single, solid board or be of frame-and-panel or post-and-rail construction.

Standard Mattress Sizes

Twin
39 in. by 75 in.

Full (or double)
54 in. by 75 in.

Queen
60 in. by 80 in.

King
76 in. by 80 in.

California King
72 in. by 84 in.

Mattress Height

Consider the thickness of the mattress and the choice of a slatted support or a box spring when determining the height of the side rails.

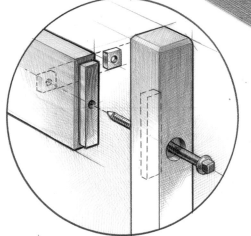

Post-and-Rail Connection

Bed bolts are the traditional method to obtain a rigid, squeak-free connection between posts and rails. The joint also must knock down for disassembly and transport of the bed.

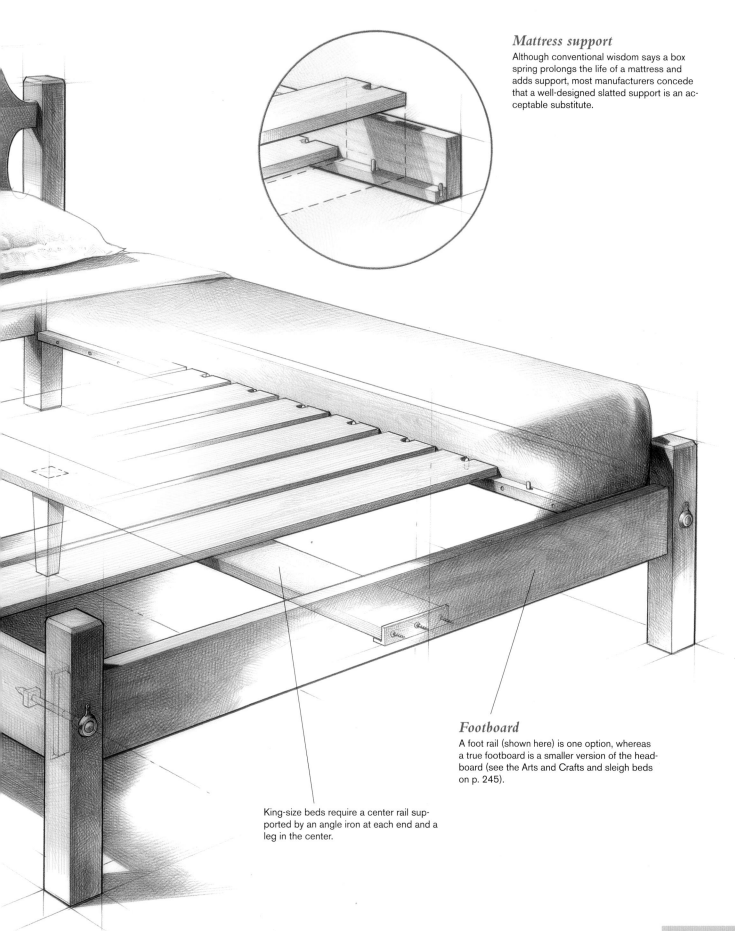

Mattress support

Although conventional wisdom says a box spring prolongs the life of a mattress and adds support, most manufacturers concede that a well-designed slatted support is an acceptable substitute.

Footboard

A foot rail (shown here) is one option, whereas a true footboard is a smaller version of the headboard (see the Arts and Crafts and sleigh beds on p. 245).

King-size beds require a center rail supported by an angle iron at each end and a leg in the center.

CONSTRUCT THE HEADBOARD

Solid Headboards Need Room to Move

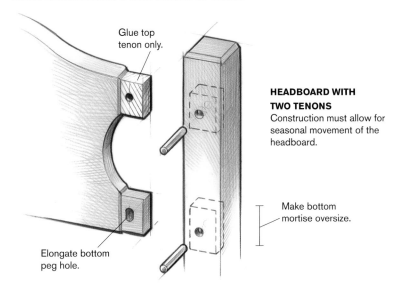

Glue top tenon only.

Elongate bottom peg hole.

HEADBOARD WITH TWO TENONS
Construction must allow for seasonal movement of the headboard.

Make bottom mortise oversize.

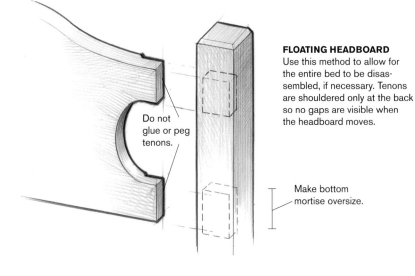

Do not glue or peg tenons.

FLOATING HEADBOARD
Use this method to allow for the entire bed to be disassembled, if necessary. Tenons are shouldered only at the back so no gaps are visible when the headboard moves.

Make bottom mortise oversize.

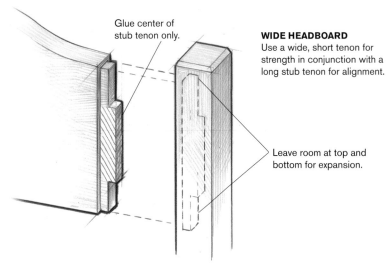

Glue center of stub tenon only.

WIDE HEADBOARD
Use a wide, short tenon for strength in conjunction with a long stub tenon for alignment.

Leave room at top and bottom for expansion.

Support the Mattress

About 80 percent of the mattresses sold in the United States come with a box spring. Full- and queen-size box springs need support around the edges in the form of wooden cleats, angle iron, cast-iron hangers, or aluminum extrusions. All of these supports are screwed to (and sometimes recessed into) the side rails. King-size box springs come in two halves for portability and need an additional support down the center of the bed that's wide enough to support both halves, with a leg in the middle of this support.

The side rails are typically 5 in. to 8 in. wide and 1 in. to 1¾ in. thick. The combined width and thickness should be enough to prevent the rail from sagging under load. I usually use 6-in.- or 7-in.-wide rails with a box spring; but to hide the box spring completely, the rails must be close to 8 in. wide. This choice is strictly a design decision.

In Europe, 80 percent of mattresses are designed to be used without a box spring and to be supported by wooden slats. I find the slatted support a little firmer, but the choice is up to you.

I use ¾-in.-thick by 4-in.-wide slats, which are thicker and wider than commercially available ones. Spaced 1 in. apart, the slats provide some flex for comfort and also allow for air circulation around the mattress or futon. Soft maple or poplar makes good slats, but avoid softwoods, which are too flexible. The slats usually rest on wooden cleats. To keep the slats from shifting, I notch the ends, fitting each slat over a dowel that protrudes from the cleat. On a king-size bed, I add a strut down the center from headboard to footboard, with a leg in the middle.

Some mattresses are designed to be used with solid platforms, which are made of plywood with support underneath to prevent the plywood from sagging. However, because these platforms do not have built-in flexibility or give, they should not be used with regular mattresses.

Design Determines Joinery

Many styles of beds are united by similar post-and-rail construction. By changing a few details, it's possible to change the look of a bed to suit your taste. Shaker beds typically feature slab headboards and foot rails. Arts and Crafts style beds have both a headboard and footboard made of slats or square spindles. Sleigh beds introduce a curve to their frame-and-panel construction. To keep the lines clean, most designs use concealed hardware. Because of their height, four-poster beds must disassemble completely. All four rails are connected by bed bolts, and the headboard floats in mortises in the posts.

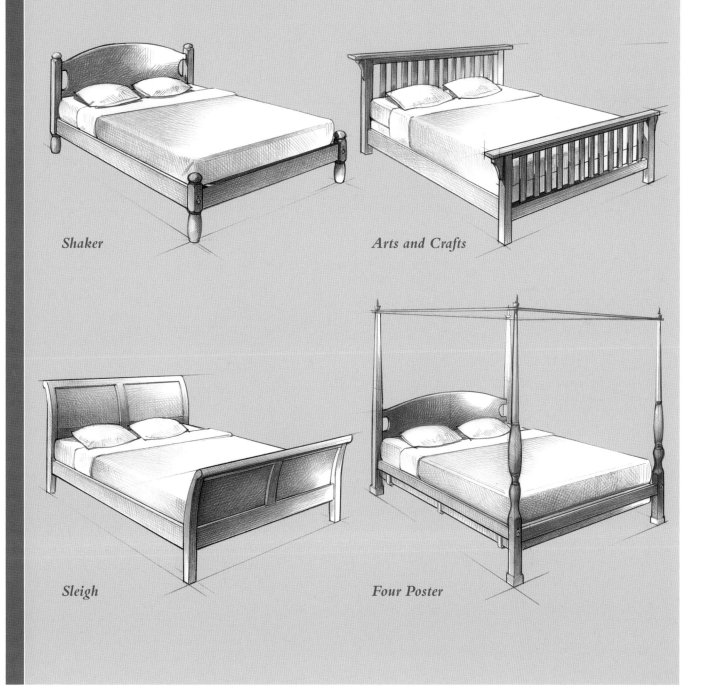

Shaker

Arts and Crafts

Sleigh

Four Poster

Headboard with Spindles or Slats

Use deep tenons. The upper tenon is lowered to avoid weakening the top of the post.

Headboard with Panel

The panel's grain can run vertically or horizontally, but in either case, the panel must be sized to allow for movement.

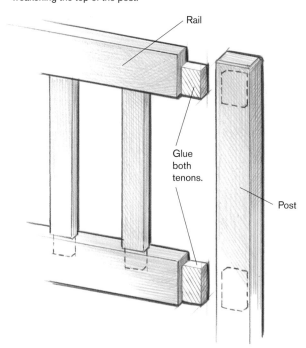

Rail

Glue both tenons.

Post

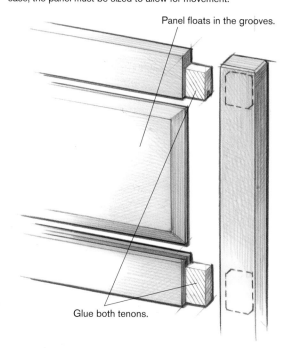

Panel floats in the grooves.

Glue both tenons.

Connect the Post-and-Rail Joints

Because the side rails support the mattress, the joints between the side rails and the bedposts are important to the overall solidity of the bed. Yet they need to be disassembled easily. This is an interesting challenge, considering that wood expands and contracts with seasonal humidity changes. Wood also can compress, either as a result of seasonal changes operating against a metal fastener, or due to the stresses placed on the bed in use. There are a wide variety of fasteners available that attempt to meet this challenge.

Bed bolts Traditional bed bolts are forged to have a square-drive head that flares out, creating a broad bearing surface on the wood. Regular bolts employ a washer for the same effect. To install both types of bolt, a counterbored hole is drilled through the bedpost and into the rail, where it meets either a nut embedded in the rail (for the traditional bed bolt) or a nut and washer in a recess. The bolt alone is not enough to hold the rail securely and to prevent rotation, so either a shallow mortise-and-tenon or a pair of dowels is needed to complete the glueless joint.

Another modern approach is to use bolts and washers with barrel nuts. This approach does not require a special wrench. Alignment of the drilled holes, however, is critical, and barrel nuts that are large enough to use with $\frac{5}{16}$-in. or $\frac{3}{8}$-in. bolts often require $1\frac{1}{2}$-in.-thick rails. There are many approaches to dealing with the bolt hole in the post: The simplest is to treat it as part of a quality joint and to leave it exposed. More likely, you'll want to conceal the hole, either with a brass cover screwed to the bedpost above the bolt hole or with a simple mushroom-shaped wooden plug, although the latter tends to work its way loose.

BOX SPRINGS NEED EDGE SUPPORT

Mattress

Side rail

Box springs need support only around the edges.

Box spring

FOR A LOW PROFILE, USE SLATS INSTEAD OF A BOX SPRING

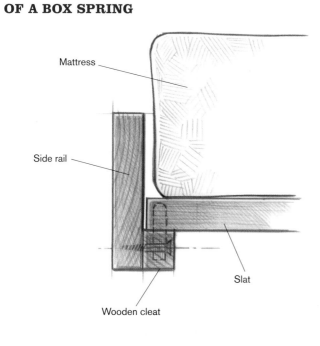

Mattress

Side rail

Wooden cleat

Slat

Wooden Cleats

An economical choice, wooden cleats are glued and screwed to the rails.

Angle Iron

Angle iron can be purchased or recycled from old bed frames. Run a rabbet in each rail, then screw the angle iron in place.

Cast-Iron Hangers

Because of their length, cast-iron hangers support a greater range of box-spring widths. They can be mounted slightly below the rail to lower the mattress height.

Wooden Slats

Slats combine the right amount of support and give for a mattress. Notching them to fit around dowels fixed to the cleats prevents the slats from shifting.

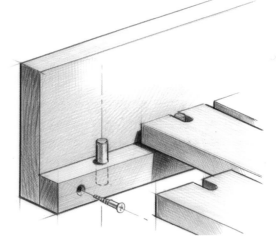

A NEW BED BOLT. Traditional bed bolts (below) have stood the test of time, but newer bolts with barrel nuts (right) are easier to install. Simply drill a hole on the inside face of the rail and drop in the barrel nut.

Brackets There are many types of two-part fasteners for attaching the side rails to the posts. Look for the most solidly made hardware. Because screws driven into end grain don't have a lot of holding power, you should glue dowels into the rails to provide some long grain for the screws to pass through. Use the largest screws possible when attaching all parts of the hardware. If the fasteners loosen up, it is hard to fix the problem. For all of these reasons, my preference is to use fasteners only on occasionally used beds.

JEFF MILLER is the author of *Children's Furniture and Design, Beds, Chairmaking and Design* and a DVD entitled *Chairmaking Techniques,* all published by The Taunton Press, Inc.

BED BOLTS ARE TRADITIONAL

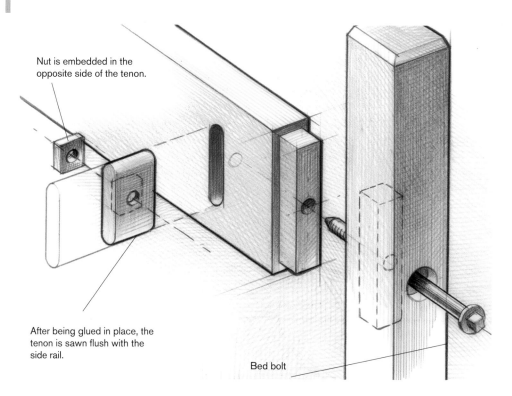

Nut is embedded in the opposite side of the tenon.

After being glued in place, the tenon is sawn flush with the side rail.

Bed bolt

Installing Bed Bolts

DRILL THE BOLT HOLE. After drilling through the post into the tenon, remove the post and complete the hole to its full depth.

A RECESS FOR THE NUT. Use a plunge router and a straight bit to cut a mortise on the inside of the rail.

LOCATE THE NUT. Fit a tenon into the mortise, insert the bolt, and give it a sharp tap to leave an indentation (above). Drill a hole at the mark and inset the nut into the tenon. Glue the tenon into the rail with the nut facing away from the post (below) and trim it flush.

ONE TIGHT JOINT. After cutting the tenon flush with the rail, insert the bolt through the post and crank it tight with the bed-bolt wrench.

Hide Bed Bolts for a Clean Look

You also can bolt a bed together from the inside of the rail, leaving no holes or hardware visible on the outside. This involves embedding the nut in the tenon of the headboard or footboard rail, then routing a specially shaped recess on the inside of the side rail. It helps to make a jig for routing the recess in the rail.

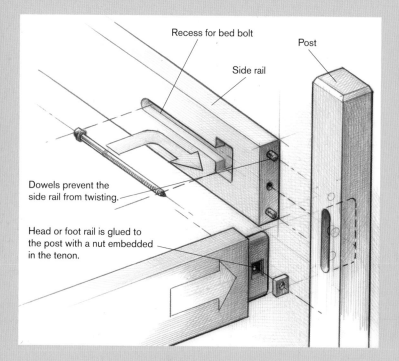

Recess for bed bolt

Post

Side rail

Dowels prevent the side rail from twisting.

Head or foot rail is glued to the post with a nut embedded in the tenon.

HIDDEN NUT. The nut is inset into the tenon on the head or foot rail and faces away from the side rails.

HIDDEN BOLT. Use a jig to rout a T-shaped slot inside the side rails (above). Then insert the bolt and tighten it into the nut embedded in the head or foot rail (left).

Installing Bed-Rail Brackets

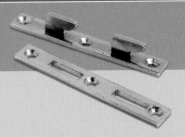

INSTALL THE CLIP PLATE. Glue hardwood dowels into the inside of the side rail to give the screws something to bite into besides end grain.

MAKE ROOM FOR THE CLIPS. The strike plate is recessed into the post. In addition, deeper mortises are required to accommodate the two clips.

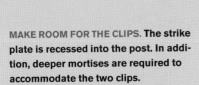

Furniture
Kids Will Love

BY JEFF MILLER

Whether it's for your children, grandchildren, or the children of other family and friends, making things for the kids in your life can be uniquely satisfying. But there are challenges as well. How do you know what will be appreciated or what will be safe? Children's furniture differs from the adult variety in many ways, much as children themselves do.

A whole set of design considerations revolves around how children see and interact with furniture. But these are opportunities—new creative avenues for designer and builder. Kids' furniture also requires a special emphasis on safety that should guide you every step of the way.

Exercise Your Creative Freedom

There are several approaches to designing furniture for children. All are fun in their own way. For example, children love having their own version of a special adult piece. It makes them feel grown up, even though they'll certainly use the furniture in some rather un-grown-up ways.

On the other hand, many successful designs have an element of whimsy, such as bold shapes and bright colors. I believe children see the world as bright, new, and

WHIMSICAL OR ALL GROWN UP.
Part of the fun in designing kids' furniture is turning the imagination loose. This anthropomorphic chest of drawers (bottom of facing page) by Vancouver furniture maker Judson Beaumont experiments with storybook shapes. You also can create replicas of adult furniture, like these Arts and Crafts–inspired chairs by Sam Norris of Burlington, Vermont.

exciting. This can be inspiring—and liberating—to adult designers. Just don't leave out a healthy measure of taste when you add in the whimsy. You can't always know what sort of playful role a child will find for a piece, but you can certainly encourage one. This is the impulse behind things like a bed with a race car, animal, or castle theme, but the play element can also be more subtle. One of my more successful designs is a "Marble Chair," which has a back that is a marble race (see the top right photo on p. 260). It is endlessly entertaining, although definitely not suitable for children under 3 years old.

Some pieces serve new roles after the kids outgrow them: A play table turns into a coffee table; a baby's changing table becomes a sideboard for the dining room.

Guidelines for Safe Construction

Foremost in your mind should always be the overall safety of the furniture. There should be no sharp edges or corners. I'm not fond of rounded-over edges, but in this case they're a very good idea.

The construction of the piece should be beyond question—the best possible joinery on strong components. A child is much smaller and lighter than an adult, but adults rarely drag their chairs all around the house

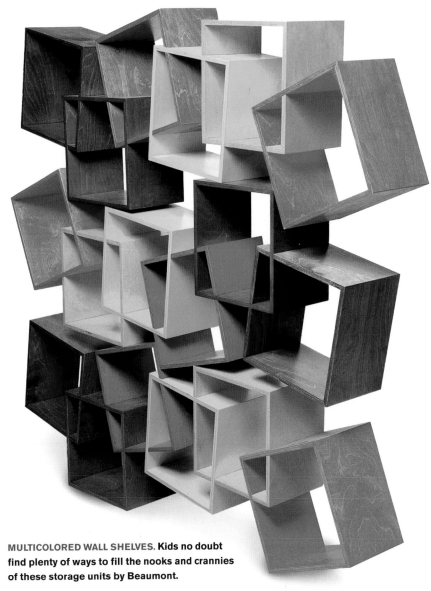

MULTICOLORED WALL SHELVES. Kids no doubt find plenty of ways to fill the nooks and crannies of these storage units by Beaumont.

and use them as step stools. Areas around joints must be almost as robust as on full-size furniture.

Consider using extra screws (and glue) for mattress-support rails, and corner blocks on chairs. Pin mortise-and-tenon joints if it will strengthen the structure. For children 3 and under, avoid loose parts small enough to cause a choking hazard.

Another issue related to younger children is the safety of the finish. Most finishes designed for furniture are considered food-contact safe once the solvents have evaporated or the various chemicals have combined. And even Consumer Product Safety Commission rules allow a little bit of lead (0.06 percent) in paint deemed safe for cribs. But I've seen how kids will gnaw on crib rails, and I, along with most new parents, would err on the side of caution and select finishes that are nontoxic.

One of the most readily available safe finishes, shellac, is actually edible, and has been used for coatings on medicines and candies. For this level of "edibility" you should probably mix your own with shellac flakes and high-proof grain alcohol or denatured alcohol (the alcohol evaporates as the finish dries). Shellac may not be as durable or protective as some other finishes, but it is quick and easy to apply. There are other commercial finishes designed to be completely nontoxic. These include oils, waxes, paints, dyes, and stains.

Quick and Easy Can Be Fun

The last time I built something fancy for my kids was before I had any. The piece was a Colonial cradle in walnut, with classic lines and tricky dovetails on a compound angle (see top right photo on the facing page). I finished it the night my wife went into labor, in a last crazy burst of nesting instinct.

Like many pieces of fine children's furniture, I suspect, the cradle has been more useful in its second life as a hopper for stuffed animals. As a cradle, the heirloom soon lost out to a parade of plastic contraptions—vibrating chairs, automatic swings—that were ugly but very functional, and the baby outgrew it in a few months anyway.

Since then I've been a busy dad, and the kids have grown like weeds. If I were their retired grandfather, maybe I could keep them in little Windsor chairs, but I just don't have the time. I save my finest woodworking for full-size things we'll use for life. But I've also made at least a dozen kid items, from beds and storage to desks and chairs.

I think of kids' furniture as quick and dirty: It's got to be quick and it is going to get dirty—the chipped paint, crayon marks, and Elmo stickers are kiddie patina. And although my stuff is not ready for the Readers Gallery, I don't apologize for any of it. There is great fun in whipping up a mini Adirondack

SAVE THE QUILTED MAPLE. Smaller kids especially are more likely to appreciate bold colors. Christiana made this bed from home-center lumber and finished it with latex paint.

chair or a child's desk in an afternoon, and then seeing it give good service for many years.

Spend an hour measuring your child and sketching up a plan, and then bang it out in Baltic birch, using biscuits, router roundovers, and water-based poly. I also recommend paint-grade pine and acrylic paint. Paint covers mistakes, cheap lumber, and easy joinery, and kids love bright colors a lot more than bird's-eye maple, in my experience.

Call it "Pine Woodworking" if that makes you feel any better. I call it fun.

ASA CHRISTIANA is the editor of *Fine Woodworking* magazine.

Cribs and Cradles

CUSTOM MADE FOR A LULLABY. Cradles like these by Miller (left) and Christiana (below) are especially popular projects for grand-dads. They share some safety concerns with cribs, from slat spacing to the fit of the bedding. Christiana made this dovetailed walnut cradle for his first daughter, but it soon became a repository for stuffed animals.

CRIB AND CRADLE SAFETY

There should be no more than 1 in. of space around the mattress.

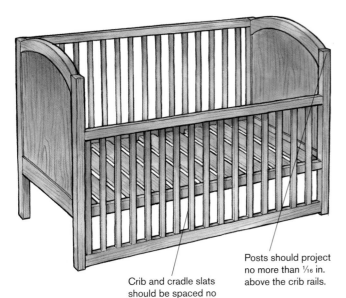

Crib and cradle slats should be spaced no more than 2⅜ in. apart.

Posts should project no more than ¹⁄₁₆ in. above the crib rails.

MATTRESS SIZES

Before building a crib, cradle, or youth bed, measure your specific mattress if at all possible. Variations from standard sizes are common. In a crib or cradle, this can be the difference between an appropriately tight fit and something that is either dangerously loose or too tight to fit.

Bed type	Mattress size
Cradle	15 in. by 33 in., or 18 in. by 36 in.
Crib	27 in. by 52 in.
Twin	39 in. by 75 in.
Double	54 in. by 75 in.

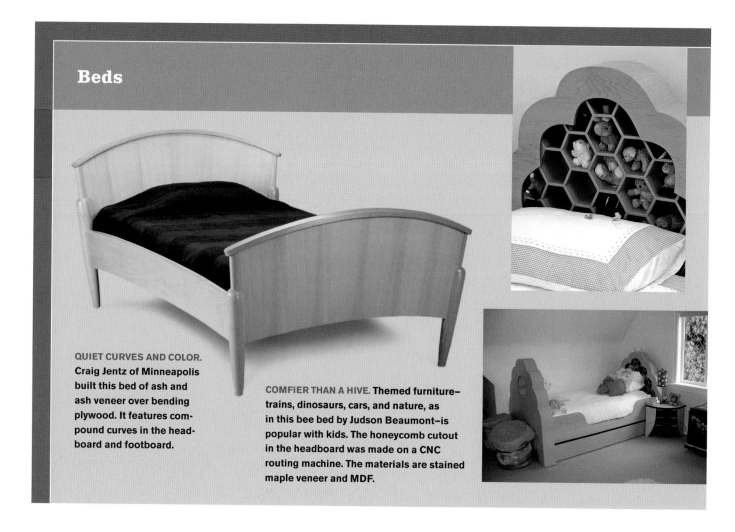

Beds

QUIET CURVES AND COLOR.
Craig Jentz of Minneapolis
built this bed of ash and
ash veneer over bending
plywood. It features com-
pound curves in the head-
board and footboard.

COMFIER THAN A HIVE. Themed furniture—
trains, dinosaurs, cars, and nature, as
in this bee bed by Judson Beaumont—is
popular with kids. The honeycomb cutout
in the headboard was made on a CNC
routing machine. The materials are stained
maple veneer and MDF.

So far, we've discussed general guidelines that apply to any piece. Here are some
specific tips for the most popular types of
children's furniture.

Cribs and cradles Cribs and cradles are
subject to many regulations, because babies
are left unattended in them and safety is
paramount. A rule that most people seem to
be aware of limits the distance between slats
or spindles to no more than 2⅜ in. This
will prevent an infant's body from slipping
between the slats (the head is bigger, and
typically won't pass through). The slats also
should be securely attached. Your best option is mortise-and-tenon joints pinned at
every tenon, both top and bottom.

It is very important that the posts or legs
on a crib or cradle stick up no more than
¹⁄₁₆ in. above the rails, headboard, or foot-

board. Anything projecting farther can snag
clothing and create a strangulation hazard.
An exception would be for high posts that
project at least 16 in. above the rails (as with
a canopied crib). It would be extremely
difficult for a child to get clothing snagged
on posts this high. Likewise, any cutouts
or shaped components must avoid potential for catching either the neck, body, or
clothing. Check the size of the mattress if
possible before you begin your project. It's
important to fit the crib or cradle well to
the mattress to prevent a child from getting
trapped between them. For the same reason,
joinery should be very secure, so there is
no loosening of the rails that would create extra space between mattress and rails.
Cribs or cradles that bolt together should
be checked periodically for tightness.

Bunk beds As you might expect, bunk beds have plenty of regulations. Any openings on the upper bunk must be less than 3½ in. in the smaller dimension. Guardrails are required on both sides of the top bunk, and these rails must be attached securely to the bed. The opening in the guardrail for the ladder should be 15 in. or less. It is also very important to secure the mattress support to the upper bunk side rails. Kids love to kick the upper bed from below; there should be no chance that the upper mattress support could come loose. The safety standards also strongly suggest that children under 6 not sleep on the upper bunk, and that a night-light be installed in any room with bunk beds. Discouraging play on the upper bunk is also strongly suggested, but good luck in enforcing that rule.

BUNK-BED SAFETY

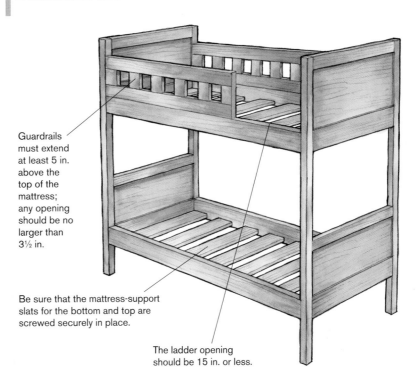

Guardrails must extend at least 5 in. above the top of the mattress; any opening should be no larger than 3½ in.

Be sure that the mattress-support slats for the bottom and top are screwed securely in place.

The ladder opening should be 15 in. or less.

Toy Chests

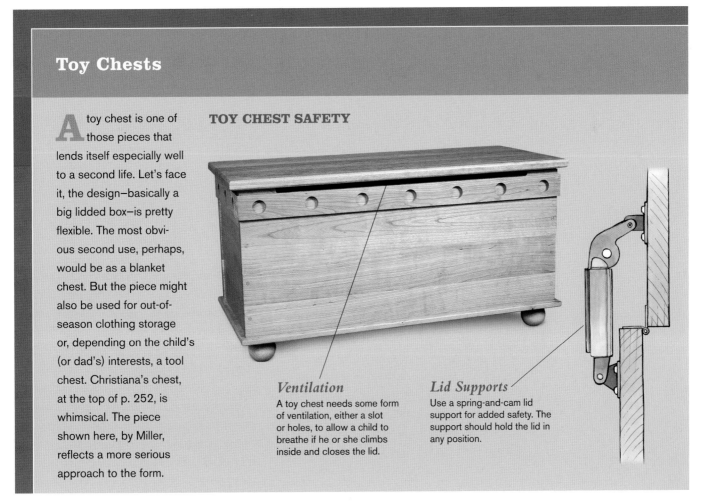

A toy chest is one of those pieces that lends itself especially well to a second life. Let's face it, the design—basically a big lidded box—is pretty flexible. The most obvious second use, perhaps, would be as a blanket chest. But the piece might also be used for out-of-season clothing storage or, depending on the child's (or dad's) interests, a tool chest. Christiana's chest, at the top of p. 252, is whimsical. The piece shown here, by Miller, reflects a more serious approach to the form.

TOY CHEST SAFETY

Ventilation
A toy chest needs some form of ventilation, either a slot or holes, to allow a child to breathe if he or she climbs inside and closes the lid.

Lid Supports
Use a spring-and-cam lid support for added safety. The support should hold the lid in any position.

AN OLD-FASHIONED PLAY STATION.
Built for a toddler, this set by Pekovich pairs a lightweight but sturdy post-and-rung chair with a bombproof table that features pinned mortise-and-tenon joinery.

KID-SIZE PROPORTIONS

Table Height

Chair Height

CHAIR AND TABLE HEIGHTS

Standard adult chair height is 18 in.
Standard adult table height is 28 in. to 30 in.

Age	Chair height (in.)	Table height (in.)
2–4	9–11	17–20
4–7	10–15	18–21
7–10	13–17	19–25
10–13	15–18	23–27
13+	18	24–30

Toy chests Toy chests, or anything with a lid that lifts up, should be outfitted with special lid-support hinges. The spring mechanism in these hinges allows the lid to remain in any position without slamming down on heads, hands, or anything else. The specific hardware will have its own installation instructions, and will often be designed for lids of a particular weight and size. Toy chests should also have ventilation holes or slots. Kids will climb into them and hide, and it's important that air can flow in and out.

Tables and chairs Sometimes, safety requirements send you into uncharted waters. For example, high chairs should have both waist and crotch safety straps—not something a woodworker encounters every day. A trip to a camping-supply store (and some good sewing-supply stores) can outfit you with appropriate nylon webbing and buckles for making these straps (changing tables should also have safety straps to secure the wriggling baby). High chairs should also be built with enough splay to the legs so that

Tables and Chairs

IMAGINATIVE TOUCHES, BOTH BOLD AND QUIET. Kids' furniture can artfully meld eye-catching shapes and bright colors, as in this desk by Jay Jones of Greensboro, North Carolina (left). Or it can be more subdued. *Fine Woodworking* art director Michael Pekovich built a more traditional desk for his son, but enlivened it with trout inlaid in silver and secret compartments. Textured end grain on the top adds a distinctive tactile detail.

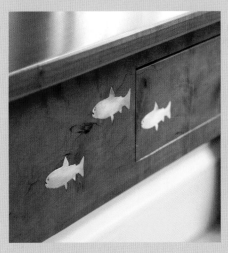

A CHANGING TABLE THAT CHANGED WITH THE TIMES. This piece by Pekovich started life as an infant's changing table but now serves as a sideboard in his family's dining room. The key is a design that's basic enough to serve more than one need.

ROCKING AND ROLLING. Miller's plywood rocker (above) and Pekovich's Arts and Crafts version (right) both have runners with a 30-in. radius, just tight enough to rock without tipping. Miller's marble chair (top right) features a built-in element of play. Grooves in the slats and uprights form a zig-zag track for a marble.

they are harder to tip over during all of the writhing, twisting, and bouncing around that happen there. Kids love to test the limits. You don't want such an experiment to end with a fall.

The trick with tables and chairs is in building them the right size. Kids will outgrow tables and chairs almost as quickly as they outgrow their clothes. I usually make children's chair seats 12 in. to 14 in. high, but my chairs are made more for play. For writing or schoolwork, the range is much wider, depending on the age and size of the child. At my local primary school, writing-table heights range from 17 in. to 25 in. for 2- to 10-year-olds. Chair seat heights range from 9 in. to 17 in. for the same age range. Play tables tend to be 16 in. to 18 in. tall.

JEFF MILLER is the author of *Children's Furniture and Design, Beds, Chairmaking and Design* and a DVD entitled *Chairmaking Techniques,* all published by The Taunton Press, Inc.

Kid-Safe Finishes

Because younger children will chew on anything within reach, Miller prefers nontoxic finishes. Shellac flakes, milk paint, and natural waxes are all good choices.

Furniture for Your Next TV

BY STEVE CASEY

THE CONSOLE IS A MODERN APPROACH. Positioned underneath a wall-hung television, consoles offer design freedom. They can be small or very large, they come with you when you move, and they don't have to be replaced when screen technology changes.

I have been designing and building custom furniture since 1978, much of it devoted to home theaters, entertainment centers, and other pieces built around televisions. Recent years have brought major changes in TV technology, creating new furniture possibilities and making my work much more interesting.

TV screens are wider than ever, but the most important change for furniture makers is in how thin the sets have become. Two types of sets have led the way. The first are flat-panel sets with plasma or liquid crystal screens. Some of these displays measure 60 in. diagonally but are only about 5 in. deep. The other type of set is the large-screen projection TV, which used to be housed in a giant cabinet but now averages only about 17 in. deep. The advantage of the latter type is that they cost thousands of dollars less than plasma or LCD sets with comparable screen sizes.

The new sets allow designers to rethink the typical entertainment center and to create cabinetry and furniture for TVs that was not practical or even possible just a few years ago. Televisions today are attractive enough that they don't have to be hidden

TELEVISIONS ARE GETTING SHALLOWER AND WIDER

The picture tube in a large traditional television requires furniture that is at least 2 ft. deep. The latest rear-projection televisions have screens as wide as 61 in. but can be housed in much shallower cabinets. A typical plasma or LCD set is slender enough to hang on the wall.

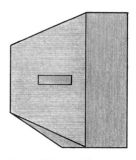
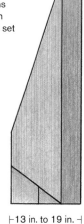
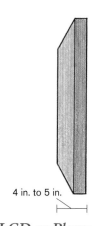

├── 22 in. to 25 in. ──┤   ├13 in. to 19 in.┤   4 in. to 5 in.

Cathode-Ray Tube   *Rear Projection*   *LCD or Plasma*

Wide-screen televisions, many of them designed to carry digital, high-definition signals, have proportions much like those of a movie-theater screen. Screen size is measured the same way, however—across the diagonal. So a 32-in. wide-screen set (bottom right) has a screen that is wider and shorter than its standard-ratio counterpart (top right).

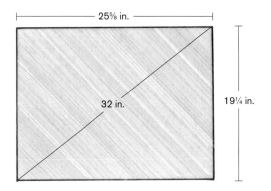

├─────── 25⅝ in. ───────┤

32 in.   19¼ in.

Standard 4:3 picture ratio

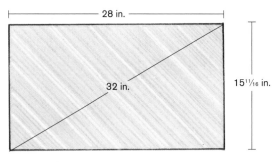

├────── 28 in. ──────┤

32 in.   15¹¹⁄₁₆ in.

Widescreen 16:9 picture ratio

behind doors in the now-too-familiar black box. Many new designs put the set on display. Here are a few ideas.

Options for Flat Screens

Because TVs now can be hung on the wall like pictures, with minimal intrusion into the room, furniture makers are not limited to "big box" solutions like armoires. Instead, we can create equipment consoles that sit beneath the screens, or mount screens into the shallow bookcase section of traditional built-in cabinets.

Console units One piece I often build to go with flat-panel TVs is the console—an ideal furniture design for housing electronic gear in small spaces such as bedrooms or apartments. Consoles support or sit underneath the TV but do not enclose it.

The console's smaller scale offers several advantages over conventional wall units. It is relatively easy to move when users want to relocate the piece or get behind it to connect equipment. Also, because the console doesn't house the TV itself, there is no need to buy new furniture if you buy a bigger set. Being of smaller scale, consoles are less expensive and take less time to build than larger wall units or full-on cabinet systems. But because they function more as pieces of furniture than as cabinetry, they create opportunities for solid-lumber construction and traditional joinery—elements that might break the bank if used on larger built-ins.

Bear in mind that consoles have limitations. The unit's height almost always will require some kind of compromise. Ideally, the piece should be low enough so that it doesn't interfere with the ideal height placement of the TV (the screen should be centered at eye level from the viewing chair). Build a console this low, however, and you'll probably have to stoop down to load your VCR or DVD player. Fortunately, this isn't an issue in bedrooms, where the screen should be much higher off the floor for a viewer perched in bed.

Traditional cabinets Flat panels can go where no large TV has gone before. A big TV in the shallow bookcase section of a traditional cabinet was not possible until this technology reached the market. The example at left below shows how little depth is needed to build a flat panel into a piece of furniture. With a standard 10-in.-deep shelf, the TV still had to come forward a few inches in order to get the screen flush with the bookcase face frame. The leftover space was used for a mounting device with an articulating arm that allows the screen to be pulled forward and swiveled (see photo at right below).

Most plasma or LCD sets need plenty of open space around them so that air can circulate and keep the equipment from overheating. It's essential to bring the screen forward and to leave a decent amount of space around the display for cool-air draw and proper convection. If you plan to enclose a plasma or LCD set in casework, consult the screen's manufacturer for its specifications on ventilation.

On traditional painted cabinets (see photo at left below), I like to use two-sided, pine-core melamine board for the closed case interiors. The melamine requires no further finishing and will take lots of abuse without showing wear. I used white inside the cabinets and black for the component rack because it complements and contrasts with the painted finish and goes really well with electronic equipment. I used MDF for the bookcase sides and backs, maple plywood for the shelves, and solid wood for the raised-panel doors, face frames, and all of the trim. On this piece I also included a cherry countertop made from veneer-core plywood with solid trim.

Solutions for LCD and Plasma TVs

MODERN TECHNOLOGY MIXES WELL WITH TRADITIONAL CABINETRY. Because it requires so little depth, a flat-panel television can mount easily inside the bookcase section of a traditional built-in cabinet (left). A commercially available mount (above) allows a plasma or LCD television set to be pulled away from the wall and swiveled, either for service or for viewing.

Projection TV: Big Screen Fits in a Shallow Cabinet

This big-screen technology offers a crisp picture for less money than a plasma set, and still is much shallower than a traditional TV. This cherry unit (right) is only 18 in. deep. Another approach uses a plywood backboard instead of a full-height case (below), making the piece contemporary, more open-looking, and easier to install or move.

Options for Projection-Style Sets

Large-screen projection TVs are bulkier than flat-panel sets but they, too, allow for much thinner and less conventional furniture designs because they have minimal depth, size, and weight. Not long ago, a projection set with a 48-in. screen was nearly 3 ft. deep. A similar set today is only about 15 in. to 17 in. deep. The furniture I build to house much larger 60-in. or 70-in. projection TVs is typically only 20 in. to 22 in. deep. The TV no longer determines an entertainment center's maximum depth; the other home-theater components do.

Familiar casework with a smaller footprint As TV displays get larger, clients are growing more comfortable with smaller furniture that shows off their TV instead of hiding it. The example in the top photo above was designed by Deborah Goldstein of Interior Motives to replace a much larger cabinet that housed a much smaller TV. When "big" television screens were only 36 in. across, the sets were heavy and deep, but took up only a small percentage of the cabinet's face area. In this unit, the screen size accounts for more than 25 percent of the cabinet's face area. Today's large-format sets, in addition to being thinner, are also quite lightweight. I no longer need to build beefed-up TV-support shelves to hold lots of weight and prevent sagging over time.

The unit is only 18 in. deep and still allows 4 in. behind the TV for good ventilation. In this space, the idea of putting a big, deep cabinet so near the entry to the room would be bad design. The television's narrow profile allowed me to scale back the support furniture for an unencumbered entry to the space while providing a large-format viewing experience.

Put the picture in a frame A contemporary approach (see the bottom photo on the facing page) frames and highlights the TV while hiding the equipment behind doors for a clean, sleek look. This design has a lower drawer base with a structural backboard attached. Using a plywood backboard instead of a full-height case gives the piece a more open look and makes it easier to install and move. With lighting and display, this kind of approach creates drama in the room.

I like to build contemporary pieces like this using plywood with a Douglas-fir core and an MDF layer just below the hardwood face veneer. The MDF layer ensures flat surfaces, whereas the fir core provides structural strength and screw-holding ability. With a few matched sheets, I can play with the grain and do wonderful matched faces and backs. The face frames are solid wood. I typically use hot-melt edge tape to veneer the door and drawer edges.

Assembling the backboard panel on the matched veneer seams gives an illusion of one seamless back even though the final piece might be three parts and 9 ft. across. I used biscuits and tight-joint fasteners to hold the panel together. The backboard did not have to be secured to the wall but is secured to the cases. This helps to prevent racking and provides a way to attach the smaller, floating shelves. Everything is held square and in place on the backboard with biscuits and then secured with drywall screws inserted from the back. All of the equipment is behind doors in the closed cases. The drawers below store DVDs, videotapes, and CDs.

STEVE CASEY builds custom furniture and cabinets in Los Angeles, California. You can view his work on the web at www.stevecaseydesign.com.

BUILT ON A BACKBOARD

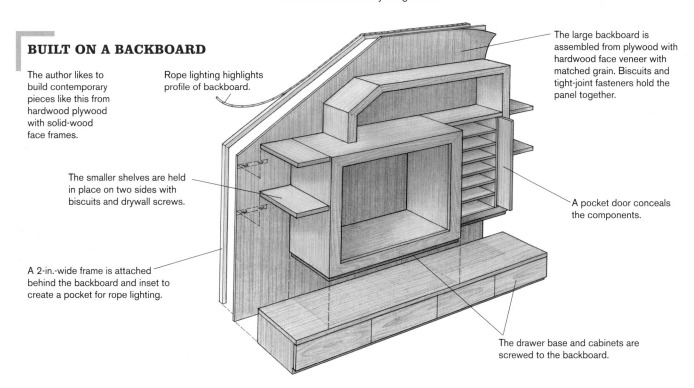

The author likes to build contemporary pieces like this from hardwood plywood with solid-wood face frames.

Rope lighting highlights profile of backboard.

The large backboard is assembled from plywood with hardwood face veneer with matched grain. Biscuits and tight-joint fasteners hold the panel together.

The smaller shelves are held in place on two sides with biscuits and drywall screws.

A 2-in.-wide frame is attached behind the backboard and inset to create a pocket for rope lighting.

A pocket door conceals the components.

The drawer base and cabinets are screwed to the backboard.

Credits

The articles in this book appeared in the following issues of *Fine Woodworking*:

Photos: p. iii by Asa Christiana, courtesy *Fine Woodworking*, © The Taunton Press, Inc.; p. iv (left) by Michael Fortune, courtesy *Fine Woodworking*, © The Taunton Press, Inc., (right) by Gregg Krogstad, courtesy *Fine Woodworking*, © The Taunton Press, Inc.; p. 1 (left) by Lance Patterson, courtesy *Fine Woodworking*, © The Taunton Press, Inc., (right) by Jonathan Binzen, courtesy *Fine Woodworking*, © The Taunton Press, Inc.; p. 2 by Steve Scott, courtesy *Fine Woodworking*, © The Taunton Press, Inc.

p. 3: Designing Furniture: A Survival Guide by Garrett Hack, issue 156. Photos pp. 3, 4 & 6 by Asa Christiana, courtesy *Fine Woodworking*, © The Taunton Press, Inc.; p. 5 by John Shelton, courtesy *Fine Woodworking*, © The Taunton Press, Inc.

p. 7: A Guide to Good Design by Graham Blackburn, issue 168. Drawings by Graham Blackburn, courtesy *Fine Woodworking*, © The Taunton Press, Inc.

p. 13: Sam Maloof on Design by Asa Christiana, issue 179. Photos by Asa Christiana, courtesy *Fine Woodworking*, © The Taunton Press, Inc.

p. 22: 9 Tips for Better Design by Michael Fortune, issue 182. Photos and drawings by Michael Fortune, courtesy *Fine Woodworking*, © The Taunton Press, Inc.

p. 30: Drafting Basics by Philip C. Lowe, issue 161. Photos by Asa Christiana, courtesy *Fine Woodworking*, © The Taunton Press, Inc.; Drawings by Vince Babak, courtesy *Fine Woodworking*, © The Taunton Press, Inc.

p. 39: Mock-Ups Quicken the Design Process by Keith Allen, issue 139. Photos by William Duckworth, courtesy *Fine Woodworking*, © The Taunton Press, Inc.

p. 42: Fine-Tune Designs before You Build by Gary Rogowski, issue 189. Photos by Steve Scott, courtesy *Fine Woodworking*, © The Taunton Press, Inc.

p. 48: Scaling Furniture from Photos by Miguel Gomez-Ibannez, issue 170. Photos by Karen Wales, courtesy *Fine Woodworking*, © The Taunton Press, Inc.

p. 55: Building Without Plans by Craig Vandall Stevens, issue 141. Photos by Jonathan Binzen, courtesy *Fine Woodworking*, © The Taunton Press, Inc., except p. 60 by Stephen Webster, courtesy *Fine Woodworking*, © The Taunton Press, Inc.

p. 61: A Short History of Design by Graham Blackburn, issue 146. Drawings by Graham Blackburn, courtesy *Fine Woodworking*, © The Taunton Press, Inc.

p. 70: Quintessential Arts and Crafts by Graham Blackburn, issue 162. Drawings by Graham Blackburn, courtesy *Fine Woodworking*, © The Taunton Press, Inc.

p. 79: Building in the Language of Greene and Greene by Thomas Hugh Stangeland, issue 106. Photos by Jonathon Binzen, courtesy *Fine Woodworking*, © The Taunton Press, Inc., except p. 79 by Gregg Krogstad, courtesy *Fine Woodworking*, © The Taunton Press, Inc.; Drawings by Maria Melschnig, courtesy *Fine Woodworking*, © The Taunton Press, Inc.

p. 86: Elements of Shaker Style by Chris Becksvoort, issue 131. Photos by Scott Phillips, courtesy *Fine Woodworking*, © The Taunton Press, Inc., except p. 87 by Dennis Griggs, courtesy *Fine Woodworking*, © The Taunton Press, Inc.; Drawings by Michael Gellatly, courtesy *Fine Woodworking*, © The Taunton Press, Inc.

p. 92: Edge Treatments Make a Difference by Will Neptune, issue 132. Photos by Lance Patterson, courtesy *Fine Woodworking*, © The Taunton Press, Inc.

p. 98: Designing Along the Grain by Paul Harrell, issue 6. Photos by Jonathon Binzen, courtesy *Fine Woodworking*, © The Taunton Press, Inc.; Drawings by Bob LaPointe, courtesy *Fine Woodworking*, © The Taunton Press, Inc.

p. 103: Understanding Wood Movement by Chris Becksvoort, issue 165. Photos by Dennis Griggs, courtesy *Fine Woodworking*, © The Taunton Press, Inc., except p. 103 by Karen Wales, courtesy *Fine Woodworking*, © The Taunton Press, Inc., pp. 106–107 by Michael Pekovich, courtesy *The Taunton Press, Inc. & p. 111 bottom by Kelly J. Dunton, courtesy *Fine Woodworking*, © The Taunton Press, Inc.; Drawings by Vince Babak, courtesy *Fine Woodworking*, © The Taunton Press, Inc.

p. 112: Supporting Drop Leaves by Chris Becksvoort, issue 111. Photos by Charley Robinson, courtesy *Fine Woodworking*, © The Taunton Press, Inc.; Drawings by Heather Lambert, courtesy *Fine Woodworking*, © The Taunton Press, Inc.

p. 119: Designing on the Go: A Coffee Table Takes Shape by Peter Turner, issue 128. Photo p. 119 by Peter Macomber, courtesy *Fine Woodworking*, © The Taunton Press, Inc.; p. 120 by Dennis and Diane Griggs, courtesy *Fine Woodworking*, © The Taunton Press, Inc.; and pp. 121–122 by Scott Gibson, courtesy *Fine Woodworking*, © The Taunton Press, Inc.

p. 124: Designing Table Legs by Graham Blackburn, issue 139. Drawings by Graham Blackburn, courtesy *Fine Woodworking*, © The Taunton Press, Inc.

p. 135: Joining Legs to Aprons by Garrett Hack, issue 161. Photos by William Duckworth, courtesy *Fine Woodworking*, © The Taunton Press, Inc.; Drawings by Graham Blackburn, courtesy *Fine Woodworking*, © The Taunton Press, Inc.

p. 142: Attaching Tabletops by Mario Rodriguez, issue 163. Photos by Mark Schofield, courtesy *Fine Woodworking*, © The Taunton Press, Inc., except pp. 145–149, top right inset by Kelly J. Dunton, courtesy *Fine Woodworking*, © The Taunton Press, Inc.; Drawings by Michael Gellatly, courtesy *Fine Woodworking*, © The Taunton Press, Inc.

p. 150: Engineering a Table with Drawers by Will Neptune, issue 130. Photos by Boyd Hagen, courtesy *Fine Woodworking*, © The Taunton Press, Inc.; Drawings by Bob La Pointe, courtesy *Fine Woodworking*, © The Taunton Press, Inc.

p. 158: An Illustrated Guide to Table Design by Graham Blackburn, issue 177. Drawings by Graham Blackburn, courtesy *Fine Woodworking*, © The Taunton Press, Inc.

p. 166: Building Bookshelves to Last by Jeff Miller, issue 190. Photos pp. 166, 169 top right, 170 bottom left & top right, 172 & 173 middle, bottom left & botttom right by Tom Begnal, courtesy *Fine Woodworking*, © The Taunton Press, Inc., pp. 167, 168, 169 top left & bottom left & bottom right, 170 top left & bottom right, 171 & 173 top by Michael Pekovich, courtesy *Fine Woodworking*, © The Taunton Press, Inc.; Drawings by Stephen Hutchings, courtesy *Fine Woodworking*, © The Taunton Press, Inc.

p. 174: Anatomy of a Chest of Drawers by Will Neptune, issue 163. Photos by Michael Pekovich, courtesy *Fine Woodworking*, © The Taunton Press, Inc.; Drawings by Bob La Pointe, courtesy *Fine Woodworking*, © The Taunton Press, Inc.

p. 185: Designing a Chest of Drawers by Garrett Hack, issue 151. Photos by John Sheldon, courtesy *Fine Woodworking*, © The Taunton Press, Inc.; Drawings by Vince Babak, courtesy *Fine Woodworking*, © The Taunton Press, Inc.

p. 191: Dressing Up a Basic Box by Roger Holmes, issue 152. Photos by Michael Farrell, courtesy *Fine Woodworking*, © The Taunton Press, Inc.; Drawings by Vince Babak, courtesy *Fine Woodworking*, © The Taunton Press, Inc.

p. 194: Graduated Drawers by Chris Becksvoort, issue 141. Drawings by Vince Babak, courtesy *Fine Woodworking*, © The Taunton Press, Inc.

p. 197: Drawer-Design Strategies by Gary Rogowski, issue 117. Photos by Vincent Laurence, courtesy *Fine Woodworking*, © The Taunton Press, Inc.; Drawings by Jim Richey, courtesy *Fine Woodworking*, © The Taunton Press, Inc.

p. 204: Where Furniture Meets the Floor by Mario Rodriguez, issue 135. Photos by Bob La Pointe, courtesy *Fine Woodworking*, © The Taunton Press, Inc.

pp. 205, 206 inset, 209 inset & 210 bottom left by Michael Pekovich, courtesy *Fine Woodworking*, © The Taunton Press, Inc.; pp. 206, 208 & 209 by Jonathon Binzen, courtesy *Fine Woodworking*, © The Taunton Press, Inc.; p. 210 inset by Boyd Hagen, courtesy *Fine Woodworking*, © The Taunton Press, Inc.; Drawings by Vince Babak, courtesy *Fine Woodworking*, © The Taunton Press, Inc.

p. 214: Sideboard Strategies by Will Neptune, issue 138. Photos by Michael Pekovich, courtesy *Fine Woodworking*, © The Taunton Press, Inc.; except p. 215 bottom by Scott Phillips, courtesy *Fine Woodworking*, © The Taunton Press, Inc.; Drawings by Bob LaPointe, courtesy *Fine Woodworking*, © The Taunton Press, Inc.

p. 225: A Back For Every Cabinet by Steve Latta, issue 192. Photos by Steve Scott courtesy *Fine Woodworking*, © The Taunton Press, Inc.; Drawings by Stephen Hutchings, courtesy *Fine Woodworking*, © The Taunton Press, Inc.

p. 234: What Makes a Chair Stand Up to Abuse? by Jere Osgood, issue 110. Photos pp. 234–235 by Dean Powell, courtesy *Fine Woodworking*, © The Taunton Press, Inc.; pp. 237 & 239 by Zachary Gaulkin, courtesy *Fine Woodworking*, © The Taunton Press, Inc.; Drawings by Bob La Pointe, courtesy *Fine Woodworking*, © The Taunton Press, Inc.

p. 241: Anatomy of a Bed by Jeff Miller, issue 175. Photos by Mark Schofield, courtesy *Fine Woodworking*, © The Taunton Press, Inc.; Drawings by Brian Morser, courtesy *Fine Woodworking*, © The Taunton Press, Inc.

p. 252: Furniture Kids Will Love by Jeff Miller, issue 194. Photos p. 252 top by Asa Christiana, courtesy *Fine Woodworking*, © The Taunton Press, Inc., bottom courtesy Storme, p. 253 top by Seth Janofsky, courtesy *Fine Woodworking*, © The Taunton Press, Inc., bottom by Adam Greaves, courtesy *Fine Woodworking*, © The Taunton Press, Inc., p. 254 by Steve Scott, courtesy *Fine Woodworking*, © The Taunton Press, Inc., pp. 255 & 260 top by Tanya Tucka, courtesy *Fine Woodworking*, © The Taunton Press, Inc., p. 256 left by Craig Jentz, courtesy *Fine Woodworking*, © The Taunton Press, Inc., inset by Mike Wakefield, courtesy *Fine Woodworking*, © The Taunton Press, Inc. & pp. 258, 259 & 260 bottom by Michael Pekovich, courtesy *Fine Woodworking*, © The Taunton Press, Inc.; Drawings by Stephen Hutchings, courtesy *Fine Woodworking*, © The Taunton Press, Inc.

p. 261: Furniture for Your Next TV by Steve Casey, issue 183. Photos by Dean Della Ventura, courtesy *Fine Woodworking*, © The Taunton Press, Inc.; Drawings by Vince Babak, courtesy *Fine Woodworking*, © The Taunton Press, Inc.

Index